LIES WE LIVE BY

LIES WE LIVE BY
THE ART OF
SELF-DECEPTION

Eduardo Giannetti

Translated by John Gledson

BLOOMSBURY

Published by Bloomsbury Publishing, New York and London.
Distributed to the trade by St. Martin's Press

A CIP catalogue record for this book
is available from the Library of Congress

ISBN 1-58234-057-9

First published in 1997 as *Auto-engano* by
Companhia das Letras, São Paulo

First U.S. Edition 2000
10 9 8 7 6 5 4 3 2 1

Typeset by Palimpsest Book Production Limited,
Polmont, Stirlingshire, Scotland
Printed in England by Clays Ltd, St Ives plc

CONTENTS

3. THE LOGIC OF SELF-DECEPTION

4. MORAL PARTIALITY AND HUMAN SOCIABILITY

PREFACE AND ACKNOWLEDGEMENTS

Who are we? Why do we believe what we believe? How are we to live? The essential problems of human existence and fulfilment have no respect for academic boundaries and cataloguing conventions. Specialised knowledge advances, and the mystery and perplexity deepen. Eliminating false answers is easier than facing the real questions. What, in the end, do we know about ourselves? Rationality guides, but does not provide the impulse; science illuminates, but does not satisfy; technological progress speeds up time and opens up a wider gamut of possibilities, but it does not weigh up different options, nor does it choose the aims themselves. The subjective universe in which we are immersed is as real as the objective world in which we work and act. The most intimate, treacherous and defining relationship that a human being has is with himself.

This book approaches the question of self-deception from four distinct and complementary angles. The first is the *identification* of the phenomenon: what is self-deception, and how is it different from the action of deceiving someone else? Another thread of the argument tackles the *explanation* of its existence. Why is self-knowledge such a challenge for human beings, and what are the basic motivations which feed our spontaneous propensity for self-deception? The third line of approach is of a *logical* nature: how is it possible for one and the same person to deceive himself? How do we carry out such feats as believing in what we don't believe in, lying to ourselves and believing the lie, or rowing backwards towards our goal? Lastly, the question of self-deception is dealt with from an *ethical* point of view. What is the place of self-deception in practical existence, both from the point of view of the projects, desires and aspirations of each individual (personal morality), and in the wider perspective of our life together in complex societies (civic morality)?

These four sets of questions on the common theme of self-deception define, with one single exception, the structure and sequence of the book. Chapter 1 is dedicated to the analysis of the repertory of deception in the natural world, the characterisation of self-deception as singularly human, and to the description of the principal forms in which it occurs. The *why* and the *how* of self-deception are dealt with in the two following chapters. While chapter 2 has as its principal focus the precariousness of self-knowledge and the factors which underlie our tendency to self-deception, chapter 3 tackles the paradoxical logic of the phenomenon, and tries to elucidate the twists and turns of self-deceiving promises, particularly in love and politics. In chapter 4, which rounds off the book, I discuss the implications of self-deception for human interaction in society, and the role of impersonal rules in the moderation and prevention of its worst effects.

The great exception – the question which does not fit in to the thematic sequence laid out above – is the discussion of self-deception in the perspective of personal morality. There is a simple reason for this. The theme of the relationship between self-deception and the values, motives and beliefs of individual conduct in ordinary life is the only one which is not confined to any specific chapter of the book, precisely because it is the thread which unites and runs through the argument, from the beginning to the end of the book. From the praise of self-deception in the first chapter (sections 5 to 7), to the discussion of the intertemporal exploitation of a person by himself in the last chapter (section 5), and passing through the epistemology of self-knowledge and the logic of self-deception in the two intermediate chapters, it is questions of personal morality which give unity to the book and define its basic orientation.

Each individual is a microcosm: a complex whole of contradictory forces, and only partially self-aware. For reasons I try to examine in detail in the book, the issues of personal ethics – who am I? what do I want to do with my life? how can I live better, in the individual and collective senses? – turn out to be especially slippery, and vulnerable to the action of a vast repertory of specious evasions in the human mind. If the propensity for self-deception is frequently a curse, this curse also seems to be a source of the bets we make about our unknowable future, and on which depend not only the greatest creative achievements of humanity, but also the savage, inexplicable hope which feeds and sustains us in our lives. Mapping, illustrating and discussing the ethical implications of self-deception in practical existence, while keeping the formation of beliefs, impulses and individual conduct as the chief focuses of the investigation, are the central objectives of this book.

A work like this is inevitably exploratory and incomplete. One can say of self-deception what Socrates said of good and of virtue, and Augustine of time: we all imagine we are familiar with it, but we are incapable of understanding it in a clear and satisfactory way. Worse than simple lack of knowledge, however, is the potent ignorance of false certainty – the cocksure belief of someone who is certain he knows what he does not know. To open ourselves to radical doubt – to the possibility that we might be seriously wrong about ourselves and about the beliefs, passions and values which govern us – is to open ourselves to the opportunity of looking again, and moving forward. It is daring to know *who one is*, so as to be able to rethink life and become *who one can be*.

The analytic philosophy of self-deception is in a way the reverse of the exhortatory therapeutics of self-help. Nothing could be further from this book than the aim of 'curing', converting or convincing anyone to change. I do not believe in the efficacy of homilies and 'cures' in the form of capsules of self-help, just as I am sceptical of the possibility of any form of 'regeneration' by means of moral persuasion. I do, however, believe in the strength of the desire of every human being to do the best he is capable of with his life; and I believe in the Socratic principle that self-knowledge – a clear and critical vision of the values and beliefs which rule our existence – is an indispensable part of the better life within our reach. I hope that the effort of exploration, the sometimes frankly provocative intention, and the innumerable perplexities of this book may in some way contribute not to reducing the frequency of our self-deceptions, but to making them less harmful and more fruitful.

Reading a book is the opportunity for an encounter. When the tone and content of the book are predominantly technical or factual, the terms of the exchange between author and reader tend to be clear and well-defined: what the one offers and the other looks for in the reading are relevant information and the tools to obtain further results. The contact between minds remains on the surface and the degree to which the contents have been assimilated is measurable.

But when we are dealing with a literary or philosophical text, whose content is essentially reflective, as is the case here, the nature of the relationship mediated by the printed word is different. Rather than a simple intellectual exchange between author and reader, the reading is the intertwining of two soliloquies, silent and separated in time: the internal dialogue of the author with himself as he conceives and writes what goes through his mind; and the internal dialogue of the reader with himself as he reads, interprets, assimilates and remembers what he has read.

As someone who spends a good part of his time reading other people's ideas and investigating what happens to them (I teach and research on the history of ideas), I never tire of asking myself: where are we, what are we looking for and what are we thinking about while we read? The testimony of the reader Fernando Pessoa represents an extreme state of an experience that, in variable degrees of intensity, is probably common to all. 'Although I have been a voracious, avid reader', the Portuguese poet Fernando Pessoa says, 'I don't remember any book I have read, to such a degree were my readings states of my own mind, dreams of mine, and, even more, the things which kindled my dreams'.

To read is to recreate. The final word is given not by the person who writes it, but by the one who reads it. The internal dialogue of the author is the seed which produces its fruit (or withers) in the internal dialogue of the reader. It is a mutual challenge, with an unpredictable outcome. There is no such thing as absolute understanding. A misunderstanding – haphazardly leafing through a text which accidentally falls into our hands – may be the beginning of something more creative and valuable than reading something straight through, but in a bureaucratic, mechanical way.

'Authors are actors, books are theatres.' The real plot is the one which goes on in the mind of the reader-interlocutor. Time spent in reading, no less than in literary creation, can be an occasion for a serene encounter, friendly and concentrated – something getting ever harder to find, it seems – with our own subjectivity.

In the internal dialogue which resulted in this book I have tried, above all, to be faithful to myself. In practice this means accepting the challenge of thinking out directly, for myself, and at my own risk, the problem of self-deception, instead of hiding under the protective mantle of what Mário de Andrade once christened, referring to a real occupational hazard amongst Brazilian intellectuals, the 'sedentary exposition of other people's doctrines'. That is why I opted to write a book which does not presuppose any sort of prior expert knowledge, and why I have tried to avoid, as far as possible, the temptation to intersperse the argument developed in the main body of the work with erudite quotations and digressions. As the flesh, however, is weak, I have liberally availed myself of the notes at the end of the book to indulge the passion of the historian of ideas.

The important thing to underline, however, is that in reading the main text one can dispense entirely with consulting the notes and references to be found at the end of the volume. The use of the notes is thus entirely optional, and depends only on the specific interest of the reader in any point addressed in the work. Perhaps the best thing to do while reading, in order to preserve the fluency of the text and the thread of the argument, is simply to ignore the notes.

The composition of a book is an opportunity for new encounters. With the exception of the preface and the notes, this book was wholly written during four stays of a month each in the Pousada Solar da Ponte, in the historic town of Tiradentes, in Minas Gerais. When I went there for the first time, at the beginning of 1996, in search of the seclusion and solitude necessary to concentrate on the composition of the book, I did not know how I would react, and what I would find on the other side. The experience, happily, went beyond my most optimistic hopes. In the serene and welcoming atmosphere of the Pousada – a little work of art set against the delightful backdrop of the town – I found the ideal surroundings I wanted to carry out my work. To John and Anna Maria Parsons and all the staff at the Solar – Suzana, Márcio, Inês, Pedro, Marlene, Bete, Mazé and Siloé – I wish to express my sincere thanks for the generous and cordial hospitality with which they received me. For my part, there remains the memory and the hope of reliving in the future days of mystical happiness and calm fulfilment, like those I was lucky enough to enjoy in Tiradentes.

Several people have read and commented, *viva voce* or in writing, on one or another of the many preparatory sketches for this book. Aware as I am that it would be impossible to acknowledge here all those who, directly or indirectly, contributed to my improving the argument, undertaking more reading, avoiding obscurities and persisting in carrying the work out, I would like to thank: Cleber Aquino, Persio Arida, Ana Maria Bianchi, Carlos Alberto Primo Braga, Antonio Cicero, Renê Decol, Angus Foster, Norman Gall, Carlos Alberto Inada, Celia de Andrade Lessa, Luiz Alberto Machado, Juan Moldau, Verônica de Oliveira, Nilson Vieira Oliveira, Antonio Delfim Netto, Samuel Pessoa, Celso Pinto, Horácio Piva, Rui Proença, José Maria Rodriguez Ramos, Bernardo Ricupero, Carlos Antonio Rocca, Jorge Sabbaga, Pedro Moreira Salles, Luiz Schwarcz, Marcelo Tsuji, Caetano Veloso and Andrea Cury Waslander.

Preliminary versions of the first three chapters were presented and discussed in academic seminars at the Institute for Economic Research at the Faculty of Economics, Administration and Accountancy of the University of São Paulo. I am grateful to the post-graduate students and other participants in these seminars for their interest and their questions and commentaries, some of which were later incorporated into this book.

I would like to offer special thanks to four close friends – Marcos Pompéia, Maria Cecília Gomes dos Reis (Quilha), Luiz Fernando Ramos (Nando) and Tal Goldfajn – who have taken an active part in my adventures along the paths and the hidden ways of self-deception. More than anyone, they were the people with whom I was able to engage in exhaustive, creative and almost uninterrupted dialogue about the ideas, lines of enquiry, investigations and perplexities that I was working on in the book.

This book is dedicated to my mother, Yone, a poet and psychoanalyst. This was the way I found to try to convey, not just to her, but to the other members of my family, the gratitude I feel for the privilege of our life together throughout these years.

I

THE NATURE AND VALUE
OF SELF-DECEPTION

1. The Art of Deception in the
Natural World: Principles

Nature has placed every living thing under the yoke of
two sovereign masters: survival and reproduction. Nothing
escapes. From the single-celled protozoon to the self-styled
Homo sapiens, the preservation of the individual and the
continuation of the species constitute the lowest common
denominator of biological subsistence.[1] Why this is so, no
one knows. What does seem clear is that the risk of extinc-
tion is common to all species, and that not all living things
satisfy the imperatives of survival and procreation with the
same ease. Environmental conditions change according to
random forces, and the powers of an organism do not
always meet the demands defined by its vital needs. Nature
can be generous, but she makes no concessions.

To talk of 'warfare' would be an exaggeration – apart
from sporadic cataclysms, there is at least as much creation
and exuberance as ruin and destruction in the natural flux

1

of life on this planet. What can be observed, however, is that the evolutionary process is marked by fierce competition and conflict, in a dispute over scarce resources. Some environments, it is true, are more demanding than others. But, if they are generously well-endowed for the preservation and reproduction of life, the very proliferation of living things that results from this auspicious fact will take it upon itself to alter the environment and tighten the pressures on each individual. When the environment becomes more demanding, the sieve of selection tightens up: the number of those who don't make it through rises. The challenge of surviving and procreating successfully in nature is a game of cunning and agility, luck and brute force – a game in which not all of those called manage to be chosen.

How far can a living thing go in meeting its biological imperatives? The question sounds puerile when we survey the natural world. Everything seems to point to the fact that nature is blind, obstinate and devoid of scruples. An organism will simply do everything in its power to satisfy its most urgent needs. It will act, driven by the intensity of its urges and satisfactions on the one hand, and constrained by the gamut of possible behaviours open to it, and by the threats and obstacles it comes across, on the other.

But while the ends pursued by all living things are essentially uniform, the means available to pursue them are enormously diverse. The repertory is extraordinary, and contains examples of the most astonishing ingenuity. The art of deception – an organism's use of morphological traits and patterns of behaviour capable of deluding and avoiding the attack and defence systems of other living beings – is a significant part of the arsenal of survival and reproduction in the animal world.

There are deceptions for all tastes. From the simplest to the most complex natural organism, the offensive and defensive use of illusion permeates the whole chain of being. The art of deception needs no conscious premeditation or intentionality on the part of those that practise it. It appears not only in the relationships *between* the members of different species (interspecies), but also, in several cases, in interactions taking place *within* a single species (intraspecies).

The first indications of what lies ahead are already manifest in the realm of molecular life. The functioning of animals' immune systems is based on the automatic operation of mechanisms that protect the organism against the invasion of harmful substances – pathogenic micro-organisms like bacteria, viruses and protozoa. The immune system has a twofold mission: detecting the presence of the invader and dispatching the right artillery of antibodies to eliminate it.

The identification of the pathogenic invader is done by recognising relevant differences between the biochemical composition of the cells that belong to the organism (and so have to be preserved), and that of the harmful substances that don't belong to it (and so must be destroyed). However, it doesn't always work. If an identification error occurs, one of two things may happen: the invader enters just as he wants and has a high old time in the insides of its host, or, as happens in auto-immune diseases, a part of the good cells of the organism is mistakenly destroyed by the disastrous targeting of the defensive battalions.

The internecine warfare that opposes pathogenic invaders and the immune system offers plentiful examples of the practice of camouflage, trickery and misinformation. Several bacteria manage to deceive mammals' immune detection mechanism thanks to the presence of a surface chemical layer that has the property of making them apparently identical to the organism's normal cells. Some viruses, like those of polio, certain types of flu and perhaps HIV, trigger the organism's defences, but only sacrifice minor molecules, using tactics of chemical camouflage to avoid the hostile fire of the antibodies on the crucial molecular targets.[2]

The African trypanosome – a parasitic protozoon transmitted by the tsetse fly and responsible for sleeping sickness – goes further. As it penetrates the human circulatory system, it displays a protein that acts as a bait, sets off the alarm-bells in the immune system and prompts a speedy and vigorous reaction. The trouble is that, when the shock-troops of the antibodies are ready to do battle and massacre the invader, the trypanosome has already changed its armour and is displaying another variant of the same protein, thus neutralising the first line of defence, and provoking the call-up of another battalion of antibodies. At the moment a new engagement is imminent, however, it is suspended by another alteration in the chemical surface of the invader. In this manner, the protein-bait and manifold surface variations follow hard on each other's heels – the trypanosome carries genes for more than a thousand analogous manoeuvres – until, finally, the infection becomes chronic and the host organism succumbs (no wonder!) to a profound lethargy.

A fertile soil for the propagation of the flora of deception

– in spite of its innocent appearance – is the vegetable realm. Some plants, like, for example, the Venus's fly-trap (*Dionaea muscipula*), exhibit a pseudo-flower that works as an ambush to attract, trap, and swallow insects. Although it is perfectly useless from the point of view of the plant's reproduction, the pseudo-flower is vital when the next meal is at stake.

Several plants, in their turn, mimic the look and smell of dry faeces to attract flies and beetles in search of food and a suitable site to lay their eggs. When they become aware of the trick, the insects begin the search again, and inadvertently pollinate the neighbouring impostors. Defensive camouflage is a ruse typical of plants growing in the harsh environment of semi-arid regions. As their only chance of escaping the hungry eye of the local herbivores is *not to strike the eye*, many species of plants in such regions end up acquiring an evasive aspect and coloration, similar to indigestible substances like dry bushes, dead branches, dry grass and gravel.

A place of honour is reserved in the flora of vegetable deceit for the delicate and numerous family of the orchids – there exist about fifteen thousand classified species. Orchids reproduce by means of allogamy: the process of fertilisation demands that the pollen on one flower should be mixed with the stigma of another. How can the distance between them be bridged? The solution is to resort to the promise of sex.

Different types of orchid have specialised in attract-ing different types of insect, seducing them with sexual stimulants that recall the aspect, coloration, and smell of their respective females. However, inciting them merely to approach the flower, attracted by the promise of sex, is not enough. For the pollination to be successful, the insect has to be stirred to get on top of the flower, feel it close and be roused to the point of a pseudo-copulation with it. Only thus will the pollen-sacs be fixed onto its body, and be carried and joined with the sexual organ of another orchid.

What is astonishing is the degree of refinement and sophistication some orchids have reached in the simulation of the attractions of certain female insects. For the bees of the *Andrena* genus, for example, the delightfulness and charm of the flowers of the *Ophrys litea* seem to surpass the allure of their real females. Given the choice, in an experimental situation, the majority of males turned out to prefer to indulge in the glorious, illusory sex of pseudo-copulation.[3] The copy outdoes the original. Deceitful advertising?

2. The Art of Deception in the Animal World: Applications

As we go up the evolutionary scale, advancing towards the animal kingdom and the intelligent primates, the repertoire of deception widens and proliferates. Unlike micro-organisms and plants, animals are not restricted to *morphological* resources – those linked to the form and external properties of the organism – in the art of deluding their neighbours. The novelty is the emergence of *behavioural* variations and strategies, that progressively tend to dominate the spectacle of deception in the natural world. Along with the mask that provides disguise, we now have the gesture that deludes the onlooker.

6

What can we expect from an insect? If morphology gets in the way, cunning solves the problem. The African bug *Acanthaspis petax* has developed a wily technique for using some ants in order to eat others. First, it hunts some isolated ants and sticks their carcasses onto its own body. Thus disguised, it sets off in the direction of the juiciest anthill in the area, goes in unmolested, and feasts happily within on the dish of its dreams. If there are no isolated ants to conceal itself with, the bug repeats the hoax, this time using fragments of earth and sand. If the Venus's fly-trap, with its pseudo-flower, is the botanical equivalent of Homer's siren song, this African bug is a biological version of the Trojan horse.

The rise in behavioural flexibility also brings into play the practice of intraspecies opportunism based on deception. This can be seen, for example, in the case of some varieties of house-fly in which the male courts the female by offering her some food as a gift. As the female attacks the food and gorges on it, the male takes advantage of this and mates with her. Nothing surprising up to now: there is no illusion or trick, just a sadly familiar exchange of equivalents. The hoax only appears at the moment when a heterodox male of the same species appears, who mimics the interested female, manages to induce an upright male into offering him the morsel, and, at the moment of coitus, grabs the food and skedaddles. With pseudo-transvestites like this one, the defrauded fly can't even get a paltry pseudo-copulation.

Another example of intraspecies opportunism based on deceit is that of the bluegill sunfish (*Lepomis macrochirus*). The normal male of this species needs to make a sizeable paternal investment to have the chance of procreating.

He prepares the place where fertilisation will happen by constructing a large number of nests where the female, duly courted, can come and deposit her eggs. The male then fertilises the eggs and guards the nests, protecting them against predators until the young are hatched.

There is, however, a well-defined variety of the male sunfish that, because it attains sexual maturity precociously – aged two instead of seven – cannot compete with others in the search for and preparation of suitable places for procreation. Of course, that doesn't stop them trying. Their trick is to infiltrate themselves at the right moment into others' nests, and unload their gametes onto any eggs that might be there. Once this incursion is over, these precocious fish lose no time: they set sail to other nests and leave the defrauded sentinels to look after 'their' offspring. While they are young, the precocious males have the size and look of the females; when they grow and attain maturity, they switch to disguising their furtive incursions by acquiring the females' coloration and demeanour.[4]

A similar short-cut, although availing itself of the unwitting aid of other species, is taken by the cuckoo (*Cuculus canorus*). Apart from its ability to imitate the vocal timbre of several birds, the cuckoo has become specialised in the art of laying its eggs in the nests of other species of birds. If the target-nest is too small for the female cuckoo to lay her egg directly in it she lays the egg on the ground and carries it in her beak to the nest, taking advantage of the momentary absence of the host. The cuckoo's secret is to lay eggs with an external aspect like those of the host's. Importantly, too, she has to take care not to abuse hospitality: *only one egg*, each time, in the stranger's nest. It seems that the caution pays off. In spite of the aggressiveness of the cuckoo chick

– when it is born it sets about destroying the other eggs and throwing its mystified 'brothers' out of the nest – cuckoos' eggs have been found in the nests of 180 different species of birds.

The analysis of the art of deception in the natural world reveals that the repertoire of illusion gravitates around two basic stratagems. There is deception by *hiding*, which is based on camouflage, mimicry and dissimulation; and there is deception by *active misinformation*, based on practices like bluff, hoaxing and the manipulation of attention.

In the first case, deception derives from a negative illusion: the discrepancy between reality and appearance here consists in not letting oneself be seen, and so inducing the other organism *not to see what is there*. This is the case of the chameleon; of furtive toads who intercept females attracted by other males; of the polar bear and all animals that practise dissimulation to avoid predators and rivals, or to get closer to their prey. In the hiding game, the more imperceptible the better.

In deception by active misinformation, the illusion is a positive one. The discrepancy between reality and appearance consists in leading an organism to *see* things, to form mistaken images or to be momentarily distracted; in short, to *see something that is not there*.

A bewildering variety of occurrences belong to this mode. Witness the case, for example, of the rattlesnake, with its hypnotic rattle casting a spell over its victim; of foxes that feign death to put predators off, and emit false alarm cries to frighten the other members of the pack and keep the food to themselves; of the false coral-snake, with its coloration, loud and identical to that of the feared poisonous coral-snake; of female insects that emit luminous signals to attract males and devour them; of lizards that dupe their predators by detaching their tails; of reptiles that swell up and mammals that let their hair stand on end to seem bigger than they are in dangerous situations; of elephants that rush into attack but don't attack, or, to give a final example, of dogs that bark and aggressively show their teeth, but, when it comes to a fight, run for it. In deception by active misinformation, the more like the real thing, the better.

There is no way of finding out what happens in the mind of an animal that deceives another – that is, if the notion of mind makes any sense here. The existence of subjective life in animals, although plausible in some cases, cannot be proved. If it is sometimes hard to know what is going on inside our own heads (even though nobody seems able to deny that *something* goes on in there), what can we say of the hypothetical subjectivity of a sunfish, a lizard, a cuckoo or a pet dog?[5]

It is difficult, too, to determine to what degree a given type of animal deception is the result of genetics, environmental pressure, the learning process or a combination of factors. What does seem clear, however, is that when we come to the human species' closest evolutionary relatives – anthropoid primates like the chimpanzees, gorillas, and orang-utans – new continents are unveiled for the exercise of deception. Behavioural flexibility helps; language – its absence, that is – sets the limit.

The inventiveness of the primates seems to be the result of a fusion of cognitive and behavioural elements – not only the ability to learn and infer, but also a propensity to improvise and experiment in the search for solutions. The detailed accounts of ethologists who have specialised in the observation and study of different groups and species of apes, in the wild and in captivity, show the versatility of their actions and reactions when faced with new situations and opportunities. In some specific cases, involving inter-actions that are both *inter* and *intra*species, the practice of deception seems to come close to conscious deliberation and premeditation.

The repertoire of deception amongst the primates includes tricks both of hiding, and of active misinformation. A young, subaltern chimpanzee, for example, has to avoid the aggressiveness of the dominant males. But this isn't going to stop him showing his true colours when he can. One way is to use his hands. When a junior chimpanzee has an erection, he is able to use his hand judiciously to hide the fact from any dominant male who might be around, but taking the necessary care that the female he's interested in may not be in the least deprived of this conclusive proof of his virility. Strategically showing and hiding the genitals is a part of the rhetoric of conflict and seduction amongst the anthropoids.

Another stratagem common in certain primates to avoid the physical aggression of any threatening-looking male is to pretend to be hurt, by ostentatiously limping, for example. When the potential aggressor is nearby, the monkey limps; as soon as he disappears from the scene, the monkey walks normally again; but, if the other should come back again, the monkey suffers a sudden 'relapse'. Consistency of character – 'if you are taking the risk of forming a new character, let it remain to the end as it was when introduced, and keep it true to itself', as Horace proposes in the *Ars poetica* (ll. 126–27) – is one of the basic rules of good narrative fiction.

Episodes of attention-manipulation and of control of the expression of emotions are also frequent. One of the favourite techniques used by students of primate behaviour is the so-called 'hidden food problem'. How does a monkey deal with a situation in which he alone had the chance to observe where a succulent bunch of bananas has been hidden?

The variations on the same story and the answers obtained in different situations, involving not only relations between monkeys, but also between them and human actors, are enough to fill a treatise. From outright solidarity to utter rapacity, everything seems possible. A commonly observed response is prolonged, manipulative, calculatedly egotistical dissimulation. A monkey is capable of feigning ignorance for hours, right near the hiding-place, so making sure that the other members of the troupe don't get to know about his precious secret. Later, when all except him are asleep, his 'amnesia' ends. The monkey furtively returns to the hiding-place, grabs the bananas, and decamps.

This all happens, of course, in silence. What if monkeys could talk? The challenge of teaching some kind of human language to monkeys has been provoking the patience and ingenuity of ethologists for generations. However, considering the effort expended, the results up to now have been derisory. The first attempts, based on oral communication, led nowhere. Although they are ready to 'monkey' practically anything men do, the anthropoids are a complete fiasco when it comes to vocalisation. Better results are being obtained with the use of communication by means of hand signs and gestures (deaf-and-dumb language). But the utmost achieved up to now has been to teach a vocabulary of about 130 sign-gestures, that are basically used, with rare and doubtful exceptions, to express local, tangible desires like 'food', 'play', 'scratch' etc. In the realm of syntax, grammar and the decontextualised use of language, the highest mark obtained so far by a simian was near zero.[6]

The curious thing about all this is that, even though it is precarious from the linguistic point of view, the competence of monkeys and apes in the use of language is sufficient to betray their strong propensity for the practice of deception. Once a certain – still rudimentary – point in the acquisition of language has been reached, they seem to realise the new possibilities open to them.

The wiles of Chantek – a male orang-utan who underwent an intensive regime learning to communicate by means of hand-gestures – are a good illustration.[7] In normal situations, Chantek was able to convey to his educators signs evincing some desire or asking for some kind of attention. Of course, his requests were not always granted. What he began to perceive with time, however, is that the use of certain specific terms – like the sign 'dirty' expressing the desire to go to the bathroom, for example – invariably produced the desired effect. Why not use the effectiveness of this gesture for other ends?

It was then that Chantek taught his teachers something completely new. He began to use the sign 'dirty', supposedly manifesting his desire to leave the room to use the latrine, but when he was led to the bathroom by his trainers, he 'lost the urge', and began happily to play with the soap and the tap. It did not take long for this discovery to be generalised. Chantek soon realised that terms other than 'dirty' – gestures indicating 'hug', 'lower down', 'be careful' or 'listen', for instance – could also lend themselves to other uses and aims, in the most varied contexts. The astute manipulation of language became, ironically, his best ruse for interrupting and getting out of an excessively boring training session.

It was in this context, finally, that the trainers managed to extract what is still perhaps the most astute expression of language yet made by an ape. It seems that, when he saw that he was about to be admonished for yet another of his mischievous games with language, Chantek, cornered and contrite, gestured in his own defence: 'Chantek good'. Self-deception?

3. The Anthropomorphic Bias in the Mirror of Nature

Nothing is everything. Time, space and condition impose, to some extent, perspectives, angles and filters. The past and the future can only be conceived from the point of view of the present; the near and the distant can only be defined from a given point; the remote presupposes and reflects what is familiar. If animals seem to us to be deprived of scruples and a moral sense as they pursue their goals, how do we, human beings, seem to *them* as we pursue ours? Anthropomorphism can be partially mitigated, but not completely eradicated. Even were an animal to speak with the effortlessness of a human being, we would still have to question, understand and interpret it. However objective it may be, human knowledge carries stamped on its forehead the indelible mark of our humanity – the strong selectivity imposed by the web of human perceptions, categories and interests.

Nature in its totality, just like history, is an inexhaustible pool – a storehouse of facts, processes and events with which one can prove practically anything or its opposite. That same nature that led a Stoic philosopher to portray it as providential and harmonious, to the point of setting it up as a moral standard and trying to live according to it (*naturam sequi*), led ancient atomists to conceive of it as a blind, implacable force, the mere self-propelled result of physical laws alien to any ethical principle.

In analogous fashion, that same nature that the Romantic exalts as the supreme fount of knowledge and virtue – 'The axioms of physics translate the laws of ethics [. . .] every natural process is a version of a moral sentence; the moral law lies at the centre of nature and radiates to the circumference' (Emerson) – leads a cosmic pessimism to see it as the lair of morbid, perverted lusts: 'the battleground of tormented and agonised beings who continue to exist only by devouring each other' (Schopenhauer). When we contemplate nature, what do we see? Heraclitus weeps, Democritus laughs. If Rousseau idolises it and kneels before it in tears, Baudelaire demonises, mocks and is repelled by it.[8] Nature is anything that is the case.

Obviously, not everything is the case. The practice of deception in the natural world is part of a whole. It is only *one* of the innumerable strategies – co-operation and open conflict, for example, are others – by which living beings face the challenge of survival and reproduction. But its apparent ubiquity in both inter and intraspecies relationships, permeating the vast chain that goes from the molecule to the primate, makes one think. How far, we might ask first of all, are we justified in talking about 'deception' in the interactions between living organisms in the natural world? Are we incurring a larger degree of anthropomorphism than advisable, given the search for scientific objectivity?

The risk of overstepping the mark in attributing human traits to non-human beings is a real one. It appears clearly, for example, in the investigation of one minefield: the subjectivity and emotional life of animals. It is no accident that many ethologists prefer to ban terms like 'anger' and 'fear' from their researches, substituting for them expressions like 'a manifestation of aggressive behaviour' and 'a defensive impulse to flee'. What at first sight may look like an overly antiseptic mode of expression may seem more understandable when one examines the excesses of lyrical anthropomorphism in speculations about the elephant's weeping, the hyena's cruelty, parrots' shyness, the boredom of grazing animals, or dolphins' happiness. The same thing can be said of imputing human social relationships to the animal world as, for instance, in the supposed practice of rape among the orang-utans or of slavery among ants.[9]

Deception doesn't go so far. Our first care is to dissociate the notion of deception in the animal world from any attribution of specific subjective configurations to those participating in a relationship, or any connotation of conscious premeditation or intentionality in the action.

Of course, in the examples presented earlier, several anthropomorphic peccadilloes were committed – bees attracted by the 'promise' of sex; 'deluded' flies; sunfish that 'don't stop trying', and so on. This type of slip-up, however, is quite unimportant. Its presence in the text simply reflects the rhetorical desire to write lively prose and entertain the reader. The fact is that all the examples given, with the possible exception of the ape Chantek, could be rewritten to eliminate any residuum of explicit anthropomorphism, that is to say, anything out of place in a description governed by the standard of objectivity associated with explanations formulated on the basis of the exclusive operation of the mechanisms of natural selection. This would not guarantee, of course, the empirical validity of the examples or the theoretical truth of the explanation, but at least it would remove the suspicion of crass anthropomorphism.

The real threat of anthropomorphic bias comes from another direction. *Deception* is a particular type of relation between two living beings – an interaction in which the morphology and/or the behaviour of one of them creates a discrepancy between reality and appearance that muddies the perceptions and modifies the action of the other. From a certain perspective, the notion of deception is strictly as human as, say, that of gravity, that is, the law according to which bodies are attracted to one another in the exact proportion of the inverse of the square of the distance between them. What we have in each case are general and abstract concepts constructed by man with the aim of organising sense experience and shedding light on a defined range of phenomena. From another point of view, however, the notion of deception really does seem to suffer from a greater degree of anthropomorphic bias than is the case with gravity or other concepts of modern science.

Suppose a world just like ours, but from which the human species has disappeared. It is not difficult to imagine that in such a world the relation of attraction between bodies will go on obeying the law of gravity: the absence of a human observer does not alter this reality. But is this the case with deception? It's doubtful. The orchid and the bee, it's true, don't need us to continue their idyll. But would there be any sense in attributing the characteristic of *deception* in a universe in which humanity no longer exists? To talk about deception – or, for that matter, co-operation or open conflict – is to impute a content to that relationship that makes sense from the point of view of what is relevant *to us*, human beings, but not, as far as one can tell, to others who participate in the relationship, or to the other beings who inhabit the planet.

To speak of the occurrence of deception in the natural world seems, then, to presuppose the existence of an external observer capable of discerning and discriminating a particular type of interaction in the relationships between other organisms. That is what gives them the meaning of deception. Unlike gravity, whose reality has no need of any external attribution of meaning, deception has no existence independent of the perspective that humanity has on life. Changes in outside temperature, to give another example, would continue to exist in the world even if there were no people and no thermometers to register them. But can we say the same thing of the occurrence of deceptions in nature? I think not. It is people who bring deception into the world, even if afterwards they find it everywhere around and within themselves. It is a human judgement, made on the basis of human experience.

As we reflect on the relationship of deception in the natural world we need also to take into account the possibility that many other things, beyond those that we know of as things stand, may also be happening. As Heraclitus long ago pointed out, 'nature likes to hide herself' (fragment 123). What seems to us deception pure and simple, on the basis of what we know about the interaction, may no longer be, if we discover something new about it, such as the existence of some concrete benefit derived by the deceived animal as it interacts with the deceiver.

What we perceive as we observe any given relationship between organisms in the natural world is based: a) on what our senses and our scientific instruments apprehend; b) on what our mental categories allow us to think about; and, c) on what our curiosity, pragmatic or idle, is looking for. Reality, however, is certainly much larger than that, and can force us to look again in an unexpected and radical fashion at a good part of what seemed cut and dried to us. Nothing, in short, rules out the risk that we might be wrong not only about details, but about the essentials, turning the network of relationships between living beings into a kind of *Othello* without Desdemona.

Suppose, for the sake of the argument, that an extraterrestrial super-scientist is conducting from space an investigation into the sexual habits of human beings. At a certain moment in his researches, he comes across a curious fact: the adolescent males of the species *Homo sapiens* get sexually excited, and many of them habitually masturbate while leafing through erotic magazines. What might he deduce from this observation? Would he be justified in concluding that young humans are usually *deceived* by photographic images that imitate the visual aspect of the females of the species, even though it is only a thin layer of ink printed on paper? To reach a hypothesis a little less absurd, the extraterrestrial would evidently need to know something about what happens in the mind of a young man excited by erotic images, and about the human faculty of being able to go along with one's own fantasies, knowing all the while that they are fantasies. Some of our hypotheses about deception in nature may turn out to be as mistaken as those of the extraterrestrial about us.

Nothing is everything. Reflected light illuminates projected light. Nature is also a mirror. As we reflect on the tangled, exuberant forest of deceptions that we find within it, nature is not only reflecting what *she*, to a great extent, possibly *is*; she is at the same time reflecting back on us what *we are*: projecting on humanity our own reflection on the world. The knowledge of the practice of deception in the natural world is a two-way street: tentatively coming to know *an other*, however distant and alien he may seem, is tentatively to know *oneself*. The return is the continuation of the outward journey. Thinking about man from nature's perspective presupposes thinking about nature from man's perspective.

The all-too-human art of deception is not the isolated, inexplicable aberration of a being who lost his innocence when he was expelled from paradise. It is the expression of our profound kinship with everything that is born, lives and dies – the continuation, by other means, and with other resources, of a vast repertoire of deceptions, both by means of hiding and by active misinformation, in the natural world. *Natura non facit saltum.* 'He who [would] understand [the] baboon', the young Darwin jotted down in his early philosophical notebooks, 'would do more towards metaphysics than Locke.'[10] True enough. The only trouble is finding out how to get rid of metaphysics in our attempts to understand the baboon.

4. *The Big Bang of Language in the Universe of Deception*

In the beginning was deception. What's harder to know is, *who deceived whom?* First Adam, ashamed of his own act, tries to deceive God: he hides with Eve amongst the trees of the Garden of Eden. Discovered, however, he admits before God the betrayal of the promise not to touch the forbidden fruit. What Adam then tries is to escape the blame by accusing Eve of having seductively offered him it. Eve, in her turn, responds to the divine questioning by pointing the accusing finger at the serpent: it had deceived her and persuaded her to try the fruit. But what did the serpent say? It told Eve that the threat made by God was a deception – they would not die when they ate the fruit, but their eyes would be opened and they would become like God in the ability to discern good and evil.

That was precisely what happened. Adam and Eve not only did *not* die, but, in the words of God himself, fearful now that they might try the fruit of immortality: 'Behold, the man has become like one of us, knowing good and evil' (Genesis, 3:22). The feelings of shame and guilt, did, it's true, contaminate the minds of the first couple; but the fruit *did bring* divine knowledge, and *did not* kill them.

Are we to conclude that God lied, then? That he tried to stifle the human aspiration to knowledge and transcendence with a false threat? Not necessarily. In the literal sense of the truth, however strange it may seem, the serpent was more honest than God. What transpires, however, is that the death which God referred to in his threat was not the sudden and literal death of the organism, but the

21

anticipation of death – the sharp awareness of the bitter condition of finiteness that links us to and tears us apart from every living thing.[11] The original deception of the Fall, then, originated, it seems, from a *misunderstanding* of the divine word. The serpent did not lie. What it did was exploit the opening provided by a spontaneous misunderstanding, that is, by the naive attribution of literal truth to a threat that was just as real. It was by this small breach – the supposed divine lie – that the serpent's cunning managed to get in and impregnate Eve's innocence.

There was more in store, of course, for the first couple's offspring. Faced by such an apparently non-malicious deception as that of Adam and Eve in Eden, a more humane and less vengeful deity could perhaps have made his the words of the crucified Christ – 'Forgive them, for they know not what they do' (Luke, 23:34) – and given them another chance. That didn't happen. After the Fall, and only because of human transgression of their limits, nature itself was accursed and corrupted. If Prometheus paid for the fire he purloined from the gods with the torture of his entrails devoured by vultures, the price of the knowledge stolen by the biblical couple fell not only on them but on the whole of humanity and the natural world. It is only from that moment on that, according to the Genesis myth (3:16–19), two universal torments begin to have sway in human existence: our *precarious survival*, by means of hard work and the sweat of one's brow, and *agonised procreation*, marked by the excruciating pains of childbirth.

To believe that a text like the Scriptures, endowed with infinite suggestiveness, can have *a single* correct interpretation is a mistake that has consumed innumerable lives in the past, and that we need not repeat. As Montaigne observes, 'to an atheist all writings make for atheism'. 'The volumes of interpreters and commentators on the Old and New Testament', says Locke, 'are but too manifest a proof of this. Though every thing said in the text be infallibly true, yet the reader may be, nay cannot choose but be very fallible in the understanding of it.'[12]

The text tempts the reader to read and interpret it. The illusion of final understanding is a seductive fruit within reach of the fallible mind: *believing is biting*. The notion that from the encounter between the serpent's truth and Eve's naive literalness was born the original mistake of the Fall is only one possible reading amongst a (literal) infinitude of others. But what the chain of deceits and incriminations in the biblical narrative of the Creation expressively reveals is that, with the entry of the human animal onto the scene, the spectacle of deception in the world takes on new colour and dramatic intensity.

The conquest of the gift of language, it is plain, represented a veritable 'big bang' in the expansion of the universe of deception. In relationships *between* man and the other biological species, as we will see, the role of language in the art of deception is necessarily limited and indirect. But when we turn to the *intraspecies* relationships of the human animal, including of course the reflections and conversations of the individual with himself, it would be difficult to overestimate the vastness of the field of possibilities for deception and self-deception that the use of language affords. It is in the parallel cosmos of human subjectivity mediated by language that the art of deception finds its true element and reaches fulfilment.

The physical universe and the biological organisms that

inhabit it don't let themselves be deceived by the linguistic cunning of human beings. It is easier to imagine that *we* hear the stars than to presume that *they* might hear us. No amount of sweet-talking could persuade a fish not to flee from its predators, or the polio virus to lodge elsewhere.

What language does permit, however, is an exchange of information and a co-ordination of actions that make us able to manipulate the natural world for our own benefit. The fisherman learns his skill and uses a bait to catch the fish. Preventive medicine pits the vaccine's ruse against polio's: when the virus penetrates the organism, it finds an army of antibodies already trained (against a bogus enemy, of course) to identify and crush it. It is no accident that the first act by which Adam affirmed his rule over all the animals – and so prepared the ground for the practice of deception en masse – was naming them.

The power of deception via physical interference in the organism succeeds in making a living being leave aside its deepest biological impulses. A plant that has its genes modified doesn't close and shed its leaves merely because autumn has come and winter is near; it traverses the seasons of the year without stopping, as if it were in the warm tropics, and goes on producing its flowers and fruits in the middle of the European autumn and winter.

An experiment with rats cuts the link between pleasure and the satisfaction of biological urges. A rat with electrodes implanted in its brain is induced to push a lever that stimulates its lateral hypothalamus with a small electric current. The activity is supposedly so pleasurable and gratifying for the rat that it will repeat it in a compulsive manner for hours and hours on end, even to the point of losing interest in eating and drinking (not to mention sex). The result: death from exhaustion.[13]

It's worth pointing out that the same principle of organic misinformation appears in several technological feats that help us get round at least some of the torments and plagues that can be laid at Adam's door. Anaesthetic, for example, suppresses the pain sensation in pain, making us no longer feel what we feel. A sleeping pill lulls the wakefulness of the person unable to sleep, infiltrating somnolence into the last hiding-place of insomnia. In the same fashion, though by another route, the contraceptive pill tricks the woman's organism, making it work partially *as if* she were already pregnant, when she really is not.

When we ask for the application of an anaesthetic or swallow certain kinds of substance we are interfering chemically – in a quite specific way – in the functioning of our organism. We are disseminating chemical information into our metabolism with the object of annulling or altering the natural processes by means of which the organism reacts to the stimuli it receives. We are, in short, practising self-deception in the most palpable and literal sense of the term.

All of this belongs, of course, to the non-linguistic repertoire of deception. The manipulation is of a physical order, and takes place in the silence of nature. The phenomenon of interference, even if not the deception itself, can be observed and measured from without, and satisfies the most demanding criterion of scientific objectivity. The maxim attributed to the atomist Democritus is valid here: 'Speech is the shadow of action' (fragment 145). It would make no difference, at least up to this point, if the whole of subjective human experience were like the music of the spheres that the Pythagorean mystics spoke of – nothing more than a harmless and enchanting fantasy haunting the objective mechanism of things.

But when we turn from relationships *between* man and natural objects (including the human body and brain) to the relationships of men *amongst themselves* (including that of a person with his own subjective life), the picture changes radically. True, the biological and the material – the subterranean force of the imperatives common to everything in existence – do not stop operating. But the overwhelming subjectivity of the human experience of life invades and completely takes over the scene. The psychological and the symbolic transfigure the plot and begin to dominate the show. On the stage of human relationships – just as in dramatic fiction itself, religious and profane – it is actions that become, to a large extent, the shadows of speech.

Although it is given enormous extra power by the gift of language, the human propensity for deception has pre-linguistic roots. The human baby learns to deceive even before it learns to speak.

A brief episode from my own experience as a father helps to illustrate the point. When my first son was a little less than a year old, I took him in my lap one morning and decided to show him that it was possible *to play with his own crying*. I simulated as well as I could the sound and facial expression of his crying, brought my face close to his shoulder, and, straight away, looked at him laughing and making fun of what I had done. The idea was to repeat this a few times, to see how he would react.

At first, of course, he stared at me with an astonished look and seemed intrigued. In a matter of minutes, however, as I repeated the same sequence and invited him to laugh with me at my own weeping, he began to enjoy the game and laugh too. The crowning moment was when he imitated what I was doing: he briefly simulated a crying expression and straight away laughed. I was euphoric. I imagined – without realising, of course, what I was doing – that I had taught my son that he could laugh at his own tears, and so to see himself from the outside, that is, to bear a little more easily the moments when some need or discomfort might make him cry.

These were merely the fond illusions of a father. In practice what happened was that he realised, even earlier than would happen spontaneously with any baby, that he had a new and powerful weapon in his hands. Soon he began to simulate his own crying, not with the idea of playing, but to affirm his will and attract his parents' attention. It seems no exaggeration to assume that the linguistic initiation of the human baby is directly associated with the perception, acquired very early on, that he can manipulate the reaction and the attention of adults by means of sounds.

In this light, the child's linguistic apprenticeship is not reduced to the bare acquisition of a technique of communication based on vocabulary, syntax, and grammatical rules. What is essentially in play is the gradual discovery by the child, by means of trial and error, of what it is possible to do, that is, how far one can go with the use of language in the satisfaction of one's desires. Experimentation in the art of deception is a central component of this apprenticeship. As Jean Piaget observes, in his classic work on the psychological and moral development of the child, 'the tendency to lie is a natural one, whose spontaneity and universality show how much it forms a part of the egocentric thinking of the child [. . .] still, at age six, the child really feels no

27

internal obstacle to the practice of lying [. . .] he lies more or less as he invents or plays'.[14]

Nothing, of course, comes from nowhere. The innocence of the human animal in its formative stages is above all suspicion. If the child *is as he is*, it is because he has someone to take after. At least on this point, it seems, religion and science are in complete agreement. If the Darwinian ape plays merry hell with the first sliver of language to come out of his hands, Adam's offspring are not far behind. Questioned by God about Adam's whereabouts, Cain replied: 'I do not know; am I my brother's keeper?' (Genesis, 4:9). The sublime idea that one can hoodwink a divine being was not born yesterday.

With the arrival of language, then, the art of deception comes into its own. To the basic repertoire of the natural world – restricted to the operation of morphological and behavioural factors in the practice of deception by hiding and active misinformation – is added that extraordinary generator of discrepancies between reality and appearance that is the linguistic factor.[15] A bare-faced lie, like the one attributed to God by the serpent, is only one end of an ample spectrum, to which belong exaggeration, subtle omissions, distortion and diversionary tactics. At the other end of the spectrum is the spontaneous, involuntary interpersonal deception, well captured in the words of Machado de Assis: 'How many wicked intentions there are that take advantage of a half-truth like this, expressed in an innocent, pure phrase! It makes one think that lying is, at times, as involuntary as perspiration'.[16] It is by this innocent tip of involuntary interpersonal deception that we approach the road that leads to self-deception.

5. *The Innocent Spectrum of Self-Deception*

Intra-organic self-deception, as we have seen, is a rough but open game. It is *chemistry* against *chemistry*: the chemical information coming from outside is introduced into the metabolism and temporarily subdues the effect of the native chemical information. If you feel lethargic and melancholy, for instance, an anti-depressant with a serotonin base may bring the relief that perhaps no effort of will, memory or conversation could bring. More than that: if it occurs to you that you feel more energetic just because you took the medicine, this may worry you a bit, but it will not put a stop to your new-found vigour.

A little more delicate is the situation in which self-deception is the result of a deliberate attempt to manipulate the environment so as to furtively alter certain habits and propensities. Suppose I have a problem with arriving on time, and that, in spite of all my efforts to be more punctual, I persist in arriving late at my appointments for lectures and talks. A possible way out would be for me to put my alarm-clock or my watch forward by half-an-hour, so as to compensate for my natural lateness. The secret of this tactic is *not to remember*. As long as I 'manage to forget' that the information I am receiving is false, all is well; but, if I begin to remember the truth every time I consult my watch, I begin to make the relevant 'discount' and am back to square one. The problem, of course, is that I can't remember to forget: the forgetting has to be as innocent as my lateness.

This type of self-deception, however, based on the manipulation of counter-information from outside the individual, is a minor and secondary ramification in the repertoire of self-deception. The main trunk is made up of *intrapsychic* self-deception, that is, where the person's mind manages in some way to manipulate and delude itself. This is a far more rarefied game – after all, it is a *mental* against *mental* classic – and it is anything but open and above-board. An underlying good faith, however absurd and unjustified it may seem to others, is fundamental.

The most extreme point in the spectrum of intrapsychic self-deception is *hallucination*.[17] Hallucination in the technical sense of the term should not be confused with sensorial illusion and reverie. It is distinguished from the first because it doesn't depend on external stimuli to trigger it: if you hear part of a melody on the radio, and think for a few moments that it was another song, you were simply mistaken; but if you *hear* part of some melody, without there having been any sound stimulus external to your own mind, you *might* be having a hallucination.

Understanding the difference between hallucination and reverie allows us to define the phenomenon more precisely. If you sing a favourite song in silence as you walk along the street and amuse yourself that way, you are engaged in reverie. But, if you *clearly hear* João Gilberto singing 'The girl from Ipanema', to the point where you get up to find out where the radio is, only to realise that there is no radio, or any audio equipment playing that song, you're having a hallucination. The auditory experience, in this case, unlike reverie, has a hallucinatory clarity.

The variety most studied by specialists in the topic of hallucination is the experience called the 'phantom limb'. People who lose a limb, like a hand or an arm, in an accident, war, or an operation, frequently go on feeling the non-existent limb as if nothing had happened. Their subjective experience denies and contradicts the new bodily reality. They continue to experience the tactile sensations of pain, itching or simple contact that they would have were the hand or arm still there.

One of the most curious varieties of this type of occurrence is the 'hijacking of the neural circuits'. There are cases when another part of the body, for example one of the sides of the face, begins to receive the tactile sense-impressions that correspond to the lost limb, the hand, let's say. When his face is touched by someone's finger, the person has the exact sensation that his 'hand' has been touched. What happens in these cases, it seems, is that the part of the brain that used to receive and process the sensorial information from the amputated hand has been in some way hijacked by the part of the brain that fulfils an analogous function for that side of the face.[18] (The erotic possibilities opened up by hijackings of this kind are incalculable . . .)

Hallucination is intrapsychic self-deception in a pure state: clear and crystalline, but far removed from ordinary life. Much more familiar than hallucination, and, happily, outside the annals of medical pathology, are some of its popular neighbours in the repertoire of self-deception: *dreaming* proper and *daydreaming*. It is arguable whether animals dream like us; the universality of dreams amongst human beings, with no distinctions as to time, ethnic group or culture, would be hard to question.

Our subjective experience of life is *bifurcated*. Everyone, when he goes to sleep, removes himself from the world in which he lives and acts, and retires to a universe all his own. When he awakes, however, he sometimes realises he has *dreamed* – he remembers, more or less clearly, perceptual, emotional, reflective and narrative experiences that he must have gone through in the recesses of the mind while he was asleep. Time, space, and common logic go to sleep: the dead visit the living; a crucifix burns in hell; the Emperor Marcus Aurelius reads a medical prescription; a nuclear missile blasts off; Pelé as a child smiles; lovers suck at one another like roots; Descartes glimpses geometrical patterns. While it is being dreamed, the dream's subjective reality is absolute. To dream that you are only dreaming is as real a dream as any other. 'When we dream that we are dreaming', says the German poet and thinker Novalis, 'then we are near to waking'.[19]

Whether or not the substance of each person's dreams obeys some general explanatory principle is of no importance here. What is relevant about dreams from the point of view of self-deception is that they are something intensely lived as *real and genuine while we are dreaming*, but it turns out that they were *just a dream* when we awake. The mind of the person dreaming plunges entirely into the subjective truth of the fiction that it tells itself.

A dream is not something that can be fabricated by the individual for internal consumption; it is an imaginary flux that 'passes through' one's mind, that is, something that one 'receives' and lives through as an involuntary occurrence, even though at bottom it is the wild fruit of the operations of one's sleeping mind. In short, when we sink into sleep, we can never choose whether this time we are going to dream or not; nor what will be the particular content of the dream or the emotional intensity that it will be invested with. This little world that might seem to belong completely to us thus reveals itself to be a strangely alien universe – a subjective world that can be delightful, indifferent, terrible, or all these things, but that is entirely closed to our conscious will and choice.

Daydreaming belongs to the waking side of life. Like dreaming proper, it consists in the creation of a subjective reality; in the attribution of a more or less evanescent reality to the machinations and confabulations of our own imagination. The capacity of the human mind to process several experiences simultaneously and keep several balls in the air seems to be fundamental here.

The vision of the impossible needs nothing more than a few notes from a melody or a moment loosed from the folds of time: someone relives a fragment of a dream as he goes down in a lift in the early morning; another converses with his idol as he drives his car and listens to the radio; the student lies on the beach with her ex-boyfriend while she takes notes on a maths lesson; a businessman clinches a contract in church; the beggar wins the lottery and is received by the Pope; under the intense midday sun a doubt assails the pedestrian ('And what if everything is a dream dreamed by someone in another world?'). 'Daydreams', says the narrator of Machado de Assis's *Dom Casmurro*, 'are like other dreams, they are woven according to the patterns of our wishes and our memories [. . .] my imagination has been the companion of my whole existence, lively, quick, restless, sometimes timid and inclined to stop short, but more often capable of covering huge areas in its flight.'[20] Experiences of this kind do not have the vividness of hallucinations or the complete conviction of the night-time dream as it is being dreamed, but their reality and presence in our everyday mental life are unquestionable.

The frequency, tone and intensity of daydreaming vary,

in all likelihood, from person to person, in the course of anyone's life. It would perhaps not be misleading, however, to suppose that the variations in the propensity and aptitude to enter this type of intrapsychic self-deception allow of some generalisations. The faculty of daydreaming seems to be more favoured by the blurred frontier between sleep and wakefulness – just after waking up or just before going to sleep – than at other moments in the day. It seems, also, to manifest itself much more frequently, freely and intensely during childhood (playing games), youth (passionate love) and senile old age (imaginary terrors and religious fervour) than during adult existence. It is difficult to determine to what extent our occupation in life creates or reinforces our personal inclinations; but there is not much room for doubt that poets and artists tend to be more assiduous and expert in the exercise of daydreaming than, let's say, neurosurgeons, engineers and economists.[21]

The capacity for daydreaming in human subjectivity benefits immensely from external stimuli and catalysts. There are, of course, exceptions. The Latin poet Horace describes, in one of his epistles, the exceptional case of an individual who was uniquely gifted in the art of daydreaming:

A well-known figure in Argos used to think that he was watching a splendid tragic performance as he sat alone excitedly clapping in the empty theatre. Apart from that he coped with the daily business of life perfectly well – a good neighbour, a charming host, kind to his wife, the sort who managed to forgive his servants and not go mad with rage if the seal of a jar were broken, who had no trouble avoiding a cliff or an open well. He was finally cured thanks to his relatives' care and expense. But when the potent drug had done its work, expelling the harmful bile, and the man recovered, he cried: 'By Pollux! You've killed me, my friends, not cured me; for now you've ruined my pleasure by driving away the illusion that gave such delight, forcing me to renounce my mind's delightful illusion.'[22]

What happened in the mind of Horace's spectator, before his 'friends' gave him the medicine, we shall never know. The difference between him and us, it seems, is that he was able, at the same time, to create, direct, stage, and enjoy, in his subjective experience, something that in normal circumstances is not only produced and consumed separately, but that also involves the work, the talent, and the good will of a large number of people. Like a sort of super-gifted medieval visionary saint, he gathered together in the stage and auditorium of his own mind everything that, with a greater or lesser power to carry us away, narrative fiction offers the ordinary spectator.

In normal conditions, of course, and in war no less than peace, the show has to go on. Where there is demand, there will be supply. In the consumption and enjoyment of art – and of narrative fiction in particular – we enter into what can be seen as a kind of sacred space and privileged time of daydreaming. 'A novel', says Stendhal, 'is like the bow, and the reader's soul the body of the violin which gives out the sound'. A good work of narrative fiction is one that *dreams a dream for us*. As we give ourselves over to the fictional transport of art, it is as if we were taking a holiday from our subjectivity, in its concrete and personal aspects. It is as if we were getting a break from ourselves so as to daydream other lives, beliefs and emotions. As we journey through the imagined subjectivity of the characters and actors who act out the plot, we temporarily lift the yoke of our mental world – 'prison of thought, is there no release from you?' – to enter into the open and enthralling world that presents itself to us.

What does the ordinary consumer of dramatic fiction look for? Diderot brilliantly answers:

It's at times when everything is false that people love what is true, it's when everything is corrupt that the theatre is at its most refined. A citizen who goes to the Comédie leaves all his vices at the door and picks them up again as he goes out. Once inside, he is just, impartial, a good father, a good friend, a lover of virtue; and I've often seen, sitting next to me, rogues who get deeply indignant at actions they would certainly have committed if they'd been in the same position as that in which the poet placed the character they detested.[23]

Empathy is a gift well-distributed amongst men. The human animal is endowed with exceptional fluency in subjectively imitating, in his own mind, the mental states and feelings of others. The poet beckons, the reader follows; the transmitter invites, the receiver plunges in.

Between the moment the lights go down at the theatre, and the moment they come up again, the spectator daydreams that he is another, as if he were being dreamed by him. It is not only virtue and goodness, which Diderot alludes to in such a masterly fashion, that move us. The human repertoire shifts, almost in the blink of an eye, from fear to happiness, from unutterable love to unspeakable treachery. From Othello to Don Juan, from Emma Bovary to Medea, from Charlie Chaplin to Woody Allen, from Falstaff to Superman, nothing that is human or superhuman seems to be alien to the worldly spectator. 'The final belief', says Wallace Stevens, 'is to believe in a fiction, which you know to be a fiction, there being nothing else; the exquisite truth is to know that it is a fiction and that you believe in it willingly'.[24] It is only in logic, not in life, that contradictions cannot exist.

Diderot's spectator is the mirror image of Horace's virtuoso. He swallows another person's fiction, sucks the juice from it, spits the leftovers into the gutter opposite the theatre, and once the play is over, calmly resumes the thread of his normal life of mediocre vices and deceptions. Once recovered from the passing trance of daydreaming, the citizen that goes out of the theatre door is exactly the same one that came in. But is he simply a hypocrite? What is the relationship, if there is one, between the sublime spectator, capable of unsuspected greatness and virtue in the darkness of the stalls, and the abject citizen, capable of so much perfidy, cunning and pettiness in the cold light of day?

In the darkness of the auditorium, while there is life on stage, there is no room for hypocrisy. The spectator is motionless, silent, and under the effect of the actions, words, sounds and images that take him out of himself. If he stops being who he is, turning, let's say, into a martyr for ecology or a *femme fatale*, there is no intention to deceive anyone in this innocent transfer. Daydreaming is a variant of intrapsychic self-deception. If the spectator

37

deceives anyone as he unaffectedly enters into a different character from his own, the logic of the situation implies that he can only be deceiving himself.

Back in the outside world, however, it is a different picture. As he takes up the chores of daily life, Diderot's citizen shakes off the momentary intoxication of his subjective holiday, and starts being himself again. His eyes are opened, but a certain innocence is gone. The *possibility* of hypocrisy and interpersonal deception is back.

The human animal, as we have seen, wakes up very early, both in biblical and biological time, to the manipulation of others by the cunning use of language. If, in the theatre, spectators identify fully and sincerely with ethical characters – just and impartial people, good fathers, good friends and lovers of virtue – but then negate that in their ordinary lives, playing out roles that would leave them profoundly indignant if they were put on stage, how are we to understand this strange metamorphosis? Are they hypocritical deceivers, acting in bad faith and calculating every act? It's doubtful. There are good reasons, as I will presently argue, to suppose that even here a summary verdict of falsity and hypocrisy would be a sign of hasty judgement, possibly far from the real cause.

The *first* reason is an argument from moral psychology. Extreme ugliness and foul smells are unbearable when we are too close to them. However bad anyone may be in the eyes of a Diderot or any other external observer, nobody can bear living with a morally repulsive image of himself for a long time.

It is plain to see: if the spectators are sincerely indignant at seeing their own wickedness played out on stage, it is because *they do not see themselves that way*. What offends and upsets in others, seen from the outside, becomes quite neutral and reasonable when it is seen and lived from the inside. The exhaust from the car or bus that we are travelling in doesn't irritate us. The fierce eyes of the snake cannot see or terrify themselves. The spontaneously partial and affectionate consideration that everyone has for himself operates like an opium that is able to make us go on daydreaming even when the theatre lights go up and the fictional rapture is over. When it takes up the threads of its own plot, self-deception innocently changes clothes and role: the good daydream of the silent spectator is replaced by the bad waking dream of the cunning man in the street.

The *second* motive to doubt the thesis of simple hypocrisy is an argument from evolutionary psychology. From a Darwinian perspective, lying and deceiving are universal, innate propensities of the human animal – mechanisms of survival and reproduction as natural as, for example, sweating or courting. The repertoire of deceit in the non-human natural world is only the preamble for the farcical epic that follows on from it.

The deceiver's great problem is that he is not alone in the world. As a child soon begins to realise as he tries and tests his first lies to his parents, nobody likes to be deceived against their will. There is always the risk of being caught, and the punishment can be severe. To achieve success, the deceiver needs others to give him *credit*, that is, it is essential that they believe in his word and in his professed intentions. His veneer of credibility and honesty cannot have suspect cracks and splits since, as Protagoras said, referring to the pressure exercised by the community on the citizen of the *polis*, 'anyone who doesn't pretend to be just must be mad'.[25] Lying is an art.

The hypothesis of evolutionary psychology is that there is an 'arms race' going on.[26] Attack and defence: just as the deceiver wants to deceive, the potential victim of the deceit wants to be prepared against it. The principal defensive weapon in this struggle consists in anticipating the manipulation planned by the deceiver so as to catch him in the act while there's still time. The art of defence is to seek out, detect and decode all the suspect signals that might indicate dishonesty and hypocrisy in those we interact with. What is happening is not, obviously, a Manichaean competition between a class made up only of hypocrites, and another of potential victims of hypocrisy. All human animals are, at some time or other, active deceivers and victims of deceit; we are all, intermittently, confronted with *both* situations.

The real evolutionary competition is between two strategies that face one another on the stage of practical existence: active deceit against action to prevent deceit. It's precisely here that self-deception, now at the frontiers of interpersonal deceit, comes back into the reckoning. The human baby, as we have seen, learns to deceive before he learns to speak; self-deception is the post-graduate course. The child soon realises that crying *that is really meant*, whatever its cause, is much more effective than superficially *feigned* crying. But there is a moment in feigned weeping, that is, in the mimicry of a feeling that is not experienced, in which the emotions corresponding to sincere weeping come to the surface and really do take over the child's mind. Self-deception has been born.

The self-deceived deceiver, sincerely convinced by his

own deception, is a deception machine more competent at his art than the cold, calculated deceiver. Any slip-up could be fatal. So that his mind should not be read and deciphered by others – so that he doesn't slip and give himself away by letting others read between the lines, with all the harmful consequences that would follow – the deceiver enters into his own lies, lets himself be carried along by them in a gradual, incremental fashion, and, finally, ends up believing in them with all the innocence and good faith in the world. He doesn't excite doubts because he has none: who could doubt him now? Horace's spectator had better look out. Diderot's spectator does in life what Diderot's actor does not do on the stage: he not only creates while he acts, but genuinely lives his role.

6. *The Splendour and Misery of Self-Deception*

Hyperbole is the enemy of precision. But it is difficult to resist a sensation of astonishment and verbal frustration when faced by the harm and suffering that man's natural propensity to deceit and self-deception can cause. The knowledge of good and evil, on the one hand, brought with it feelings of shame and guilt at our own selves and expelled humanity from Eden; the advent of language and technology, on the other, has dramatically altered the relative positions of strength in our dealings with the natural world. Individually as well as collectively, the human animal has become a miracle and an enigma in his own eyes. He has conquered the divine privilege of knowing his own potentiality and the tragic prerogative of becoming his own worst enemy.

41

Consider, for example, the labyrinth of deceits of what was perhaps the most terrible collective experience yet lived through by a human community – German Nazism. While Hitler confided to an intimate colleague his 'quite special secret pleasure of seeing how the people around us fail to realise what is really happening to them', the Mephistophelian Goebbels, Minister of Culture in the Third Reich, boasted of playing on the psyche of the German people 'as if it were a piano'.

Others, better educated, heard the music of their own self-delusions. While the existentialist philosopher Heidegger actively co-operated with the Nazi authorities in the attempt to ward off bourgeois degradation of the dignity of *Dasein*, the conductor Furtwängler, the brightest star of German classical music at the time, had other plans: he sincerely imagined (or so it seems) that he would be able to soften the regime's harshness by bombarding the Nazi chiefs with brilliant performances of the immortal works of Bach, Beethoven and Wagner.[27] I wonder: what would Diderot have said when faced by the grotesque scene of an audience of SS leaders being transported by Furtwängler's baton to the playful, bucolic world of the 'Pastoral'?

The *whole* can be equal to, more than or less than the sum of its *parts*; but it is inconceivable without them. The collective does not exist on its own; it is the combined result – often with new properties – of the interaction of a large number of smaller groups and individuals. Collective self-deception on a large scale, like the Spanish and Portuguese Inquisitions, Nazism and Soviet Communism, is the synthesis of a myriad of synchronised individual self-deceptions. The madness of the whole is the result of the confluence of the follies of the parts. It is in the microcosm of the individual that we find the cradle and the habitat of the repertoire of self-deception in all its astonishing diversity.

At the same time, the evil of self-deception is not limited to the harm that – isolated in the individual or joined together in society – it can cause to others. If the risk of the calculating deceiver is being detected, with consequent punishment and disgrace, in the case of self-deception the principal victim is often the actor himself. Imagine a middle-aged man, a poet, who looks back, contemplates the life he has lived up to now, and doesn't recognise himself in what he did and what he was:

> I lived, I studied, I loved, and even believed,
> And today there's not a beggar I don't envy because
>   he's not me . . .
> I made of myself what I did not know,
> And what I could have made of myself, I didn't.
> I put on the wrong carnival costume.
> They recognised me straight away for someone I
>   wasn't and I didn't deny it, and lost myself.
> When I wanted to take the mask off,
> It was stuck to my face.
> When I took it off and saw myself in the mirror,
> I had already aged.
> I was drunk, and no longer knew how to put on the
>   costume I hadn't taken off.
> I threw the mask away and slept in the wardrobe
> Like a dog the management puts up with
> Because it's harmless.
> And I'm going to write this story to prove that I'm
>   sublime.[28]

The poet's experience dramatises and takes to an extreme a possibility that is common to everyone: is this life *mine*? This is not a *local* self-deception, restricted to a particular blind spot in a person, like, for instance, the case of a mother who idealises her son in spite of all the evidence to the contrary she has at her disposal – evidence that she would have no difficulty in assimilating if it had concerned her neighbour's son.

On the contrary, it is a *global* self-deception: the experience of waking up from one's own past as if from a bad dream, of radically losing familiarity and ease with oneself, of living a lie one cannot escape from. When he contemplates his life from a point of view defined by the present moment and present feelings, the poet can find himself no longer, having lost his own self. The road one has travelled along up to now is nothing and has led nowhere. I am no longer who I never was, but I do not know how to be anything else.

The poet, of course, may be wrong – only pretending that the pain he really feels is pain. Tomorrow, the past is another day, yesterday's bottomless melancholy vanishes with dawn, and from the abundant fountain of another deceit a new elegy can spring. This does not, however, eliminate the reality of global self-deception in human existence. It matters little if the poet really lived what he portrays; the important thing is that the nerve that has been touched really does, unavoidably, touch us. As a professional in the art of daydreaming, the poet's mission is not to believe in what he feels, but to make us believe we feel what we don't feel. Or do we?

Nobody determines beforehand and from beginning to end the road he will travel in life. The most we do is opt for certain stretches of road, with greater or lesser daring, as we go along. It so happens that, at each new stretch of the road, we come across new realities and unknown possibilities that not only alter our expectations of the future, but may put the journey already completed into a new light and perspective. Knowledge modifies what is already known.

That is the reason why everything that we live through, all our past experience and the image we have of ourselves, are at best provisional constructs, subject to more or less drastic revisions according to the character of what we discover and experience on our way through life. Literature shows, and everyday life confirms, that critical experiences along our way – a serious illness, a deeply felt loss, a spiritual conversion, an emotional crisis, an accident, a great professional challenge, a profound therapy – can force us to a deep revision of the value and meaning of our past and our beliefs about ourselves. No human being, on the empty morning of a hopeless day, can eliminate the risk of repeating to himself in silence (without feigning) the poet's lament: 'I made of myself what I did not know, and what I could have made of myself, I didn't.'

The *negative* value of self-deception is real. As I will try to show in detail in the following chapters, with examples from many diverse origins and traditions, the human propensity to self-deception is the source of immense mischief and harm in public and private life. Before embarking, however, on the analysis of the evil of self-deception, it is worth asking: *is that all there is?* Might there not also be a fertile element, the ally of life and creation, in the talent for deceiving oneself?

Turn the question the other way round. What would

happen if self-deception were completely banned from human existence and society? What would it be like to live in a world in which objective truth always prevailed? A world in which nobody ever deceived himself (local) or was deceived about himself (global)? Let's leave the universe of sleep and fictional spell-weaving on one side – who could deny the benefits of diving periodically into the fictions of dreams and art? – and concentrate instead on the positive value of self-deception in practical existence.

Imagine an already middle-aged man who earns his daily bread as a minor clerk in a small accountancy office. Seen from outside, in the mediocre routine of his day, he is the same as everybody and nobody: dust on the way to dust, a member of the herd resigned to fulfilling with no particular distinction the lowest common denominator of biological subsistence. However, under the placid exterior of a monotonous, grey existence is hidden the underground man – the secret life of someone who since childhood, and for no apparent reason, nurtures with astonishing obstinacy wild fantasies of greatness and literary creation.

The fire of that passion consumes his soul; the desire to consummate it blinds him to everything else. Faithful to himself and to the overwhelming call that impels him towards the infinite world of poetic creation, he takes no care for his prosaic future. He doesn't complete his studies, doesn't learn a trade, doesn't embark on a career. The years go by, some poems are published, but fame and recognition, in a time of cultural impoverishment, only exist in a hypothetical posterity. Finally, there comes a time in his life, as in the course of any existence, at which the certainties of that long intoxication we call

THE NATURE AND VALUE OF SELF-DECEPTION

youth begin to fade. A swarm of doubts surround and
attack the poet:

> Make use of time!
> But what is time, for me to make use of it?
> Make use of time!
> No day without some lines . . .
> Honest, superior work . . .
> Work like Virgil's or Milton's . . .
> But it's so difficult to be honest or superior!
> How unlikely to be Milton or Virgil! . . .
> Make use of time!
> My heart is tired like a real beggar.
> My brain is ready like a burden left on one side.
> My song (just words!) is the way it is, and is sad.
> Make use of time!
> Since I started writing five minutes have passed.
> Did I make use of them or not?
> If I didn't make use of them, what will I know
>   of other minutes?![29]

What moves a creator? What sustains and pushes forward someone who cuts himself off from the world and
from worldly pleasures to compose verses that no one
reads, and place a formidable, irretrievable bet on the
nulla dies sine linea command? Cold reason is cruel: the
probability of this confused middle-aged man turning out
to be a new Milton or Virgil is infinitesimal.

'Men have, in general, a much greater propensity to
overvalue than undervalue themselves,' says Hume in his
down-to-earth manner. In adolescence, his friend Adam
Smith adds, common sense flies right out of the window:

'The contempt of risk and the presumptuous hope of success are in no period of life more active than at the age at which young people choose their professions'. And, so that not even the consolation of originality should be left to the untiring efforts of the poet, the icy voice of Mephistopheles whispers in his ear: 'Go, my original, your glorious way! – / How truth would irk you, if you really sought it / For who can think of truth or trash to say / but someone in the ancient world has thought it?'[30]

Everything, in short, conspires to make the poet give in, to make him coldly and soberly look at his existence and see it as an unforgivable waste – something to be thrown out like a fistful of useless verses. Nevertheless, he does not give up. He doubles his bet and clings to the infinitesimal hope of a remote probability, as if to a thin branch hanging over the precipice of his life. He uses the absurdity of his own inexplicable ambition as the raw material of poetic creation. He keeps his faith in his youthful passion with a spider's tenacity and the ardour of a recent convert. As the years go by, he builds his work anonymously, stone by stone, doubting and starting over again, without applause, without prizes, without a seat in the academy. Self-deception?

The swarms of doubt, like the serpent's words, were right: honesty is hard, a good part of the time has been wasted, and he has not become Milton or Virgil. But if he had opened himself up to this truth, if he had believed in it instead of defeating it in thousands of ever-renewed struggles, what would have become of him? Álvaro de Campos, of course, the heteronymous dream of an obscure clerk, would have committed an unreal and anonymous suicide when still young, and in that case the poet who was not Milton or Virgil would never have become Fernando Pessoa.

Human rationality is based on two essential operations: the calculation of means and the analysis of the ends. It allows us to determine whether procedure x is the most suitable means to achieve objective y, and it helps us to identify all the costs and benefits associated with getting or achieving y. Objectives that at first sight may seem attractive often turn out to be undesirable in the light of what we would have to give up to reach them or of other goals we could try to attain. Rationality, then, is a vital instrument when we want to avoid unnecessary mistakes – to eliminate any disparity between means and ends, or errors of judgement regarding certain ends. It's not heaven, but it saves us from innumerable hells.

The problem is that calculation and prudence – the analytic sobriety and psychological acuteness of rational thinking – make us irremediably *sceptical* and *niggardly* in the face of human ambitions of greatness and creativity. Choose any daring, innovative project in art or science, in politics or religion, in the fields of sport or business: there is always a profusion of impeccably logical and objective reasons not to embark on it.

'All great attempts are hazardous,' Plato reminds us, 'and the proverb is only too true, that what is worthwhile is never easy' (*The Republic*, 497 *d*). To gamble on creativity, in any field of human endeavour, is like entering a gigantic lottery. The cost of the bet has to be paid at the point of entry, and often carries with it the best part of the hopes and energies of youth. The chances of success, however, are tiny, and for everyone who wins a prize there are a multitude of losers. 'Thus conscience doth make cowards of us all, / and thus the native hue of resolution / is sicklied o'er with the pale cast of thought.'[31] I think, therefore I hesitate.

Under the frozen glare of reason, means go cold and ends waste away. But the creator *doesn't give up*. A strange force, stronger than himself, illuminates, irradiates and enflames his mind. The subjective certainty of victory that pushes him onwards, though it may be false for the majority, speaks louder than the depressingly objective probability of failure. 'If the fool would persist in his folly he would become wise'. Many, it's true, give up; some perhaps do so when they ought not to. Human capacity for self-control and perseverance, just as for self-knowledge, is limited. *Knowing*, as Aristotle suggests, in opposition to Plato's optimism, is not a sufficient condition for *doing*: 'I see the better course and approve of it, but I follow the worse.'[32] The creative person, however, persists. The wrong *ex ante* can become the right *ex post*.

The prodigious Goliath – a gigantic warrior with bronze armour, and terrifying helmet, shield and spear – challenges any nobleman or soldier of the Israelite army to single combat. No one dares answer him: the troops' morale collapses. There appears a boy named David who accepts the challenge of facing the giant. Everyone doubts and mocks, but no one stops him. Armed with five smooth stones, a sling and the innocent faith that God is at his side, the boy David hits the head of the Philistine giant right at the first attempt – there'd not be much chance of another! – and knocks him to the ground, dead. The Israelite army gets its courage, takes back the initiative and defeats the enemy (Samuel I, 17). As Cromwell said: 'Truly I think he that prays best will fight best'.[33] If prudent cowardice arises from rational calculation, from David's self-deception – his inexplicable certainty of victory and his boyish temerity – a human miracle is born.

Obviously, luck is not everything. Talent, intelligence and strength of will count for a lot. But how can anyone be reasonably certain beforehand that he has the luck or the merit of possessing them in adequate proportions? Consider, for example, the following picture.

At a certain point in his life, a French stockbroker called Paul Gauguin decided to give up a well-paid job in the financial market, abandon wife and small children, leave everything and everybody, and go and live out his passion for painting and the sensuality of the tropics in the remote islands of Tahiti.[34] The exact details of the example, of course, are of little importance: we could just as well be talking of a candidate for Christian martyrdom in the Middle Ages; of a German philosopher in self-imposed exile in Victorian London or Venice; or to someone aspiring to the Nobel prize in biochemistry in our own time. The relevant question is: what could justify the daring and sacrifice in family terms of a decision like that?

Whatever the answer is, it will be divided into two parts. The gamble considered *before* the selection of the prize-winners is one thing. Another, the bet *after* the lots are drawn, and the awarding of the prizes. Gauguin had the luck or the wisdom to be Gauguin. It's not difficult to justify his fabulous gamble in the light of what came out of it, even though the recognition of the inestimable value of his work in Tahiti only came about, as in so many other cases, many years after his death. But what about before?

The problem is that Gauguin, *at the moment of the gamble*, was not yet Gauguin – and no one could have known with a minimum of certainty that he would be. To justify his decision only with hindsight and in the light of the success of his enterprise is avoiding the question. The miracle of a genius like Gauguin cannot be foreseen. If all aspirants to artistic immortality had a sober and realistic vision of their probability of success, very few gambles like his would have been made, and the basements of the history of art, it's true, would not be jammed with anonymous Gauguins in unknown Tahitis. But what about the actual artist? Wouldn't he too have disappeared, along with the crowd of deluded gamblers? His family might have preferred it that way. But what about humanity?

'The mistakes human beings make are what make them deserving of love.' The biggest error of all would be never to err. Condemning all those who lost their bets, only because with hindsight they did lose them, would mean condemning Gauguin to not risking everything to become Gauguin. The worth of the genuine search, however pathetic or self-deceptive it may turn out to be *a posteriori*, doesn't depend on the result attained. The gamble is valuable in its own right, whatever the number drawn out of the hat. The illusory belief that we will manage to achieve a lot (or the impossible) is often the necessary condition for us to achieve at least a little (or the possible). 'If people did not sometimes do silly things, nothing intelligent would ever get done', Wittgenstein wrote in a working notebook.[35] Without the *ex ante* self-deception of the many, humanity would be deprived of the improbable miracle of the *ex post* genius of the few.

The diamond of immortality is the unforeseeable gift of mortal coal.

In the economy, as in art, the bias of uncertain certainties is fundamental. Economic activity is the privileged sphere for the exercise of instrumental reason. But how far can it take us? Consider, for example, the decision to invest, that is, to tie up one's own money or that of others in setting up a new business, buying equipment, training a labour force, or the creation of a new research lab.

A rational decision would be one based on a complete survey of all the relevant information, so as to eliminate as much as possible any uncertainty about the viability or the return of the investment being considered. But how can this be done? How much information is needed to make a rational decision?

> The information you have is not the information
> you want.
> The information you want is not the information
> you need.
> The information you need is not the information
> you can obtain.
> The information you can obtain costs more than
> you want to pay.[36]

Knowledge, it is true, reduces ignorance; but the awareness of ignorance grows too. The fact is that if all potential entrepreneurs acted like prudent calculators, and only made new investments when they had in their grasp everything they need to be reasonably sure that they won't lose on their bets, the entrepreneurial spirit would dwindle and the economy would go into serious depression. The hiatus between rational calculation and entrepreneurial action is filled by what Keynes called *animal spirits*:

> Most, probably, of our decisions to do something positive, the full consequences of which will be drawn out over many days to come, can only be taken as a result of animal spirits – of a spontaneous urge to action rather than inaction, and not as the outcome of a weighted average of quantitative probabilities. [. . .] Individual initiative will only be adequate when reasonable calculation is supplemented and supported by animal spirits, so that the thought of ultimate loss which often overtakes pioneers, as experience undoubtedly tells us and them, is put aside as a healthy man puts aside the expectation of death.[37]

The protective blindness of the entrepreneur filters out the uncertainty and lends extra brightness to the prospect of success. Keynes's animal spirits – the subjective certainty that moves people to undertake great enterprises, bypassing rational calculation and making them forget things they know but can't remember – seem to contain a generous input of self-deception.

The limits of cold rationality and the positive value of self-deception appear clearly, too, in situations of acute adversity. The gift of successfully lying to oneself can help keep the flame of life burning in moments when survival hangs by a thread. The seriously or terminally ill person who gives in and surrenders completely to the overwhelming probability of imminent death is practically dead. But the patient who, in spite of all the evidence to the contrary, keeps in his heart the blind, firm, unshakeable conviction that he is going to overcome the illness seems to increase his objective chances of recovery.

The poignant account of the Italian chemist and writer Primo Levi, of his experience as a Nazi prisoner of war in the hellish, absurdly degrading atmosphere of Auschwitz, underscores the survival value of the protective blindness associated with certain kinds of non-rational belief:

> The non-agnostic, the believers in any belief what-soever [. . .] better endured the trials of the concen-tration camp and survived in a proportionately higher number [. . .] It was completely unimportant what their religious or political faith might be. Catholic or Reformed priests, rabbis of the various orthodoxies, militant Zionists, naive or sophisticated Marxists and Jehovah's Witnesses – all held in common the saving force of their faith. Their universe was vaster than ours, more extended in space and time, above all more comprehensible. [. . .] They looked at us with commiseration, at times with contempt; some of them, in intervals of our labour, tried to evangelise us. But how can you, a layman, fabricate for yourself or accept on the spot an 'opportune' faith only because it is opportune?

The radical mobilisation of the survival resources of the organism in situations of extreme adversity helps us understand the almost total absence of suicides in the concentration camps. When one is fighting desperately, every hour of the day, to preserve the minimal conditions for biological survival, there is no room for the 'luxury' of a depression. It was only after the liberation, when the ex-prisoners could finally breathe, look back and reflect on the horrors and humiliations that they had borne in the camps, that many of them entered a chronically depressive state. It was only from that moment on that, paradoxically, a large number of survivors of the camps gave way to suicide.[38]

Death is the edge of freedom. It is not the aim of life, but its end point. Dying deprives us of a universe of possibilities ahead of us: everything that still *might be*, but in fact will not. Loss, however, travels with us from the beginning of the journey: everything that *might have been*, but wasn't. Living is making choices – it is betting on a certain stretch of an unknown road and depriving oneself of all the alternatives that are eliminated as we go on our way. The man who goes to sleep like a dog the management puts up with is a vivid example of how the loss that comes from the wrong turnings and mistaken choices of a life can outstrip the final loss represented by death. 'Was the world always this way, or is it only now that it's become such a sad place for me?' There's no need to die to lose life.

But while there is life, not everything is lost. The darkest hour is just before dawn. To repent and feel remorse for a life wasted is to go into mourning for a past that has not been lived. Temporary depression is the condition of spiritual growth – it's the hibernation of a life that retires into itself and prepares to return renewed. From the extreme limits of pain, as in childbirth, there bursts forth indescribable happiness, a flood of love. 'For a second, unsuspected, unheralded birth / redeems the suffering of the first, / and time shines forth again.'[39] From death in life, life is born again, like the *giesta*, the flower that grows on the cold ashes of Vesuvius. If the human animal expelled from paradise was punished with the awareness of death and the shame of being who he is, he also received from nature the gift of a stubborn and inexplicable hope: the saving, shining hope that protects us from thinking and living to the full the absurd weight of our mistakes and the certainty of our end: a happiness with no reason for existing.

7. Self-Knowledge, Moderation and Self-Deception

The temple of Apollo at Delphi, the religious and geographical centre of the Greek world, had two stone inscriptions. One of them, as we will see in chapter 2 (section 4), recommended the unceasing search for self-knowledge: 'Know thyself'. The other inscription established a norm to be observed in human life and society: the principle of moderation summed up in the maxim 'Nothing in excess'.[40]

While the first motto makes a demand of a cognitive nature, directed towards the ideal of seeking the truth about oneself, the second has an essentially practical, prudent aim. Any kind of arrogant, immoderate zeal (*hubris*) has its corresponding retributive justice (*nemesis*). The road to excess – the exacerbation of human aspirations and passions – goes beyond the limits of our mortal condition, offends the divine or natural order of things, and, for that reason, cannot end happily.

The juxtaposition of the two Delphic mottoes makes one think. On the one hand, the search for self-knowledge and the principle of moderation strongly *complement* one another. There is a profound internal relationship between them. The man who knows himself recognises his own limits, and so does not overstep his capacities or condition. At the same time, the person who is capable of soberly identifying and examining his own emotions and desires succeeds, to some degree, in seeing them from the outside and distancing himself from them, which reduces the risk of them coming to tyrannise his mind or attaining an excessive power over his actions. No false subjective certainty will lead him to try to be someone he is not, or let him be swallowed up by his own passions.

Lack of self-knowledge, on the other hand, favours excess. Overestimating oneself, an overpowering self-belief, and an inordinate concentration of the will show us that the individual is, in some way, *outside himself*, that is, he has lost his footing in his own internal reality. The overwhelming and unassailable certainties that move him endanger his awareness of limits and his sense of proportion. 'To desire something violently', observes Democritus, 'is to become blind to the rest' (fragment 72). When judgement is short-sighted, actions are distorted. The worst excesses of public and private life spring from ignorance of oneself. If men really did strive for self-knowledge, they would naturally become more balanced and temperate in their enthusiasms and ambitions. 'Know thyself', in short, is the great epistemological ally of 'Nothing in excess' in the realm of practical existence.

There is also, however, a powerful *tension* between the two Delphic principles. This tension can be separated into two basic questions, both of which follow from the same conceptual operation.

The first is the result of the application of the principle of moderation to the neighbouring recommendation for self-knowledge: to what extent does 'nothing in excess' also apply to 'know thyself'? Is it possible to go too far even in the search and attainment of self-knowledge? The second question turns the modulating mechanism of the principle of moderation on its head: to what extent does the motto 'nothing to excess' apply reflexively to itself? Is it possible to overdo it, going too far in the attempt never to go too far? Might there not also be risks in sinning by *excess of moderation* in practical existence?

These are issues that send us straight to the question of the value of self-deception in human life. If the complementarity between self-knowledge and moderation brings to light the dark, menacing side of self-deception, the tension in the relation between the two Delphic mottoes points in the opposite direction, that is, towards what self-deception has, not just of benefit and value, but even of necessity, for our lives.

The human condition cannot bear too much self-knowledge. Imagine, for example, that a new medicine – an ultra-modern and sophisticated version of the drug that 'cured' Horace's spectator – allowed us to suppress all the epistemological and psychological barriers that make self-knowledge so precarious and slippery. When we take the pill of self-knowledge, all the defences, fissures and biases of the mind disappear. Where there once was a labyrinth, dark and resistant to introspection, there now appears a clear, precise and detailed map of all the streets, tunnels, alleyways and parks of the internal mental flux. No part of the mind can any longer lie to other parts, play practical jokes on them, lead them astray or pretend not to understand them. What would be the subjective life of someone who has banished the possibility of intrapsychic self-deception? Of someone incapable of deceiving himself?

Endowed with a perfect objectivity about what happens in its subjective experience, the human animal 'cured' of self-deception would never allow himself to enter into the fictitious and illusory constructions of his sleeping or waking mind. On plunging into the universe of sleep, he doesn't dream; on emerging to fulfil the lowest common denominator of biological subsistence, the same thing: no daydreaming in art or practical existence. Resistant to Keynes's animal spirits, and to any fantasy of creation – any achievement or greatness that he is incapable of explaining to himself – he only invests his time in rational projects, in which the probability of success is mathematically secure and certain.

When he acts, there is total transparency. He always knows, exactly and in each case, what his real motivation is, what he is doing and aiming at, what he can realistically expect from any given action. The momentary impulse never has sway over the neutral vision of the long term. Averse to any kind of excess or recklessness, dancing or fasting, in emotional life as in creative work, he perfectly understands Solomon's advice – 'He that trusteth his own heart is a fool' (Proverbs, 28:26) – and never lets himself get involved in the self-deception of the poet-lover who says, 'If one cannot love unconditionally, love is already in a critical condition.'[41]

In the mind of the man 'cured' of self-deception there would be no place for any thought about himself, his future, and his ability to change things, that did not satisfy the most rigorous test of realism and objectivity. No belief, emotion or subjective experience hidden from self-examination; no illusion, comforting or not, would find shelter in the austere setting of its frozen rationality. Any excessive attribution of value would be immediately suspect. Belonging to the natural world like the insignificant and absurd being that he genuinely knows himself to be – nothing more than an ephemeral and fortuitous concatenation of accidental circumstances in the infinite ocean of matter – what kind of hope or sense can he find in existing?

Without self-deception, in short, what is the human animal but a 'healthy beast, a future corpse that breeds'?[42] The pill of self-knowledge and the radical 'cure' of self-deception transform the human being not into a model of virtue and wisdom, but into a monster from which all other men – not to speak, of course, of the 'cured' man himself – would run as from a terrifying ghost. Bored and solitary in his impeccable nihilism, the result of maximum logical and cognitive rectitude, his only way out now would be to try to find in an intraorganic self-deception the chemical antidote to neutralise the 'cure' and give him back the gift of intrapsychic self-deception.

Nothing in excess. The threat of *hubris* followed by *nemesis* also haunts the 'know thyself'. Human survival, procreation and creation have demands that go beyond the biological realm and our capacity for understanding. The spontaneous happiness of being alive and all creative activity depend on non-rational dispositions that Apollonean self-control, the source of morality and objective knowledge, undermines and cannot satisfy. The human animal demands that his life make sense: personal, collective, and cosmic. When it

LIES WE LIVE BY

imposes limits on the Delphic principle of self-knowledge, the principle of moderation sets itself limits – without overdoing it, of course.

2

SELF-KNOWLEDGE AND
SELF-DECEPTION

1. Knowledge: Familiarity v. Objectivity

It doesn't matter what it is: ask yourself whether you know
something, and you'll have serious reasons to begin to
doubt. First, we should ask: *what is knowing?* It depends,
of course, on how demanding we are. If, for example,
you spend an afternoon visiting a historic town, you can
come back home and say that you know it. If you spend
several months in the same town, you will notice that the
changes of climate, the shifts in your own mood and
everyday little surprises have the ability to reveal angles
and facets that were unknown to you. But if you spend
some years in the town, studying its past, researching into
the development of its buildings and town-plan, and trying
to understand the historical meaning of what happened
there, you will be astonished at the vastness of what is still
unknown. With the advance of knowledge, the unknown
expands. 'Doubt grows with knowledge'.[1]

Tautologies and truisms apart, no knowledge is final.

Whatever the object of enquiry – a forest or an industry, a classic text or a neurotransmitter – one thing is certain. However much you know of it, it will always be possible to *know more*. And since, by definition, nobody knows what is still unknown, the unknown can have a peculiar property. For it is not always the case that getting to know more about something is just a matter of discovering things that merely add to the pre-existing stock of knowledge. The tension between new and old – between the existing stock and fresh findings – generates surprises and anomalies. The new knowledge generated can radically alter our understanding of the nature of pre-existing knowledge and of its truth-value. Knowledge modifies what is known. The unknown is a ticking time-bomb, ready to implode (or not) the edifice of established knowledge – a threat pulsating in everything that we take for granted.

There is no such thing, then, as complete certainty. To say that there was would be to deny that the unknown is unknown. It would be to suppose *a*) that the final and impassable frontier of knowledge has been reached, or, at least, *b*) that what remains to be known is necessarily 'well-behaved', that is, something that can be added on to what is already known, rather than subverting it. The first hypothesis implies a complete dogmatism; the second prejudges, unjustifiably, what by its very nature cannot be known.

For anyone in search of knowledge, then, and not the comfort of opinions well rooted in the soil of belief, surprises and anomalies are valuable finds. The discovery of a surprising fact leads to the search for more facts and stimulates the formation of hypotheses and theories that might be able to explain it. The mind open to knowledge works with its radar on the alert, ready to find anomalies. Surprise is the fuse that lights knowledge, a window half-open onto the unknown. Faced with it, thought comes alive and awakes from dogmatic slumber. 'A difficulty is a light; an insurmountable difficulty is a sun'.[2]

Removing the possibility of final knowledge and affirming the hypothetical character of all knowing does not mean, however, that we fall into the extreme opposite notion, that nothing is or can be known. Between the drugged Scylla of dogmatism and the disheartened Charybdis of radical scepticism lies the notion that knowledge, though contingent and not always cumulative, does not just exist but admits of gradation; knowing is a matter of degree. It is not the sleep of stone, but neither is it the vertigo of the whirlpool. The very notion that in the face of any object of knowledge it is always possible *to know more* presupposes the existence of some criterion that allows one to compare and order the supposed knowledge. The question is: on what basis? What criteria are we to adopt?

From the perspective of *common sense*, knowledge has to do with *familiarity*. What is known, according to ordinary language, is what is familiar. If you are accustomed to something, if you have dealings with it and operate habitually with it, then you can say you know it. The unknown, by contrast, is what is strange. Degree of knowledge, in this perspective, is a function of degree of familiarity: the more familiar, the better known. That is the origin of the formula: 'I know = I am familiar with it as a certainty'.[3] But if the object manifests some kind of abnormality, if it has different aspects or behaves in a different manner to what I am used to, I lose the certainty I had and realise that I didn't know it as well as I thought. I have to

LIES WE LIVE BY

tame it, to pacify the imagination again. As I readjust my expectations and familiarise myself with the new aspect or new behaviour, I recover the sense of knowing it.

From a *scientific* point of view, however, familiarity is not only defective as a criterion for knowledge; it hinders the search for it. The subjective sensation of knowing associated with familiarity is illusory, and inhibits the questioning curiosity that knowledge is born from. The familiar does not have the property of being known just because we are used to it. What we are used to, on the contrary, often turns out to be the most difficult thing to really get to know.

Just because I am completely familiarised with the faculty of sight, for example, does not mean that I know anything about the processes and mechanisms that allow me to perceive things. Humanity, of course, lived for thousands of years with the subjective experience of sight – the sensation of seeing what we see – without anyone realising they knew nothing about it. It was only from the moment when some men lost familiarity with sight and began to see it as a problem – as something strange and alien demanding some type of explanation – that knowledge of the phenomenon began to go beyond square one. Familiarity blinds one.

In the scientific approach, *objectivity* takes the place of the pre-reflexive sense of familiarity as the criterion for knowledge. The degree of knowledge is a function of the degree of objectivity: the more objective, the truer it is. The ground zero of knowledge, in this perspective, consists of the permissive and relativist 'anything goes': 'Right you are, if you think so!'. The highest point is the objective truth that retains its validity even when it is not believed in: 'Truth is what it is, and goes on being true, even if people think the opposite.'[4]

Let's go back to the example of sight. The pre-Socratic philosopher Empedocles dared to tear the veil of familiarity and made serious enquiries about what happens when we perceive things. The essence of his original conjecture was the thesis that, when we see something, it is our eyes that act and illuminate the objects that are seen. The sensation of seeing is a consequence of the fact that, in vision, beams of light or something equivalent are emitted by the eyes, descending on things and making them visible. Blindness means that the light irradiated by the eyes has ceased to flow. Other investigators, however, were not persuaded. The coup de grâce – simple and devastating – was dealt by Aristotle. If Empedocles' thesis was in fact correct, so that the eyes projected shafts of light onto things, there would be no problem seeing in the dark![5] After Aristotle's remark, any theory of sight that aspired to greater objectivity would need to explain why this does not happen.

What makes a theory or proposition more objective than another? What is deserving of belief? Being certain is not enough. The starting-point in the analysis of the concept of objectivity is the realisation that the act of believing should not be confused with the act of identifying and critically examining the reasons that lead us to believe what we believe.

The drive towards a more objective cognition is linked to the analysis of what can justify, or not, our belief in something. Tradition and authority, for example, do not pass muster. A theory or a proposition does not become more or less objective because of *who* states or defends it, but because of *what* it states or defends. The knowing subject may be more or less objective in his knowing. His ideas and conclusions may be more or less believable. The objectivity, however, is not *his* property. It is an attribute *of whatever it is* that he conceives, elaborates, registers, and offers to others' public appraisal.

What, then, does objectivity consist in? The fundamental idea is to eliminate from the search for knowledge everything that does not belong to reality *as it really is*. Knowledge will be the more objective the more independent it is of the cognitive subject, and this is as valid with respect to the individual characteristics of the person knowing as, at one extreme, with respect to the culture, the society, and even to the specificity of the biological species that he happens to belong to. The ideal of objectivity is the complete annulment of bias and subjectivity in the search for knowledge.

Subjective truth, based on the assent of the knowing subject, should not be confused with objective truth, which is independent not only of the acquiescence, but of the perspective, constitution and individuality of any knowing subject. To arrive at an understanding of the world *as it is*, we have to relinquish our own world – we have to transcend our own personal, partial, unreasoning, and limited point of view, to try to understand it, as far as we can, from outside, free of any kind of interference. We have to conceive of it *as if* we didn't exist.

2. *The Double Expulsion of Subjectivity*

The ability to eliminate subjectivity and any type of bias in the search for knowledge is not of the nature of an instantaneous fiat. It is rather a process of attaining growing degrees of objectivity: a progressive and asymptotic, though not a linear movement, whose object is to reach objective truth like a moving point in infinity. Many of the principal discontinuities in the history of science have been the result of more or less sudden advances in the human capacity for transcending the limits of its natural epistemic condition, and revolutionising the current dominant modes of abstraction.

On the other hand, it is important to recall that different traditions in the evolution of modern science developed different strategies for approaching the common aim of objective knowledge. A mapping of those strategies, though inevitably brief and schematic, allows one to identify the two main currents in the evolution of an objective conception of reality: Baconian empiricism and Cartesian rationalism.

The human mind, in Baconian epistemology, is the natural soil of errors, fantasies, illusions and insidious false images. Everything conspires to remove it from true knowledge. As Heraclitus' cautionary warning puts it: 'The eyes and ears are bad witnesses for men if they have barbarian souls'. That is why we must take every precaution to avoid the takeover of the mind by the 'idols' that 'pervert and infect all the anticipations of the intellect'.[6]

Bacon's idols – of the *cave* (local prejudices), the *theatre* (philosophical systems), the *market* (linguistic terms) and the *tribe* (human nature's sub-rational passions) – are permanent threats to the objectivity of knowledge. We can defeat them in isolated battles, but our victories over them – and over the idols of the tribe in particular – will never be final. The great imperative of Baconian philosophy is identifying and suppressing everything that diverts the mind from an objective apprehension of the world. Its basic thrust is the determination to transcend all the biases, idiosyncrasies, subterranean desires, philosophical dogmas, linguistic fetishes and all-too-human weaknesses that flourish in our subjective lives. The empirical evidence open to public scrutiny is the fundamental safeguard of the mind against its barbarous vices and crooked offshoots.

In the hands of the Baconian scientist in his laboratory or in the field, aggressive experimentation is a weapon to harass nature with, to prod it from all sides and make it confess its secrets. As Bacon put it: 'The faculty of wise interrogating is half knowledge'. The observations and evidence collected by the senses are the original sources of knowledge, and the guarantee that it will produce the practical results that give it legitimacy. The usefulness of knowledge in the solution of problems and the improvement of human life – and not some kind of naive verification criterion – is the definitive test of truth.[7] It is by its fruits that we put the tree of knowledge to the test. But the ever-present spectre of deception and self-deception in the gathering, processing and interpretation of the empirical evidence dogs the Baconian experimenter as insistently as it afflicts the Cartesian cogito.

In the rationalist tradition, empiricism's *not everything is what it seems* gave way to the radical thesis that *nothing seems what it really is*. It was this decisive step, originally sketched out by the pre-Socratic Greek atomists and elaborated by Cartesian philosophy, following the advances and conquests of physics in the seventeenth century, that revolutionised the bases of the scientific concept of objectivity.

What is real? In the atomist philosophy of Democritus, the world as we apprehend it through the senses is not the world *as it is*. All our impressions and sense-perceptions are caused by the action of things on our senses, but the knowledge thus generated is of an inferior ('bastard') quality in relation to 'legitimate' knowledge, based on complete abstraction from what is sensory and transient.

The real, in this perspective, is what remains in place when no one is there. It is everything that would go on existing in the universe even if there were no philosophers or beings with sense-organs to apprehend it. The analysis of the physical basis of perceptions shows that our senses, however well disciplined they may be, are like barbarians, that is, excitable and deceiving, and that underlying the illusory information that they bring us is the objective reality of atoms in movement. (An ancient legend says that Democritus blinded himself so as to be able to think better.) Although they differ from one another in size and format, the atoms ('indivisible particles') of which the world is made are devoid of sensory qualities (colours, sounds, smells, textures etc.). In the seminal Democritean principle – 'Opinion says hot or cold, but the reality is atoms and empty space'[8] – lies the embryo of what would become, twenty-two centuries later, the conception of objectivity in Cartesian rationalism.

Cartesian philosophy takes up and extends the theory of knowledge of the Greek atomists, and turns it to good account. The demand for the greatest possible certainty and the most absolute objectivity in the search for knowledge requires in the first place the 'removal of superfluous rubbish'. The Cartesian cogito arms itself with systematic doubt and banishes from the mind anything that might lead it into error or obscurity. By doubting our own existence, we reach the end of the line and the beginning of knowledge: the indisputable certainty *that we are doubting*.[9] Doubt about the nature of the world, in its turn, leads to the search for a concept of reality that avoids the trap of appearances that deceive, and overcomes the limitation of partial points of view and individual idiosyncrasies. The Cartesian project aims for the elaboration of a conception of the real free to the greatest possible extent from the unreflective judgements and notions that surround us, and free of the peculiarities and particular contents (memories, desires, sensations etc.) that inhabit our minds.

The result of this effort of abstraction is a concept of reality in which the objects of the physical world are endowed with extension, shape, weight and movement – the irreducible 'primary qualities' of everything that exists and occupies space – while everything else is removed to the common grave of the 'secondary qualities' that inhabit every person's subjectivity.

It's not only beauty that's in the eye of the beholder. All sensations of pain and pleasure, everything that we think, feel and dream, all our sensory perceptions of light, colour, sound, tastes, smells, heat and cold, in short, everything that is mental does not belong to objective reality and is related to it in the same way as, to take up an analogy suggested by Descartes in *Le monde*, the *name of a thing* is related to *the thing itself*. The heat is not in the flame, the sweetness is not in the sweet. If someone lightly draws a feather across your armpit or the sole of your foot, you will feel a ticklish, itchy sensation. The reality, Descartes says, is the action of the feather on the skin and nerves, and the whole chain of measurable neurological processes that this action unleashes. Its subjective effects – our intimate experience of this innocent friction – are no more than mental itching.[10]

Nothing is what it seems. The fear of being tricked by false appearances and of being deceived by his own mind led Descartes to set up doubt as a method, and unquestionable truth as an aim. What guarantees us that this whole cognitive enterprise is not itself another deception? The guarantor of the reliability of human reason, according to the author of the *Meditations*, is in the last instance a non-deceptive divinity whose existence, he says, can be demonstrated *a priori*. But if the source of the legitimacy of Descartes' cognitive strategy were limited to this theological (un)certainty, his conception of objectivity would have been no more than another speculative hypothesis or a mere philosophical curiosity. However, that was not the case. The model of radical abstraction sketched out by the Greek atomists and perfected by modern philosophy has revealed itself to be astonishingly fertile in the history of science.

One of the keys to the scientific success of Cartesian abstraction was its encounter and happy conjunction with the recently discovered analytic geometry. On the one hand, the primary qualities of the *res extensa* – extension, shape, weight and movement – lend themselves admirably to mathematical measurement and manipulation. At the same time, the discovery of analytical geometry (an achievement to which Descartes' mathematical genius was decisive) demonstrated the possibility of relating in a rigorous fashion the sphere of numbers and equations, in algebra, with the universe of spatial forms, in geometry.

For the first time, this allowed numerical formulae and geometrical figures to function as two languages, capable not only of communicating with each other, but also, what is more crucial, of being translated into each other, with analytical geometry acting as the master key to the process of translation. The meeting of a *res extensa* eager to be quantified, on the one hand, with the voracious appetite of the tools of analytical geometry, on the other, opened up a wonderfully productive vein in the search for knowledge.[11] The drive towards objectivity set off by this achievement has revealed itself to be one of the most powerful and uncontrollable forces ever discovered by humanity. The practical and intellectual repercussions of the particular type of abstraction on which it is based are far from having been exhausted.

Cartesian rationality's particular conception of objectivity is clearly more ambitious and reductive than that of Baconian empiricism. The experimental side of modern science does not have the formal sophistication of the mathematical tradition, nor does it aim to reduce everything that exists in the universe to physics, and everything that is physical to its irreducible primary qualities. Its strongly reductive vocation, however, though it is less ambitious in theoretical terms and has a more pragmatic aspect, is unambiguous. It also pursues – in its own way and with its own weapons – the same ideal of maximum objectivity and the complete openness of the results. The common denominator between the deductive stance of Cartesian mathematical rationalism, on the one hand, and the inductive approach of Baconian pragmatic experimentalism, on the other, is the double expulsion of subjectivity from the domain of scientific knowledge.

Firstly because, on both sides, the mind of the knowing subject has to be disciplined and purged of all the vestiges of his subjectivity, that is, of everything that removes him from the path of the most absolute objectivity in the cognitive act. Our mental world – subjective and personal – is an obstacle on the way to the knowledge of the world.

And *secondly* because, in the two traditions, the abstraction that presides over the search for knowledge leads to a conception of reality in which there is no room for the mental, that is, to the constitution of an objective universe ruled by its own laws, indifferent to human will, and deprived of inner experience. What is publicly observable has to be explained by what is publicly observable. What can be demonstrated has to be demonstrated on the basis of accepted premises and by means of publicly examinable procedures. There is nothing external to our mind that corresponds to our subjective experiences of what goes on inside it. There is no room for our world in the world.

3. Self-Knowledge: the Limits of Scientific Reductionism

Up to this point, we have examined the question of the knowledge of the world outside our minds. Self-knowledge transforms the subject into an object. The goal is the objective truth not about *what* presents itself to be known, but about *the mind that* inspects the unknown: the knowing subject who knows, knows that he does not know, and wants to know more. What happens when this knowing subject turns from external nature to look at his inner, subjective experience?

If the intention is to produce reliable knowledge, the first thing to do is to examine oneself as objectively as possible. So nothing could be more natural than mobilising in the search for self-knowledge all the cognitive arsenal of controlled observation, experimentation, inference and construction of models, in short, all the apparatus created and perfected by modern science with the aim of increasing the degree of objectivity of knowledge. Armed to the teeth, the subject inspects himself as an object and enquires: how far can the rigorously scientific approach to self-knowledge take us?

The answer, like the enterprise itself, is paradoxical. From a certain angle, and in a certain sense, the search for objective knowledge about ourselves – the strictly scientific understanding of human beings about themselves – has not only made startling progress; it promises to transform and revolutionise our self-understanding and self-image in an even more radical way. Nobody can say, at this point, what lies in store and how far we can go along this particular road.

But, on the other hand and in another sense, the project of submitting human self-knowledge to the rigours of a scientific approach comes up against a serious intrinsic limitation – a deficiency inherent in its own internal constitution and that no amount of scientific advance, at least on the pattern of what has happened up to now, seems capable of overcoming. This limitation, identified and brilliantly analysed by the American philosopher Thomas Nagel, makes of the scientific approach – a splendid highway for the objective knowledge of the world – a real dead end when it comes to contributing to the advance of self-knowledge, that is, when what is at stake is not the world *as it is*, but rather *our world*.

Let us look once again at the problem of visual experience. From Empedocles to the electromagnetic energy of photons hitting the optic nerve, the progress is plain to see. Better yet: recent advances in the field of neuroscience (cerebral anatomy, physiology and chemistry) allow quite a rigorous mapping of the processes linked to visual perception. What happens, for example, when you go to the top of a mountain, gaze at the landscape and see, for example, a green valley surrounded by mountains? A scientific description of the phenomenon, not cast in over-technical language, might be the following:

Think of viewing a favourite landscape. Far more than the retina and the brain's visual cortices are involved. One might say that while the cornea is passive, the lens and the iris not only let light through but also adjust their size and shape in response to the scene before them. The eyeball is positioned by several muscles, so as to track objects effectively, and the head and neck move into optimal position. [. . .] All these adjustments depend on signals going from brain to body, and on related signals going from body to brain. Subsequently, signals about the landscape are processed inside the brain. Subcortical structures such as the superior colliculi are activated; so are the sensory cortices and the various stations of the association cortex and the limbic system interconnected with them. As knowledge pertinent to the landscape is activated internally from the dispositional representations in those various brain areas, the rest of the body participates in the process. Sooner or later, the viscera are made to react to the images you are seeing, and to the images your memory is generating internally, relative to what you see.[12]

Eyes, body and brain interact in a complex manner and, at the end of the process, that is to say, in fractions of a second, you realise that you are *contemplating a beautiful landscape*. The knowledge of the intricate movements underlying the sensation of seeing something is not directly accessible to us. It is the result of an enormous effort of scientific investigation. The direct experience of the onlooker – what he has access to when he looks at the landscape – is the visual sensation associated with it, or, more specifically, the particular mental image that he forms as he observes the sky, the valley and the mountains. But what is this? What is the nature of the *subjective* visual sensation of someone who is seeing something? What can a scientific approach – in particular that of neuroscience – tell us about this?

It would be difficult to deny that the subjective image of the landscape in the mind is related in some way to the neurological configuration underlying it. The existence, or not, of a one-way causal relationship between the cerebral and the mental is an open question, and one on which the advance of scientific knowledge can throw new light.

But what seems really inconceivable is the notion that subjective experience is identical to the corresponding objective configuration in the brain, or can be reduced to it in some way. It is not, and cannot. There is an unbridgeable gap between the *seeing from outside* of the scientific standpoint and the *seeing from inside* of the person who feels, thinks and sees. However much the objective analysis of neurological processes advances, how-ever much observation techniques like magnetic resonance, electroencephalography and neuro-visualisation in general are perfected, the scientific knowledge generated will con-tinue to be inescapably *external* to the experience of the person being investigated.

Let's go back, for a moment, to look at the green valley. I am seeing the landscape and internally living that moment. I am overtaken, for example, by a diffuse and radiant feeling of hope about the future; by a sense of fatigue and sadness gnawing at my stomach; by the face and the presence of someone I loved, and has gone; by a pang of guilt because I'm not working – the particular content of the experience doesn't matter. If a super-scientist were looking at me in that exact moment – an investigator gifted with inductive and deductive faculties far superior to those of any Bacon or Descartes that has existed on the planet, and furnished with everything that the most sophisticated medical technology will provide in the future – what will he be able to know about me?

Doubtless he would have a detailed model and a com-pletely up-to-date map of the chemical and electrical changes going on in the billions of nerve-cells of my brain. More than that: he might, perhaps, be able to predict exactly the *physical* movements of my eyes, limbs and body in space. But would the super-scientist be able to know what I am feeling and thinking at that moment, what is going on in my mind and in my own internal experience? Would he be able to know what it's like for me, from my subjective and personal point of view, to see that landscape and be immersed in this or that experience?

It's quite probable that he would not. And the reason, as Nagel argues, is the fact that my personal subjective experience is closed inside my mind in such a way that it cannot be apprehended by any other observer, and this, independently of the greater or lesser sophistication of his perceptual apparatus.[13]

My subjective life – everything I feel, think, dream and perceive – is locked inside my mind with a kind of inwardness that differs in kind from the way in which my neurones are inside my brain, and this latter, in its turn, inside my head. If a neurosurgeon opens my brain, he will be able to observe objectively what is inside it. The mind, however, cannot be opened, nor the mental directly examined. Even if someone succeeded in projecting on a high-definition screen an image completely identical to the one I see as I contemplate the landscape, he would still have *his vision* of my vision of the valley, not *my own vision*.

But if the focus of cognitive interest is not just the visual image, but the hope, fatigue, nostalgia or guilt that invade me when I contemplate the landscape, we can see that not even that is possible. For what we have in these cases are internal experiences, that is, mental processes that, because they are still more remote from any type of existence independent of the experience of the person having them, don't even lend themselves to a hypothetical visual projection of what passes through the mind. The scientific notion of objectivity, in short, condemns the investigator to a cognitive stance that makes of the object of knowledge a surface phenomenon, empty of experience and deprived of subjectivity. There's nothing wrong with this, of course. The problem is that the world we live in – the world lived from within – belongs to another world.

A curious by-product of this argument, it's worth noting, is that it allows one to see Empedocles' theory of vision in a new light. The vision *seen from without* is not the vision *seen from within*. The objective light of the photons can stay exactly the same – the photometer proves that. Moods, however, are capricious, and 'between contentment and disillusionment, in the fickle balance, there is hardly any distance'. If I am gloomy and melancholy in that moment, the landscape I see goes dark – colours go pale, the sky is parched and the sun drained of vigour. But, if happiness and expansiveness lighten my heart, the sun explodes in colour, the sky beckons and light invades the world.

Things objectively looked at may have weight, volume, atomic structure and everything that scientific instruments can succeed in measuring. But human subjectivity is sovereign in its domains, and will not give up its prerogatives. Did the landscape change, or did I? A luminosity that is experienced does not reflect the light as measured. It is true that no one can see in the dark. But the light that really matters and the luminosity of things seen, as Empedocles intuited, depend greatly on the mental state of the person seeing.

The basic conclusion of the argument on the gap between the objectivity pursued by science and the subjectivity of human experience is that one should not expect from the progress of science what it cannot offer. The scientific knowledge of man and of human action bids fair to advance much further, which is fine, but what one can expect from it – and this, as much from the point of view of self-knowledge as in the realm of ethical reflection on how to live – seems fated to be very little.

Although the road ahead may be long and uncertain, nothing rules out the possibility that science may one day show in a convincing manner – no knowledge is final – that *nothing is as it seems*: just as primitive man lived in a dream-world in relation to natural phenomena, so we still live in a dream-world in relation to ourselves, and know little or nothing about the real causes of our actions in ordinary life. The progress of science may reveal that much – or, at the outside, the totality – of what we imagine *we are doing* by our own will and initiative in our lives is, in truth, *being done in us* by the autonomic functioning of the nervous system and by a succession of physio-neurological configurations in our brains. If this happens one day, something that cannot be foreseen, our self-deception with respect to ourselves will have been cosmic. It will not be the first time, however, nor probably the last, when man will have seemed absurd and inexplicable in his own eyes.

Up to this point, then, in spite of the uncertainty, there is nothing to quarrel with. The serious mistake is to imagine that the advance of science, based on the mode of abstraction peculiar to it, will bring answers to questions it has no way of formulating. It is not just the fact, important in itself, that the mind is not the same as, nor can it be reduced to, the brain. It is the vital realisation that everything that most interests us in the search for self-knowledge – the subjective universe within which our existence takes place, and in which we are thoroughly plunged – does not lend itself to the methods

82

developed with enormous success by science to deal with the observable world *as it is*.

We live, inescapably, immersed in subjectivity. The fundamental questions concerning self-knowledge – who am I? what do I really want? what should I do with my life? what's the meaning of all this? – lie outside the scope and the essential project of science. To imagine that it might one day be able to satisfy our demand for self-knowledge, that is, for values and existential meaning, is like hoping that a fax transmitter will one day be able to interpret the meaning of a text, or that someone blind from birth should enlighten us on the nature of colours.

4. *Dialogue, Maieutics and Self-Knowledge*

Know thyself. The exhortation/challenge inscribed on the portals of the principal temple of the Greek world, the oracle of Apollo at Delphi, is not a motto coined by Socrates, but it admirably expresses the essence of his philosophy.[14] The Socratic enterprise is born of an open rejection of pre-Socratic reductionism and proposes a fundamental reorientation in the aims and strategy of the search for knowledge. While his predecessors, like Democritus and Anaxagoras, essentially tried to investigate the make-up of external nature and its ruling principles, searching for objective explanations for what is permanent and transitory in the *kósmos*, Socrates proposes that the study of the natural world and of man as a natural being has a minor importance when compared to the real mission of philosophy, which is to know and transform us as moral beings.

Why self-knowledge? 'The unexamined life is not worth living' (*Apology*, 38 *a*). Socrates sees a world gone astray around him, and conceives a world of possibilities in front of him. To the blind, feverish, bewildered life of his fellow-citizens, he opposes the ideal of another life – of a life ruled not by the ephemeral glitter of false values like power, prestige, carnal love and wealth, but by the ambition to be better than one is, by the ceaseless endeavour to perfect the soul. Self-knowledge is the road that leads from one type of living to another. If the mistaken, unreflective life is the inevitable consequence of a self-satisfied lack of self-knowledge, ethical life presupposes man's determination and capacity to search continuously and incessantly for the truth about himself. The internal link between the imperative for self-knowledge and the idea of the ethical life in the Socratic enterprise is clearly spelt out in Guthrie's commentary to the *First Alcibiades* (128 *b* – 129 *a*):

> One must understand the nature and purpose of anything before one can make, mend or look after it properly. So in life, we cannot acquire an art of self-improvement unless we first understand what we ourselves are. Our first duty, therefore, is to obey the Delphic command, 'Know thyself', for once we know ourselves, we may learn how to care for ourselves, but otherwise we never shall.[15]

How can someone become better – live to the full extent of one's potential, and raise oneself to the fullness of a human existence – if one doesn't know *who one is*, and *what one's aims are*? Knowledge of oneself modifies what is known. Socrates argues that the individual not only refines his capacity to discern between right/better and wrong/worse in questions involving moral choice as he advances in the search for self-knowledge – 'There is much more risk in buying learning than in buying food' (*Protagoras*, 314 *a*) – but he also begins to act according to the appropriate knowledge. Socrates' conclusion, shared by Plato but rejected by Aristotle, is that *knowing* is the necessary and sufficient condition for *doing* – he who knows makes no mistakes – since the knowledge of what is right from the ethical point of view is always followed by the right action. The validity of this equation, as we will see later (chapter 4, section 5) is doubtful. For the moment, let's concentrate on the Socratic notion of self-knowledge.

How does Socrates proceed? A clear appreciation of the fragility of the printed word as a means of moral persuasion and the fear of being misunderstood led Socrates never to lay down his thought in writing and to opt for live dialogue as a means for communication. The dialogic method, adopted by the philosopher, is one of progressive approximation to truth by means of a lively exchange of questions and answers (*élenchos*). The dynamics of the exchange follow, in most cases, a defined pattern.

At no moment does Socrates present himself as the bearer of a positive creed or a doctrine to be impressed on the mind of his interlocutor. The essence of the *élenchos* consists in a double movement: to overcome ignorance and get light out of darkness. The mind of the other is the locus of action. The Socratic interlocutor is urged to recognise a double self-deception: he imagines and is confident he knows what in fact he does not know, but he also knows more than he imagines he knows. While

Socrates in his role as an 'irritating gadfly' nags at the wound and pulls at the veil covering false knowledge, provoking doubt and perplexity in whoever listens to him, Socrates in his role as the 'midwife of truth' opens up the person's mind, and brings knowledge into the open that was latent and hidden in his thought. 'Those who frequent my company [. . .] have never learned anything from me; the many admirable truths they bring to birth have been discovered by themselves from within.' (*Theaetetus*, 150 c–d). *Maieutics* is the art of bringing to birth.[16]

The Socratic confession of absolute ignorance – immortalised in the dictum 'I only know that I know nothing' (*Apology*, 23 a–b) – contains an obvious element of exaggeration and ironic mischief (*eironeía*). Whether rightly or wrongly, Socrates thinks he knows many things, not all of them trivial: he is confident he knows that the world around him is not as good as it should be; that the philosophical life is the *télos* of the well-educated soul; and that a reflective death is worth dying.

The point, however, is that sincere doubt never leaves him. The element that ends up predominating, at least in the most clearly Socratic dialogues of the Platonic corpus, is the inconclusive character of the search and the extraordinary difficulty of finding *terra firma* in the art of self-knowledge. In the *Phaedrus* (229 e – 230 a), for example, Socrates reacts to the suggestion of undertaking an investigation in the manner of pre-Socratic science, to shed light on a supposed enigmatic occurrence in the natural world, by quoting the Delphic motto once more, and admitting to complete ignorance about himself:

I myself have certainly no time for the business: and

I'll tell you why, my friend: I can't as yet 'know myself' as the inscription at Delphi enjoins me to do; and so long as that ignorance remains it seems to me ridiculous to inquire into extraneous matters. Consequently I don't bother about such things, but accept the current beliefs about them, and direct my inquiries, as I have just said, rather to myself, to discover whether I really am a more complex creature and more puffed up with pride than Typhon, or a simpler, gentler being whom heaven has blessed with a serene, un-Typhonic nature.[17]

Also, in the moments preceding his execution by the orders of the Athenian courts, Socrates reaffirms his confidence in the superiority of the philosophical life and the immortality of the soul, but warns not only of his own fallibility – 'If you [Simmias and Cebes] take my advice, you'll care little for Socrates but much more for the truth' (*Phaedo*, 91 *b–c*) – but also, in a wider sense, of the precariousness of all mortal knowledge. The ins and outs of the argument, the pathos of the last moment drawing near, and the surfacing of doubts and uncertainties as the dialogue progresses, lead the philosopher to an attitude not of sceptical despondency, but of sober hope: 'Let's not admit into our soul the thought that there's probably nothing sound in rational arguments; but let's far rather admit that we're not yet sound ourselves, but must strive manfully to become so' (*Phaedo*, 90 *d–e*).[18]

The fundamental orientation of Socratic philosophy is not the search for self-knowledge as an end in itself, but as a road that leads to and becomes part of the perfecting of a person's existence. Self-knowledge is the basis of all the Socratic virtues – moderation, cool courage, justice and intellectual consistency – just as the lack of it is the source of the worst moral aberrations.

External dialogue, led by the philosopher, is the intermittent occasion for a change in the mind of the interlocutor, which, if it is successful, would give rise to an *inner* dialogue which would, this time, become permanent and capable of sustaining him in the ethical life. The strategy on which Socrates bases himself to develop the dialectical fencing-match of his conversation consists in touching a sensitive nerve, and digging out each person's false certainties. The recognition, on the part of the interlocutor, of his inconsistency and of his lack of self-knowledge is the equivalent of surrender in the process of bringing to birth.

Know thyself: the type of knowledge demanded by the Delphic command is not to be confused with the search for an objective knowledge like that which has been brought to us by neuroscience or the nuclear age. As we will see, it would be difficult to establish with a minimum of certainty the existence of reliable progress in self-knowledge in the Socratic sense, from the Greek enlightenment to our own days. If scientific knowledge of the external world is never final, the knowledge that we have of ourselves seems to be condemned for ever to its initial stages. The mere existence of Socratic maieutics – not to speak of the plethora of therapeutic approaches in psychology that are directly or indirectly indebted to it – is a powerful testimony to the opacity of the human mind to each individual. Unlike the positive knowledges that time assimilates, destroys and overtakes, the Socratic injunction of self-knowledge has the property of being always in need of starting over again.

5. Introspection and Self-Deception: Epistemology

Monster or angel, Caligula or Francis of Assisi, each person is protagonist in his own plot. Others see and hear us, judge and interpret our acts and words. But they have no access to what goes on in our minds while we act, write and speak. Here, everything is inference and analogy: an effort of the empathetic imagination. However much we try to live the inner experience of another person, someone suffering from hunger or giving birth for example, the centre of gravity of our minds will go on being our own subjective experience: our mental simulation of what it would be like to live through someone's hunger or birth-pangs. No one can move from within himself. When it's a case of each person's mental processes and states, it is not only the neuroscientist, with his sophisticated clinical paraphernalia, that is condemned to see from the outside – it is the whole of humanity, apart from the subject himself.

Each individual, therefore, is uniquely situated to know about himself, and to examine the contents of his own mind. The cognitive authority of the subject – of the assertions he makes in the first person singular – appears with the greatest forcefulness in cases involving the occurrence of simple perceptions and sensations. If I am feeling heat, pain, sexual desire, or drowsiness, for instance, it is difficult to imagine that I might be mistaken about this, or that someone might be able to correct me on the point.

It is true that I can be mistaken about the specificity of the sensation, or not find the right word to describe it – the ability to discern internal perceptions and name them has an element of learning analogous to what happens in the case of external sensory impressions. But, even if I am, to take an extreme situation, dreaming or hallucinating a given sensation, all that anyone can do is try to wake me up or show that its cause is imaginary; not that it doesn't exist or that I don't feel it. When I wake up or stop hallucinating I see the self-deception for what it is, but the reality of the sensation while it was being lived remains unassailable.[19]

The cognitive problem of introspection appears in an acute form, however, when what is at stake are not simple contents, like a toothache, but the search for self-knowledge in a wider sense. Each individual's privileged access to his own mind – his thoughts, desires, fantasies, emotions, values and intentions – continues to exist, but the certainty of the simple perceptions and sensations has gone.

The basic questions of self-knowledge – who am I? what do I really feel, desire, and believe? what do I want to do with my life? – seem to contain an intractable element that makes them singularly slippery and unsuited to reliable treatment from the cognitive point of view.

Of course there are exceptions. Sartre, for example, with the conceit of those who know themselves well enough to be able to pontificate about others, thought it 'easy enough to describe Baudelaire's interior life'.[20] Others, however, beginning with the poet himself, were not possessed of the same easy aptitude. From Montaigne to Darwin, Calvin to Nietzsche, Teresa of Ávila to Diderot, Adam Smith to Dostoevsky, and from psychoanalysis to socio-biology, the basic conclusion of those who have devoted themselves seriously to the search for self-knowledge seems well summed up in Wittgenstein's sentence: 'Nothing is so difficult as not deceiving oneself'. It is symptomatic that Nietzsche – the thinker who, according to Freud, went furthest and most courageously down the road of self-knowledge – finally concluded:

> That which, from the earliest times to the present moment, men have found so hard to understand is their ignorance of themselves! Not only in regard to good and evil, but in regard to what is much more essential! The primeval delusion still lives on that one knows, and knows quite precisely in every case, how human action is brought about [. . .] Actions are never what they appear to us to be! We have expended so much labour on learning that external things are not as they appear to us to be – very well! the case is the same with the inner world! [. . .] So we are necess- arily strangers to ourselves, we do not comprehend ourselves, we have to misunderstand ourselves, for us the law 'Each is furthest from himself' applies to all eternity – we are not 'men of knowledge' with respect to ourselves.[21]

How are we to explain the difficulty and precariousness of self-knowledge in the natural epistemological condition of men? Why is it that, when we turn to look at our minds and try to understand ourselves, we encounter so much opacity? Obviously, I do not pretend to give a satisfactory answer to a question that will probably go on providing material for controversy while there are still philosophers in the world ready to controvert. 'Don't explain yourselves if you want to remain in agreement',

Diderot wisely recommends. Nevertheless, I believe that it would be worthwhile to examine in more detail some of the main obstacles in the way of self-knowledge, keeping in mind its relevance for the analysis of self-deception and its close links with it.

The epistemology of introspective self-knowledge is marked by several peculiarities and anomalies, which can be analysed separately. Consider, as a beginning, Montaigne's striking account, taken from his own experience:

> Not only does the wind of chance events shake me about as it lists, but I also shake and disturb myself by the instability of my stance: anyone who turns his prime attention on to himself will hardly ever find himself in the same state twice. I give my soul this face or that, depending upon which side I lay it down on. I speak about myself in diverse ways: that is because I look at myself in diverse ways. Every sort of contradiction can be found in me, depending on some twist or attribute: timid, insolent; chaste, lecherous; talkative, taciturn; tough, sickly; clever, dull, brooding, affable, lying, truthful, learned, ignorant; generous, miserly and then prodigal – I can see something of all that in myself, depending on how I gyrate; and anyone who studies himself attentively finds in himself and in his very judgement this whirring about and this discordance. There is nothing I can say about myself as a whole simply and completely, without intermingling and admixture.[22]

Nothing is the same as anything else. The shades of colour may be Montaigne's alone, but his problem is universal.

Self-knowledge modifies what is known. In the observation of the external world, in normal circumstances, the object has an existence separate and independent from the subject, which opens up a space for us to try to understand it *as it really is*. In introspection, things are never like that.

The internal perception we have of our mental states and processes and of the kind of person we are does not happen via our sensory organs, as in the apprehension of external reality, but via a reflexive mental process that is an integral part of our own mind. When this process is activated, it ends up modifying and creating a new internal reality. However much I try to get outside myself and find an external point of view that will allow me to have trustworthy and unbiased knowledge of my mental/emotional life or of my own character, there is no way I can avoid submitting the object of my introspection to my subjectivity. The observation of oneself interacts and is crudely mixed up with what is being observed. The interpretation is the text.

The problem of the interference of the subject with the object, it's worth pointing out, is not exclusive to introspective self-knowledge. The uncertainty principle in quantum physics and in the special theory of relativity describes situations in which the properties of an object – like, for example, the energy and position of a particle – do not possess definite values until they are observed and measured. The observer determines the observed; measuring fixes the measurement.

But in the case of introspection it is not just the degree of virulence of the uncertainty principle that is unusual. The nature of the interference is also different from what is found in the problematic areas of physics. The contamination of the cognitive process doesn't happen, so to speak, from outside in, like a virus that moulds an organism, but from in outwards, like an antibody secreted by the organism, and which makes it immune to any serious claim to objectivity. The principle of uncertainty here goes through a kind of mutation or 'quantum leap' in which the floating mental states of the observer – the internal circumstances and particular configuration of his subjectivity at the moment of introspection – powerfully interfere in the act of cognition.

Some suggestive, though inevitably indirect, empirical evidence of the interference of mental states in the intro-spective process appears in experiments on the recognition of one's own voice based on electrodermal activity.

Our mental processes – sensations, emotions, thoughts etc. – have the power to provoke, by means of subtle glandular secretions, alterations in the capacity of our skin to offer resistance to the passage of a small electric current. When we hear a recorded voice, for example, whichever voice it may be, the electricity conducted by the skin increases. When we hear a recording of *our own voice*, the dermal conductivity increases even more, and that is objectively registered and measured by an instrument called a polygraph.

The surprising thing is that when we are asked to identify a recorded voice, and to say whether or not it is our own voice, our answers are on average *less* correct than those registered by the polygraph. What has been discovered after exhaustive tests is that the errors in identification are not accidental, but are closely related to the mental state of the subject. While states of depression and low self-esteem tend to lead to us making mistakes, and failing to identify the voice even when it is ours, states of euphoria and high self-esteem tend, on the contrary, to make us mistakenly recognise as ours voices that do not belong to us.[23]

The interference of subjectivity is manifest here in the variations in the capacity to identify one's own recorded voice correctly. The self-deception is in the inconsistency between the answers offered by the electrodermal conductivity and measured by the polygraph, on the one hand, and those given orally by the subject, on the other. It is as if the body knew correctly, without being aware that it knows, what the mind doesn't know, though it thinks it does.

In the experiment, however, the voice, though our own, comes from outside. Imagine now what happens when it's a question of recognising and trying to understand not something single and external, like one's own recorded voice, but the cacophony of silent voices that inhabit our mind; when what is involved is the kaleidoscopic multitude of mental/emotional states and processes whose very linguistic designation is problematic.[24]

Choose your own account: original sin, alienation, the unconscious, the selfish gene. The maps differ, the metaphors shift and the theoretical solutions proliferate in the history of ideas, but the experience of the internal labyrinth is essentially the same: 'The human heart has so many crannies where vanity hides, so many holes where falsehood lurks, is so decked out with deceiving hypocrisy, that it often dupes itself.'[25]

The difficulty of introspective self-knowledge and the propensity to self-deception seem to be the consequence not just of powerful psychological processes (as I will argue in the next section) but also of factors inherent in the epistemological situation of the knowing subject. Such factors increase the vulnerability of self-knowledge to interference originating in the mental states of the person (*the principle of acute uncertainty*) and they seriously restrict the margin for the adoption of cautionary and preventive measures against the risk of serious contamination.

Our conclusions about ourselves, whatever they may be, are the product of one part of our mind interacting with other parts along paths and in ways that we understand little of. Therefore, whatever conclusions we may reach as we explore the streets, tunnels and buildings of the internal city in which we were born – and which we will never be able to leave until the end of our days – there will also be good reason to keep the windows of doubt ajar, and the atmosphere well ventilated.

A simple and easily generalisable illustration can help to make the nature of the problem clearer. Imagine someone, me for example, resolves at some point in his life to *question his own honesty*. I divide myself: I want to know who I am. I ask myself: have I been honest with myself, or have I cheated, lied, and cunningly beat a retreat every time embarrassing questions surface in my consciousness?

The question in itself, it would be nice to believe, exudes honesty. 'Here is someone', I could say to myself with some satisfaction, 'seriously committed to examining the recesses of his mind and settling his accounts with himself.' This is a simple trap for the naive. Nobody needs to persuade himself of his own honesty more than the dishonest man. Why this sudden urgency to know if I am honest or not? The crowning success of dishonesty is the intimate and sincere belief – the agreeable, invigorating conviction – that one is, all things considered, honest. The question in itself gives no sign, then, of commendable honesty. What it does is awake a hint of suspicion. 'Here is someone who needs a fishy settling of accounts in order to convince himself of something.'

When the first trap has been dismantled, the question remains. How are we to know? 'No one should be judge in his own cause.' Why not follow Aristotle's excellent recommendation and ask for an outside opinion, given by someone not as biased towards me as I myself am? But, so that the impartial judge can tell whether or not I am usually honest with myself, he has to know what I am really like inside – what I've been thinking, how I came to believe what I believe, how I faced fears and dilemmas, why I acted when I did, how and why I took some of life's tricky decisions etc.

It wouldn't be necessary, of course, to recount absolutely everything I know about myself, just the essential. All that would be needed is an open, courageous confession, a frank testimony, honest to the marrow, in the style of autobiographies that promise us to open everything up, tell all, put the finger in the wound, but with one crucial difference. It would not be a public confession, with one eye on the reader, suffering the terrible ambiguity of calling attention to oneself to confess to the world, in cold print and impeccable prose, the weaknesses, lapses and the vanity of the author. No. It would be a private encounter, and strictly in secret; an opening of oneself to another, closer to the confessional or to the couch than to autobiographical confession as a literary genre.

The strategy of confession, however, comes up against a serious problem of circularity. Suppose that I am, at bottom, dishonest with myself. If that is really the case, then the confession will not be reliable. I will be able to lie without realising it, spontaneously forgetting a crucial detail here, there unwittingly omitting a piece of relevant information. Confessing is recounting; recounting is selecting; selecting is weighing; weighing is judging: my confession will be the more or less polished reflection of the biased and covertly fraudulent verdicts that make up my dishonesty. But the whole problem is that I don't know, and have no way of knowing, if this is so. If I have to tell everything to a neutral interlocutor to know whether or not I am honest with myself, this is clear proof that I mistrust myself. But, if I mistrust myself to the point of having to look for an external verdict, how am I to trust the confessional story I tell?

The quality of the introspection on which the confession and the external verdict depend is indeterminate. If I could fix and know its degree of veracity, the idea of asking for outside help would be superfluous, and there would be no need for me to go to the effort of looking for it. But, since this is not possible, the result of the introspection will be in doubt, and any verdict given based on it will be doubtful.

What's more, the last word will go on being mine, in any case. The authority of any external verdict will always depend on my own assent! If my interlocutor says I am honest and have nothing to worry about, I can conclude that my story must have been flawed, or that they have been very lenient with me. But if he says, on the contrary, that I am dishonest and am no more than an inveterate opportunist where I myself am concerned, there is nothing to stop me leaving with the sincere feeling that I have given the wrong impression or that they were too hard, puritanical and strict with me. Are these honest conclusions?

With the illusion of external verdict out of the way, I

come back to myself and to the initial question. Familiarity hinders knowledge. But in the case of introspective self-knowledge, it is not merely an at times suffocating familiarity – 'I'm tired of my own imagination' – that harms the cognitive process. What does the real damage is the complete absence of a term of reference.

No human being will ever know what it is to be another human (or any other kind of) being. Internal experience of oneself is *the only one* and is *all* that each person can have. If I want to know whether or not I am usually honest with myself, there is no way I can move, however briefly, into the subjective intimacy of another person, so as to get a minimum of contrast and perspective in relation to my own mind. It is as if the privileged access I have into my own mental processes were paid for – more than paid for, extorted from me – by a total exclusion from the direct experience of any other manifestation of subjective experience but my own.

I can join with the Stoic philosopher Epictetus and say, without fear of error: 'Do they speak ill of me? Ah, if only they knew me as I know myself!'[26] But, if other people's ignorance of me comes as a relief, the isolation and the precarious knowledge that we have of ourselves generate perplexity and apprehension.

The analysis of the epistemology of introspection suggests that we should be cautious when it comes to fixing our own beliefs. Am I honest? Any clear-cut, assertive reply is either contradictory or highly suspect. If the reply is a resounding *no*, it carries within it the seed of its own negation. After all, how can someone as dishonest with himself as that accept himself honestly as such?[27] The optimistic conclusion is: I'm not so bad after all!

But if the reply is a radiant *yes*, full of self-confidence, the alarm-bell rings, and the whiff of self-deception can be smelt already. Introspection is *one step* inside: I divide myself and try to observe myself attentively. It's one part of myself trying to monitor and know the others. But when I analyse this movement, I am taking a *further step* inside. Now, I want to examine myself in the introspective act, that is, to observe myself in the act of observing myself: am I being honest when I confidently answer that I am honest?

There are plenty of epistemological reasons for doubt. The initial question – am I honest? – reveals that I mistrust myself. But, if I mistrust the mental *whole* being observed, why should I trust in the *part* of my mind that has been invited to distinguish itself from the others and observe them? What are the credentials of that thing in me that tries to know and judge the rest of me? What protects and secures me against the potential opportunism of the observer? Nothing. Before accepting any verdict, it is necessary to ask the same questions of the *part* as we ask of the *whole*. Who guards the guardian? What audits the auditor? It's an infinite regression. The shining sun of certainty fills me with doubt. When dishonesty is weak and anaemic it wants to *seem* honest; when it is strong and bursting with life, it convinces us that it *already is*.

6. Motivation and Self-Deception: Moral Psychology

From a scientific perspective, one aimed at the ideal of the greatest possible objectivity, the validity of a theory or a forecast is confirmed (or not) by the public, observable

SELF-KNOWLEDGE AND SELF-DECEPTION

course of events. The occurrence of a lunar eclipse or the functioning of the hypothalamus are natural processes that do not depend on what the person examining them may be thinking or feeling.

Human subjectivity, however, which we know of by means of introspection, does not lend itself to similar treatment. The validity of our knowledge of our experiences and character depends entirely on our internal capacity for discernment, and cannot be refuted by anything outside our mind. Melancholy apart, the poet's observation is perfect: 'We are our memory, we are this chimerical museum of inconstant forms, this pile of broken mirrors'.[28]

Lived subjective experiences, whatever they are, have the same epistemological status as dreams. Only the person himself is able to recall them, and even for him, there is no way of reliably distinguishing between what has been lived through in the recesses of the mind, on the one hand, and the memory of that experience, on the other. What did I feel as I looked at that landscape? If remembering modifies what is remembered, what can I do about it? Remember again!

This peculiar characteristic of our natural epistemological condition does not perpetually condemn us to self-deception, but it does make us extremely liable to it. Every attempt at self-knowledge is affected, to some degree, by the principle of acute uncertainty. The feeling analysed is not the feeling felt ('it's tiring to feel when you think'). The desire that is meditated and reflected upon is not direct, immediately felt desire, and may make it undesirable. If, for some reason, we become conscious that we are doing something – singing, kissing or reading for example – then we are not entirely doing it. Our mental states and the fluctuating contours of our mood heavily affect our self-image, and the beliefs we have about ourselves. The best protection against the ever-present risk of self-deception – always supposing, of course, that it is worth protecting against – is to try to elucidate and understand its internal mechanisms and the dynamic of the ways it affects our mental processes.

The epistemological argument (as set out in the previous section) describes the barriers and pitfalls on the road to self-knowledge, and our resultant liability, in principle, to self-deception. The moral psychology approach tries to determine the predominant direction and the particular content of the deceptive beliefs we create about, or for, ourselves.

Epistemology is the bed of the river, psychology its waters. The principle of acute uncertainty opens up self-deception's flank to attack, but the invasion is led by forces whose nature is psychological. If the epistemological side of the problem has a universal nature, and one possibly inseparable from the human condition, the psychological dimension is contingent and peculiar to concrete human beings, though it may be possible to speculate about the existence of statistically dominant patterns in the pre-reflective world of practical existence. The challenge is to discern, identify and analyse these patterns.

How are we to understand the propensity for self-deception? The reflections of the 'underground man' portrayed by Dostoevsky provide a good starting-point:

> In every man's remembrances there are things he will not reveal to everybody, but only to his friends. There are other things he will not reveal even to his friends, but only to himself, and then only under a pledge of

secrecy. Finally, there are some things that a man is afraid to reveal even to himself, and any honest man accumulates a pretty fair number of such things. That is to say, the more respectable a man is, the more of them he has.[29]

The situation described, we may note, has something paradoxical about it: how can one and the same man *have* memories and fear to reveal them, not to others, but to himself? If someone fears to reveal something to himself, then he doesn't know what it is; but if, as Dostoevsky's narrator says, they are 'remembrances', then they have already been revealed to the person, and there is no reason for him to fear them.

The paradoxical logic and the apparent violation of the principle of non-contradiction in the concept of self-deception will be taken up in chapter 3, and for this reason will not detain us now. Let's suppose that the last class of memories – those we hide from ourselves – has in some way been forgotten by the subject, and look, not at the *how*, but at the *why* of self-deception. What do we fear we might come to know about ourselves? What forces internal to the person may be motivating such a fear?

The concentric circles of concealment described by the 'underground man' have a common centre. In each individual's mind there are things he prefers others not to know, and, nearer the centre, things that intimate friends mustn't know. But there are also things that he himself – the alert centre that determines what others should or should not know – *prefers not to know*. Self-deception, from the psychological point of view, is the continuation of interpersonal deception by other means.

The basic idea here is that the centre needs, in some way, to protect itself in order to preserve or appreciate the value of its own existence. There is an interested resistance, on the part of the knowing subject, which filters not only the knowledge that others might have of his mental processes, but which also blocks, to some degree, the access that he himself has to what happens in his mind. To lower one's guard – to allow the collapse of this resistance that protects the centre – would imply a double loss: the loss of respectability in the eyes of others, and loss of respect in one's own eyes, that is, of that inner sensation that one is 'honest and respectable'.

There is a great deal at stake. The natural epistemological condition of man makes our mental life opaque to reflection. But the source of the shadows and echoes that, to a greater or lesser degree, distort the image we form of ourselves is of a psychological and moral nature. Whatever the value-yardstick relevant in each particular case, the individual wants to seem to others – and principally to those that matter – better than he knows himself to be.

However, the opinion of others, no matter how important it may be for each person, becomes empty and insipid if it is not well rooted in the opinion we have of ourselves. When one's own light is missing, reflected light neither shines, nor warms us. Other people's opinion is, at bottom, our own: it's the opinion we have of the opinions of others about us. *Seeming good* – being on the lookout and taking care that we are respectable in the eyes of the world and that we earn others' approval – is not enough. What is decisive is that *one should feel and believe oneself to be good*. The vital point for the individual alone with himself is sincerely to convince himself that he is honest in what matters within, and, all things considered, deserving of approval both from himself and others. The fulcrum of self-deception is not in each person's attempt to seem what he is not. It resides in the capacity we have to feel and believe in good faith that we are what we are not.

Nothing explains everything. The waters of self-deception flow from many springs. If the desire to think well of oneself frequently leads us into self-deception, the same can be said of the symmetrically opposed possibility of a morbid propensity for self-condemnation, or to contempt or repugnance for oneself.

The hypothesis here, however, is that in normal conditions of temperature and pressure the powerful, persuasive force of self-love – the tendency, up to a point natural and healthy, to protect the centre against what might threaten or harm it – prevails. In the words of Sophocles in *Oedipus the King*: 'It is sweet to keep our thoughts out of the range of hurt' (lines 1390–91). The partiality associated with the inflation of self-love, on the one hand, and the mental effervescence sometimes brought about by appetites, passions and motivations that carry us away in practical existence, on the other, are factors of the first order in the moral psychology of self-deception.

The subjective experience in which we are immersed is not a controlled experiment, nor does it lend itself to the experimental method. In these circumstances, how are we to make clear and evident the deceptions we nurture and the lies we tell ourselves?

A first approach can be tried in the history of science itself. The ever-renewed struggle against the Baconian *idols of the tribe*, like the sceptical impulse that cornered the Cartesian cogito, bringing it to the final certainty of *not being able to doubt the doubt,* bear witness to the fact that, even in the austere realms of the search for scientific knowledge, there is an interested resistance operating in the recesses of the cognitive process – a silent, insinuating preference for ourselves that may compromise the objectivity of the results. A concrete and well-documented example of how the propensity to lie to oneself is a constant threat in the undercurrents of science is Darwin's account of his incessant struggle to resist the rising tide of self-love and control his own thinking.

The ideal of objectivity demands of the knowing subject a discipline which is not merely technical and intellectual. Ethics is indispensable. The *good conduct* of the mind in the attempt to know requires, amongst other things, the honesty of not thinking one knows what one doesn't know, the respect for evidence and a readiness not to make things easy for oneself. The young Darwin's notes, posthumously published as his 'metaphysical notebooks', reveal the biologist's determination to observe himself, and to discipline the mind in the search for objective knowledge about the natural world.

The clear recognition of the existence of treacherous underground currents under the placid surface of the conscious mind is a constant note in the young Darwin's reflections: 'The possibility of the brain having [a] whole train of thoughts, feeling & perception separate from the ordinary state of mind, is probably analogous to the double individuality implied by habit, when one acts unconsciously with respect to [the] more energetic self.'[30]

Darwin's need to submit his own mind to stricter standards of self-discipline and the repeated experience of the difficulty of doing so led him to implement, in his scientific practice, what he would years later call his methodological 'golden rule', namely: every time he came across some empirical fact or argument contrary to what he was inclined to believe, he should not rely on his memory, but should force himself to set it down *straight away and in written form*. For the spontaneous tendency of his memory, Darwin would point out in his *Autobiography*, was to thwart his desire to advance knowledge, and to obliterate from the field of conscious attention, without him realising it, anything that might threaten what was already supposedly known. The spirit of Darwin's golden rule stands out with crystal clarity in Wittgenstein's advice to an ex-student: 'You can't think decently if you don't want to hurt yourself.'[31]

The reverse of the readiness to fight against the rising tide of self-love in the search for knowledge is the capitulation of the mind that gives in and lets itself be dragged away by the gently ebbing tide of self-deception. When the depths begin to move and impose themselves, logic founders, and the intellect, however formidable it may be, is a mere plaything on the moving waters of belief.

This was how Boyle, one of the fathers of modern chemistry, had the rare privilege of dying in a state of euphoria over the 'discovery' of the alchemical formula for transforming base metals into gold, leaving the secret of this unique treasure in the care of an intrigued friend (Locke).[32] It was also how Hobbes reached his memorable mathematical 'proof' of the squaring of the circle, though he still had to defend it, come hell or high water, from questioning and malicious attack from the 'envious' Oxford geometricians.[33] And how Hegel managed to conceive the inconceivable, and transform the fossil evidence for extinct biological species into 'examples of primitive art', so as to keep intact the foundations of the monumental Gothic nightmare that is his *Naturphilosophie*.[34] In the gap between the desire to know and discover, on the one hand, and the self-deceived belief in the supposedly known and the discovered, on the other, there hides the difference between the meritorious and the grotesque in the annals of science.

If self-deception in the world of intellectual speculation is merely ridiculous, self-deception in practical existence can be tragic. Religious fervour, for example, often mobilises the best and most elevated parts of a man, to put them at the service of what is worst and most odious. From the same source from which sacrifice and genuine self-denial arise there seems to come, too, the barbaric blindness that sanctifies, in the eyes of the believer, the brutal persecution and extermination of our fellow-men. An analogous combination of greatness and perversity – of a 'divine' superstructure of belief at the service of the 'devilish' infrastructure of action – seems to accompany, *mutatis mutandis*, the most aberrant cases of ideological enthusiasm and political fanaticism. The degree of blindness, in these cases, is a direct function of the strength of belief.

A recurrent pattern of conduct in Lisbon during the Inquisition shows how far the self-deception of religious fanaticism can go. The sentences handed down by the *autos-da-fé* contained a clause by which any heretics who made a convincing retraction received the 'privilege' of being hanged before being thrown to the flames. For the devout public, however, such indulgence was inappropriate. Seized by a divine fury and an urgent thirst for justice, the faithful often rode roughshod over the authorities' decision, kidnapped the heretic and guaranteed to everyone the incomparable public spectacle of the heretic being burned in the flesh.

Can there be a more deplorable example than this of how the diabolical pleasure in another's suffering can make itself pass, in the believer's subjectivity, for the most pious, unblemished good faith? The context and the particular pretexts change, but the primary motivations and the patterns of conduct remain at bottom the same. It is sombrely ironic and disturbing that Himmler, the Nazi leader responsible for the carrying out of criminal acts on a large scale, like the programme of extermination in Poland, was known by his peers in the higher echelons of the Nazi party as 'our Ignatius Loyola'.[35]

What can one say when faced by the insane monstrousness of atrocities like these? The best thing to do, perhaps, is always to remember that the distance that separates us from the repetition of extreme situations of persecution, oppression and cruelty may be less than we would like to imagine. There is a secret thread linking the tragic self-deception of communities taken over by insane images of justice, regeneration and superiority, on the one hand, and the pedestrian, prosaic self-deception of the everyday individual, on the other. Both seem to have a lot to do with the innumerable partialities that affect, to a greater or lesser degree, the perceptions we have of ourselves, and the judgements we make about our own motivations. Collective self-deception on a large scale is the tragic and grotesque result of a large number of self-deceptions, synchronised with each other on the individual level.

There are extreme situations that, seen from outside and from a long way off, seem to us – as they in fact were –

absurd and inexplicably inhuman. But they did not seem so in the eyes of all those who, inside and nearby, lived through them, justified them to themselves, and acted within them. These were terrible, cowardly people, fearful and sinister, but as human as any others. The experience of situations of extreme adversity in human history – war, famine, epidemic, hyperinflation, tyranny, panic, catastrophe etc. – reveal, with rare exceptions, behaviours and character traits that give the lie to the illusions we nurture about ourselves in times of peace and normality.

The uncomfortable question is: how many of us would have been 'the others', the inexplicably inhuman ones, neglectful and cruel? How any of us would have acted as they acted in analogous circumstances? It is probable that the most suspect and dangerous ones are, precisely, those who do not have, or allow themselves to have, any doubt. The worst blind man is the one who is convinced that he *sees*. There is nothing easier than to point out the mistakes, prejudices and fanaticism of others, while remaining blind and insensitive to our own.

The move from the micro- to the macrocosm of self-deception – the secret thread joining in the same plot the individual reality of the partiality everyone has for themselves and the collective result of a strange, wicked world – appears in a clear and unintentionally suggestive form in the poem 'Travelling in a comfortable car' by Berthold Brecht:

Travelling in a comfortable car
Down a rainy road in the country
We saw a ragged fellow at nightfall
Signal to us for a ride, with a low bow.

We had a roof and we had room and we drove on
And we heard me say, in a morose tone of voice: 'No
We can't take anyone with us.'
We had gone on a long way, perhaps a day's march
When suddenly I was shocked by this voice of mine
This behaviour of mine and this
Whole world.[36]

The traveller/protagonist looks back, reflects, and doesn't recognise himself in what he did. Two moments, two voices: the first, that denies help when the moment to give it offers itself; and the second, which recounts what happened and doesn't recognise himself in the other voice. There is the audible voice, in inverted commas in the poem, and which disgusts us; and the silent one that narrates, expresses remorse, condemns this wicked world and wins our sympathy as it castigates the other.

The problem, however, is the relation *in time* between these two voices. We can ask: does the situation described in the poem mark the conversion of the traveller? Does it reveal the definitive transition from a selfish voice that dies (the first) to the generous one that is born and takes the other's place (the second)? Or does it rather illustrate a pattern of strategic alternation between two voices that are apparently opposed, but at bottom are like Siamese twins? To what degree do the sincere emotion and the subtly comforting reflection of the second voice guarantee that the other voice has truly been silenced, and that, next time, things will be different?

Our feelings and our self-image have the remarkable property of adjusting themselves, without us realising it, to the circumstances surrounding us. It is more than easy, it is downright pleasant to imagine oneself firm, generous and sympathetic in the abstract, when the temptation of not being so is remote, and the challenge merely hypothetical.[37] Why not bask in the sunshine of self-approval and of a generous image of ourselves, when the storm is far off? But the weather can change. And, when it does – when the concrete opportunity at last offers itself to prove in practice that we are everything we imagine ourselves to be – the voice we hear is often no longer our own. Actions speak instead. And what our actions say is not always what we are used to hearing, in silence, when the future is something still open, its promise is a generous one, and its challenge, remote.

At bottom, it's as if, taking up the car metaphor again, the driver turned off the headlights at crucial moments, when he is really being tested, and left only the moral tail-lights on. When we're past the riskiest part of the journey – past the moment when the character is really put to the test – the second voice comes on stage to express surprise at the other, repair the damage, and restore the status quo for the self-image. Thus, the headlights and tail-lights alternate strategically all along the road, assuring us of the worst of two worlds: evil's good conscience.

The car is comfortable and the world is a strange place. But the conflict between the two voices in the poem is, perhaps, more apparent than real. For they can perfectly well be complementary, inseparable aspects – two sides – of the same voice: the good voice while the opportunity of doing good is comfortably distant and the bad voice at moments when it is uncomfortably at hand. 'Time', says Guimarães Rosa, 'is the magician of all treacheries'. [38] Further along life's path, the exposed nerve of another dilemma on another dark, rainy road is going to demand definitions: action or omission? Will it be different next time?

7. Deceiving Others as One Deceives Oneself?

Doubts cannot lie. Ask yourself whether you know yourself and you will have serious reasons to begin to doubt. Familiarity blinds us. The epistemological peculiarities of introspective self-knowledge, on the one hand, and the insinuating presence of powerful psychological forces, on the other, make the search for knowledge of oneself a formidably difficult and slippery task. What is astonishing, however, is the almost irrepressible human propensity, present in each of us to a certain degree and in certain sensitive spots, for shutting the door on doubt and quite innocently losing the key. Self-deception is not the simple ignorance of not knowing and recognising that one does not know. It is the illusory, unfounded claim to self-knowledge – imagining that one knows without this being so, the convinced belief that seduces and confuses, the feverish faith that carries one away, the cocksure certainty of knowing something that is not the case.

Of course, there are gradations. The ignorance inherent in the human condition cannot be defeated in its entirety – what would we say if someone said he knew himself perfectly? – but it can be mitigated. The Socratic 'know thyself', like the ideal of absolute scientific objectivity, is a moving point in infinity, a compass in the labyrinth that is life lived and seen from within. The road that it points to, however, only points to an end we must approach with humility, recognising the legitimacy of doubt and starting over again when necessary.

If the asymptotically objective truths of science are shallow, but progressive, the openly subjective truths of self-knowledge are deep, but condemned always to return to their beginning. If scientific knowledge is never final, the knowledge we have of ourselves seems bound to be eternally incipient. Every victory is partial, every conquest, provisional, and every certainty, suspect. Extreme and aberrant situations of self-deception – episodes apparently far from common experience – provide valuable clues about the poisonous clouds and intoxicating gases that surround every human heart with their radioactive charge.

Consider, for example, the phenomenon of intoxicating self-love that we call *vanity*. There are more and less vain people in the world. An extreme case, and a picturesque one, is the *Stalin paradox*.

When he was revising his official biography for publication, the Soviet dictator ordered the following sentence to be inserted: 'Stalin never let his work be affected by the least shadow of vanity, presumption or idolatry'.[39] The paradox hits you in the eye: to deny vanity in such a way is to affirm it to the skies! When he denies his own vanity publicly and categorically, Stalin ends up revealing to the world that he was possessed by it to a crushing degree. The question is: who is the dictator lying to: himself or the reading public?

The hypocrite is calculating – he measures the effects of his actions and puts himself in another's position so as to get his aim right. If Stalin was only being hypocritical, that is, if his intention was cynically and deliberately to trick the reading public, he would very probably have realised the contradiction he was falling into, and would not have said what he said *in the way he said it*. By denying his vanity as he does, the dictator reveals that he is so dominated by it that he cannot even admit to himself that he is like that. He needs to lie to himself to avoid contempt for himself. The self-deception here is so great that it impairs the intelligence and the ability to deceive others.

Everyone's life is lived from the inside. Every individual, from the most self-centred and anthropocentric to the most altruistic and eco-centric, is the protagonist of his own plot. However much he tries, nobody manages *to be another* for himself. However, in the eyes of the rest, *we are the others*. There is a conflict between the vision we have of the world and of ourselves, taking ourselves as the point of departure, on the one hand, and the vision that others have, beginning from their own internal and individual perspectives, on the other. The worst excesses of self-deception in practical existence are often linked to the partiality caused by the excesses of the first point of view (internal to the first group of persons) to the detriment of the second (internal to the second). However bad he may be in others' eyes, nobody is able to bear a disgusting, repugnant image of himself for any length of time.

Partiality in judgement comes from the depths. It is unpleasant, but it is a biological fact: the smell of our own excrement doesn't offend us as much as that of others. Bad smells come from other people's shit. Take away every man's mad preference for himself, Erasmus says provocatively in his *Praise of Folly*, 'and he'd stink in his own nostrils, find everything about himself loathsome and disgusting'. 'What use would it be to know myself?', Goethe says along the same lines: 'If I knew myself, I'd start running'.[40] It's no wonder that the 'underground man' is afraid, and prefers not to know.

But the Stalin paradox, it's worthwhile insisting, only takes to the point of paroxysm a partiality that, in light, homeopathic doses, is inseparable from the natural condition of man. 'However much I examine my vanity,' as the poet Carlos Drummond de Andrade perceptively pointed out, 'I can't see in it the same disagreeable tone of the vanity of other people, all of which is just a further stage of vanity.'[41] In the mature sobriety of this disarming perplexity lies, perhaps, the best antidote for the poison of inflated self-love.

The man who hates himself is unable to love anybody. The Christian commandment to 'love thy neighbour as thyself', rests on the premise of self-love, which is realistic, and proposes that we extend to others, and, in the end, to everyone, the love we feel for ourselves. The problem is that loving everyone equally is the same as loving no one. Distributing love in a rigorously egalitarian fashion would mean destroying it. Whoever says that he loves his neighbour as himself is either not thinking what he is saying, or is lying – he eats and sleeps regularly while there are hungry people round the corner.

But, just as the Christian ideal of loving your neighbour comes up against a logical and practical impossibility, the analysis of self-deception shows that here, too, there are limits. If self-love comes first, self-deception, so it seems, is not far behind. As we will see in the next chapter, self-deception, in contrast to interpersonal deceit, cannot be deliberate, planned or wilfully carried out. It is logically impossible to deceive one's neighbour as oneself.

3

THE LOGIC OF
SELF-DECEPTION

1. *Squaring the Circle*

There is something in the concept of self-deception that smacks of squaring the circle. Deceiving someone else is no problem: morality suffers, but logic is unhurt. The spoilt child whimpers, the seducer turns on the flattery and swears eternal love, the demagogue promises, the tax-evader tricks the authorities, the author *manqué* plagiarises, the wily football star writhes in pain on the pitch. The art of manipulating others for one's own benefit may have a more or less sophisticated plot and may be risky, but it contains no mysteries. No contradiction or logical short-circuit is involved. The credulity of the victim is the great ally – the easy, cheap credit – of the deceiver.

When I deceive *someone else* I try to manipulate his beliefs and behaviour by means of signals that falsify reality. Simple lying is a good example. If someone shows me a *circle* and asks me to tell somebody else what I have seen, I can perfectly well lie and say that it was a *square*. As the other person has not seen, and trusts in me, he believes me. The information asymmetry that exists between us is what allows me to make the circle a square in my interlocutor's mind. Self-deception is not like this. The logical sting of the lie we tell ourselves, whatever it is, is something much more delicate, a real acrobatic solo without the safety net of informational asymmetry: the squaring of the circle *in my own mind*.

At first sight, the notion of self-deception comes up against a severe contradiction. For me to deceive myself successfully, on the proposed model, I have to lie to myself, and, on top of that, believe in the lie. But how can someone simultaneously believe and not believe in something? How can I willingly accept the lie I try to tell myself? How can I know, for example, that it was a *circle* I saw a little time ago, and, at the same time, manage to convince myself that in fact it was a *square*? It would be like believing what I don't believe, or pretending not to know what I do know. When I try to lie to myself, I know what I know, I know that I am lying and thus I lose the credit that my interlocutor, in the example of the interpersonal lie, had placed in me. It's like trying to tickle oneself: it doesn't work. You can't square the circle.

Can we conclude, then, that self-deception is merely an incoherent chimera, the logical equivalent of the square circle in geometry, of the philosopher's stone in chemistry, or of perpetual motion in physics? Unless I'm much deceived (or self-deceived), I don't think so. The paradox of self-deception – the apparent violation of the principle of non-contradiction implicit in the idea of believing one's own lies – in no way invalidates the reality and the effectiveness of the innumerable mechanisms by which, in the most varied situations of ordinary life, we manage to deceive ourselves. The raw nerve of the contradiction is not in self-deception as such, but in the idea that it can be analysed on the model of simple lying or deceiving someone.

Nobody is a fool. If we managed to lie to ourselves as much as we wanted – without hindrance or limits – there would be nothing we couldn't sincerely believe in. Our bodily needs – eating, drinking, sleeping and looking after our health – would still have to be looked after. But satisfying the demands of the imagination would be as easy as breathing.

Why go to the movies or watch television? Everyone could print for himself the false currency of subjective gratification. Some would live in a permanent state of grace, others would have multiple orgasms as they day-dreamed. Out of modesty, of course, and out of fear of others' incomprehension and envy, no one would need to know; but I would live quite certain in my mind of being the first man to understand the Old Testament and of having composed, in another life under the cloak of anonymity, *The Creation*, attributed to Haydn.

If lying to oneself were as easy as breathing, how many people would feel sincerely that they were superhuman gods in the private Olympus of their own subjectivity? In contrast, however, to what Nietzsche's formula – 'the abdomen is the reason why man does not easily take himself for a god'[1] – might make us think, the root of the difficulty seems to be higher up, not, that is, in the worldly demands of the abdomen, but in the limits established by logic for fixing beliefs.

Obviously, there are limits to what we can make ourselves believe. As the poet said, 'it's hard to have visions when you're eating shit'. The open lie, if it comes into play, is self-defeating. Lying presupposes the *hidden intention* of falsifying reality, and this, independently of the truth-value of what is said.[2] But, whether true or false, the open lie, silently told by a person to himself, fails because it carries the explicit aim of falsifying stamped on its forehead. In the end, it's as if one of your closest friends took you into the corner of the room and said: 'Look, I trust you as I would my best friend, so I'm going to let you into the secret. What I'm going to say now is a lie, that's right, a lie, something not even I can swallow, but it doesn't matter: you've got to believe in me!' With all the good will in the world, it's asking too much.

The dynamics of squaring the circle in my own mind differ from those that lead to the analogous effect in my interlocutor's mind. Self-deception is incompatible with the conscious intention of deceiving oneself. By its own reflexive and self-referring nature, it cannot be deliberate or planned in a calculated way, as in the most obvious examples of bluff, trickery, fraud or deceiving others. The notion of willed, deliberate self-deception – in the sense that the liar plans and calculates his next lie – is a logical contradiction.

The *internal hypocrite* that dwells inside us is a different animal from the *social hypocrite* that prowls around and lies in wait for us. Subtly seductive and ingratiating, but cunningly sly and oblique, he knows that 'the best way to persuade consists of not persuading'.[3] The lie that we silently tell ourselves doesn't so much lie as it seduces. It acquires the semblance of truth, the better to lie.

The peculiarity of self-deception as a mental phenomenon comes from the fact that, unlike interpersonal deceit, it is an intrapsychic occurrence. It's not a matter of mind

X deceiving mind Y, but of our own mind deceiving itself about some specific thing (local self-deception) or deceiving itself, in a wider sense, about itself (global self-deception). In the concrete situations of ordinary life, of course, the squaring of the circle of self-deception – obviously, a stylised and extreme example – can take on the most varied forms and contents.

There are cases in which the identification of self-deception comes from the person himself. To this category belong confessions like that of Thomas de Quincey, for example, reflecting on his own involvement with drugs ('I well knew the risks, but grievously underrated their urgency and pressure'); or that of Francis Bacon during the parliamentary inquiry that condemned him for corruption ('My soul hath been a stranger in the course of my pilgrimage').[4]

In other cases, the occurrence of self-deception is attributed to someone by an outside observer. This happens in situations like that of someone terminally ill who sincerely refuses to accept the diagnosis of his illness, right up to the moment of death; or of a candidate to public office who believes himself, with the best of intentions, and in complete good faith, capable of fulfilling promises that as a voter or an impartial observer he would never believe in.

The difference between deceiving someone else and deceiving oneself, it's worth stressing, resides in the fact that self-deception is a passive occurrence; that is, closed to conscious inspection and subject to a peculiar logic. There is no room in it for the deliberation, the bad faith and the cold calculation characteristic of the clearest cases of interpersonal cheating and deceit. If the light of conscious attention guides the social hypocrite – one lie leads to another, and one must take great care not to be caught in the act – it is fatal to the underground, anonymous work of the internal hypocrite.

The Duc de La Rochefoucauld – always a subtle observer of the wiles and the non-rational mechanisms of the human psyche – suggests a smooth transition from interpersonal to intrapsychic deceit: 'We are so used to disguising ourselves from others that we end by disguising ourselves from ourselves'.[5] But a more thorough examination of the two phenomena reveals a critical discontinuity between them. Unlike interpersonal deceit, self-deception excludes awareness and deliberation. The lies we tell others *can be* – and frequently are – chosen and premeditated. Those we tell ourselves *never are*. No one chooses the intimate disguise or the secret lie he deludes himself with. Self-deception flourishes in the dark. The whole operation, like an undeveloped piece of film, cannot be exposed to the light.

This does not mean, of course, that every time there is interpersonal deceit, this happens on purpose. Any baby learns to use the power of crying and sulking on its parents' nervous system long before it knows what it is doing. As we have seen in chapter 1 (sections 1 and 2) the natural world provides an inexhaustible spectacle of strategies of camouflage, mimicry, guile and deceit in the struggle for survival and reproduction. The verbal relationships between adults are no less varied. Machado de Assis's warning in *Dom Casmurro* is on the nail: 'How many wicked intentions there are that take advantage of a half-truth like this, expressed in an innocent, pure phrase! It makes one think that lying is, at times, as involuntary as perspiration.' The problem, however, as Machado's hero-narrator comes to realise in the same novel, is that in self-deception the logic of the situation is different: 'But what I could hide from the world, I could not hide from myself, since I lived closer to myself than anyone.'[6]

Interpersonal deceit, it's true, is often involuntary. But nothing in its internal logic implies that it must necessarily be that way. On the contrary: when it goes beyond a certain degree of complexity, it begins to demand an ever-more alert attention on the part of the deceiver, on pain of being exposed to public contempt. The social hypocrite who carelessly misses his footing in the act he is putting on, allows cracks to appear in the consistency of his role, or gets tied up in the web of his own lies, loses credit and is busted.

In the case of self-deception, however, the opposite is true: the essentially involuntary and spontaneous character of the process is indispensable to it. If for any reason the torch of conscious attention illuminates it and the lie is shown up for what it is, the self-deception loses its appeal, withers away and perishes. The real circle that was there originally returns, and the belief in the squared circle fades away like the images of an exposed film.

Trying to *force* self-deception is the reflexive equivalent of trying to *compel* someone to believe in something: it doesn't work. The straitjacket, electric shock and psychotropic drugs; solitary confinement, the rack and the firing squad; the carrot and the stick; the fires of hell and the promise of paradise: faced by the stubborn mind of a man, there is no power on earth that doesn't have to confess its impotence. The mutilated flesh suffers, the audible voice repeats what it has to and the body simulates as it takes part in an enforced ritual, but no one sees what goes on in the silent mind of the victim. The citadel of belief is impregnable. For good or evil, someone who decides to believe in something cannot be mentally prevented from doing so. Like Dostoevsky's gambler, nothing stops him. He is capable of betting his last rouble of self-confidence and self-love in the overwhelming confidence that salvation lies in the next roll of the dice.

The grotesque fiasco of experiments in ideological indoctrination and 'moral regeneration' in the twentieth century bears witness to the precariousness of attempts to force religious faith or the 'common good' into the citadel of belief. It is probable that the unparalleled violence of the Chinese 'cultural revolution' and the meticulousness of the political policing in the ex-Soviet Union – even the use of simple photocopying machines by the average citizen was under strict vigilance – helped not to break the muffled, cynical resistance of the people, as those in power wanted, but rather to exacerbate it. 'He who's convinced against his will is of his own opinion still'.

The result is that decades of intense indoctrination and absolute control over the means of communication did not make 'good Marxists' out of the Russians and the Chinese. What seems to prevail in these cases is a kind of Newtonian law of repressed emotions: to every repressive action there corresponds an equal, contrary reaction. The return of the repressed, when the flood-gates are opened, is an embarrassing spectacle. Nothing of this, however, would have taken the Stoic emperor Marcus Aurelius by surprise. Pressed to install the ideal Platonic *pólis* by the force of his political authority in second-century Rome, he reflected: 'Never hope to realise Plato's *Republic* [. . .] Who can change the opinions of men? And without a change of sentiments what can you make but reluctant slaves and hypocrites?'[7]

The impotence of power is not restricted to the throne, the political platform, the university chair or the pulpit. The same type of muffled resistance to pressure from above tends to prevail in the dynamics of self-deception. Willing does not imply being able to. The human mind is capable of virtually miraculous achievements when it's a question of betting on the imponderable or spontaneously squaring the circle. But it is also impervious to openly intrusive and calculated interference in the process of belief-formation, wherever it may come from. When the citadel of belief is at stake, the central authority – external and internal – does not always have its way. If I want to convince myself of something I don't believe in, or get rid of something I can't help believing in, the most I can do is look for *indirect mechanisms* that may lead me to the desired belief. And although the repertoire is extensive, there are narrower limits than we imagine to what can be achieved.

2. The Limits of Propitiatory Behaviour

The main route for triggering involuntary mental and physical processes is to adopt the right propitiatory behaviour. Consider, for example, the difference between *blinking* and *crying*. The first is simple: we blink thousands of times a day, and whenever some object suddenly comes close to our eyes. This happens with no effort, spontaneously, in the silence of nature. More than that: all that's needed is a brief pause to notice that I can, in the blinking of an eye, turn off the automatic pilot that controls the opening and shutting of my eyelids and turn them into obedient servants of my conscious choice and will. I blink to find whether I am awake, I wink to signal complicity, and I blink repeatedly to hold back unwanted tears.

But in the case of weeping, things get more complicated. The working of the lachrymal glands is unpredictable, and does not share the exemplary obedience of the eyelids. I weep when I weep and not when I want to. I don't cry when I ought to, and do cry when I ought not to. A heavy cold or a piece of grit make my eyes water – a casual observer might think I was crying – but laughter can have the same effect. If I try to submit the secretion of tears to the dictates of my will, I soon find out that the edicts, orders and royal decrees of my conscious will do not work. 'But why should I cry now?' The only way out is to try and take myself by surprise, from behind, but without remembering what I am trying to do; to try to get round my system and manipulate it, putting myself in the right situation to get the desired effect.

Physical interference is a dirty trick, but, within its limits, infallible: slice onions or inhale tear gas, and it's no sooner said than done. For an unreflecting neuroscientist, the case is closed. Weeping is a secretion, and that's that.

Others, however, will ask questions: 'But is this really *weeping*?' 'Language is deceptive,' a psychologist would object. 'Not every apparent watering of the eyes', he would argue, 'corresponds to the subjective experience of weeping. When I speak of weeping, I think of tears, true enough, but above all of the unrestrained emotion of the person weeping, whether it's from sadness, happiness or whatever it may be for. What we have here is no more than a mechanical secretion, a pseudo-weeping, like glycerine tears shed in a bad soap-opera.'

True enough. The point, however, is that there is nothing here that a more refined neuroscientist can't assimilate. 'In fact', he might say, 'everyday language confuses two different things. If we project side by side, on a high-definition screen, what happens in a person's brain as he slices onions, and what happens there when someone is weeping out of unhappiness, we will see that they are completely distinct neurological states, even though both of them end, like so many things in this life, in lachrymal secretion. If you want to reserve the word *weeping* only for the second kind of event, the one that makes the lights on the screen corresponding to certain neural networks go brighter, I have no objections.'

With this misunderstanding out of the way, the question still remains. One way or another, if we consent to restrict what we mean by crying a little, the physical solution *à la* onion or tear gas can be excluded. The problem is *really crying*: how can we rescue the sovereignty of conscious will and choice, when it is undermined by the stubborn refusal of the mind to listen to appeals and commands to immediately start weeping?

Again, we have to try coming from behind. Involuntary processes can't be affected by direct choice, but that doesn't mean they are immune to the possibility of being eased along the way, and indirectly provoked. If I want to sweat, I take physical exercise or I go to the sauna – it's as easy as lying, and no one can say that it's not authentic sweating. If the challenge is to weep, and, more than that, to unleash in myself the subjective experience associated with physical weeping, the way forward is to do everything in my power to induce and predispose myself to this state.

There are two possible routes to get there: one of them we may call *situational transference*, the other an *introspective plunge*. Neither of them, of course, guarantees the effectiveness of the chemical agents that cause mechanical weeping. But, on the other hand, both bring the promise of genuine experience, able to satisfy the humanist psychologist as well as neuroscience's scanner. The two strategies, however, come up against the same kind of recursive pattern that makes propitiatory behaviour, in the generic situation of self-deception, such a subtle art.

In *situational transference* you identify, based on previous experiences, the external contexts and surroundings that have the knack of making you prone to weeping. For example: situations of desperate human misfortune or of pain or suffering with which you can strongly empathise are enough, in a good number of cases, to trigger weeping. The difficulty is that, though the world may always be full of this type of situation, it would be extremely artificial, not to say cynical and repugnant, to use them with the deliberate intention of testing a speculative hypothesis. The very enormity of the idea, if it were carried out, would almost inevitably ruin any chance of achieving the original aim. At most, we might have a slight shiver of shame: maybe not even that.

The most obvious candidate for giving us the desired situational transference is, no doubt, art. Books, plays, films, religious rituals and songs often take us close to more absorbing emotions, and thus may bring about the desired effect. English even has a specific term – tear-jerker – to denote this particular vein of artistic production. In my own case, and, it seems, in that of the majority of people I know, cinema and theatre are the art-forms with the greatest power of bringing on the tears. If I want to cry tonight, but without having to try anything more introspective and painful, my best chance is to look in the entertainment listings and gamble on the power of my chosen film or play to effect the situational transfer.

The rocky road to the gushing rapids is the *introspective plunge*. I can force myself to spend the night reopening barely healed wounds from my past, reliving painful details from the unhappiest episodes of my life, taking skeletons out of cupboards and invoking angst, in the semi-darkness, with that special close friend, also prone to melancholy. A good bottle of vodka, a cigarette and a Beethoven late quartet, to really tear the heart-strings, would be just right too. Will I make it? My emotional state and the mood of the day will count for a lot. But apart from that, and in a general sense, it's impossible to say. The unavoidable fact is that the great problem in the whole enterprise – the Achilles' heel of any kind of action meant to favour beliefs or mental states – is the element of premeditation that, to a greater or lesser degree, contaminates the process.

The *sine qua non* for the success of the operation is managing to sincerely forget what I am trying to do. The net effect of the trip to the cinema, just as much as of lugubrious self-absorption, will crucially depend on my ability to abstract from the artificiality of the project and enter unconditionally into the emotion of the moment – the borrowed plot of situational transference or the rekindled drama of the introspective plunge. If for some reason I can't manage to switch off from the true motive that has brought me to the cinema to watch this film, or that makes me spend the night incubating unhappiness, the intermittent awareness of the premeditated character of it all will stop the ship setting sail, and the wind will drop. It would be as if someone put the light on in the theatre every ten minutes while the play is on stage, or as if your mobile phone rang at the very instant the emotion was about to come to the surface. It's no accident that we can't tickle ourselves.

The secret of situational transference in art – and particularly in the cinema and the theatre – is that it makes us forget ourselves and feel without feeling. But the real Archimedian fulcrum that lifts the whole thing off the ground is something stranger yet. Art has the ability not only to make us forget and feel, but to make us *forget that we are forgetting*, and to make us *not feel that we are feeling without feeling*. It's this second element – the squaring of the circle implicit in forgetting that we are forgetting and not feeling that we are feeling what we are not feeling – that is thwarted by the intermittent awareness of premeditation.

When, for whatever reason, the interruptor of conscious attention doesn't switch off and the internal lights of the alert mind insist on blinking and whirring, the transference and the plunge are enfeebled, or unconvincing. The wind doesn't blow, the periscope of awareness is stuck, and won't go down into the depths. It's like praying without faith, having sex without the urge, or working like a dutiful automaton; it's like mass for the unbeliever, a carnival ball for the melancholy, a voodoo ceremony for the rationalist. However, not everything ends in tears – the psychologist's radar lights up as it detects a prospective client, while the neuroscientist's screen loses its thrill and excitement.

From faith to sleep and love to weeping, the same principle affects any attempt to rule from above, or self-induce, beliefs and emotional or mental states which cannot be willed. Anyone who convinces himself against his own will can't change what he feels, however much he struggles to do so. If you want to be more natural, then you mustn't recall it at every instant. If you want to sleep but can't, you need to lull your attentiveness to the fact until the waves of sleep cover your mind. When Kant discovered that his old servant, Lempe, was taking to drink and stealing, he felt that his confidence had been betrayed, dismissed his employee, and made a categorical decision to forget him. He took the notebook he kept for things he had to remember, and scribbled: 'The name Lempe shall be forgotten forever!' Wittgenstein avoided this typically Kantian slip when he observed: 'But for someone broken up by love an explanatory hypothesis won't help much – it will not bring peace.'[8]

The mental switch that turns surrender and self-abandonment on and off is an unpredictable creature. We cannot always choose the position of the key. Rather than merely impotent, the meddling finger of the conscious will is, often, counterproductive. Our repertoire of propitiatory actions is very diverse, but it is subject to recursive, inhibiting restrictions. The use and abuse of external chemical and fictional agents is intimately linked to the delicacy and difficulty of operations of this type. 'It is one of the demands of nature', Goethe rightly points out, 'that man, from time to time, should anaesthetise himself without going to sleep; thus the taste for smoking tobacco, drinking liquor and smoking opium.'[9] Some, it is true, seem to be self-sufficient. But since the gift attributed to Rousseau by Baudelaire – 'Jean-Jacques managed to intoxicate himself without hashish' – is doubtless very rare, the markets flourish.

'Three fourths of the demands existing in the world are romantic,' John Ruskin observed in 1870, 'founded on visions, idealisms, hopes, and affections; and the regulation of the purse is, in its essence, regulation of the imagination and the heart.' The passage of time and the growth in man's productive capacity have confirmed the accuracy of Epicurus's prophecy in the fourth century BC: 'The wealth demanded by nature is both limited and easily procured; that demanded by idle imaginings stretches on to infinity.'[10] The imagination eats up the stomach. The escalation of recourse to chemical and fictional catalysts in the contemporary world – the frenetic and insatiable search for situations and mental states that bring the waking anaesthesia of double forgetting – is overwhelming evidence of the demand for processes that will allow us to at once control and let go, to keep hold of and loosen the reins of our own selves.

3. *The Paradox of a Death Foretold*

To lie to oneself and believe in the lie requires talent. It's not enough to forget you are lying, and feel what you're not feeling. Squaring the circle requires you to go one step further. For the lie to *stick*, you have to forget you are forgetting and not feel that you are feeling what you don't feel. The feigning poet, master in the art of transferring himself entire and plunging wholeheartedly into the abysses of his own deep self and other selves, is a consummate artist in the acrobatics of self-deception. True, he feigns, but he 'feigns so completely that he even feigns he is feeling the pain that he really feels'. However, he is not alone. The hypocritical reader, Baudelaire's brother, is his twin. If the dramatic actor acts and weeps without feeling, the spectator feels and weeps without acting. The one is the photographic negative of the other. As Pessoa would say: 'Feel? Let the reader feel!'[11]

In practice, what makes the lies we tell ourselves more palatable and easily digestible is the fact that there are lies, and lies. The simple lie, like the one that makes a circle into a square, is an extreme case. The past is endowed with greater or lesser malleability in the human memory, but it cannot be other than what it was. Of course, the facts can be revisited, reinterpreted, and even criminally adulterated. But the simple fact that they are treated as *facts* means that, in some way, they are there. The past is a piece of charred wood; the future is the promise of a fire.

When you admit that the past existed and that a succession of facts, whatever they may be, brought us to this point, there is the implicit recognition that now it's too late to change them. If I've just seen a circle and admit to myself that I have seen it, that imposes limits on the fixing of my beliefs. Only the passage of time, the underground wish to believe the opposite, and who knows, the appearance of a new theory about 'ellipsoidal squares' – a sort of geometrical version of Soviet 'proletarian biology' – may one day alter this fact in my memory.

But when the *future* is at issue, it's a different story. If there is something irremediably closed when we look at the past, there is something peculiarly *open* when we glimpse the future. The sentence preceding this one is a brute fact – only as long as the book is not printed can it be reread, kept, corrected or cut (it wasn't!). The next sentence, however, which asks for a moment of your time, is about to be created – what it needs to say is that, until this exact moment, it wasn't yet written, but was extracted, word by word, from a virtually infinite universe of semantic and grammatical possibilities defined by language. The sentence before this one, which has just emerged from nothingness, only asks me to read it and not be too easy on it. The next sentence, however, is still in the air. It questions me and hides in the vacuum of what has not yet come into existence. It makes me stare into space, shut my eyes for a moment or pray.

What *was* or *wasn't* cannot be changed. Nobody knows for certain what *will* or *won't* be. In the subjective experience we have of time, futures that have not been undertaken (sentences that have never been written) belong to the tree of the past in a manner different to the trunks and branches that have been lived (written sentences). Future branches (sentences still to be written) don't yet belong to this tree, but to the future. Nothing rules out the possibility, however, that we may be wrong – that is, that the future may be, in reality, as closed as the past.

Nothing happens without a cause. For an intelligence like the one conjectured by the French mathematician, the Marquis de Laplace, capable of knowing all the causal laws that operate in the universe, and the state at any given instant of all the objects that compose it, nothing is uncertain – the past and the future are equivalents. They are only two words – separated from each other only by our human ignorance of the second of the two – for a single undifferentiated temporal flux. The universe would then be a book, ready and printed, in which everything, down to the last detail, was always written, and in which a tiny, tortuously written footnote would give an account of an odd species of sublunary bipeds that one day dreamed that it had an active stake in the flux of existence, and had participated as a partner in creation's formative processes.[12]

Laplace's conjecture, it's worth noting, doesn't imply a deterministic universe, in which only what does in fact happen can happen. It is equally compatible with the notion of a probabilistic world, one, that is, in which the events – whether past or future – are distributed and happen according to the objective probability that they will occur; a world, that is, in which more things could happen than in reality do occur.

If in the determinist universe an omniscient external observer is able to foresee what will necessarily be the case, in the probabilistic one he knows the distribution of the objective frequencies of all possibilities, and, thus, he will be able rigorously to foresee the probability of each one occurring through time. The book is not written in advance, but what is finally printed in it doesn't involve human co-authorship. What the Laplacean conjecture rules out is the belief that the human animal is genuinely choosing what he does or fails to do in life.

However, whether or not we accept the idea of a universe closed to human choice, there is no way we can assimilate it into our reality. Laplace's omniscient intelligence transcends the human condition and, what's more serious, seems to get ever more and more out of reach, as the advance of scientific knowledge brings more questions than answers, more perplexities than certainties. If that footnote about *Homo sapiens* is written anywhere, one thing is certain:

if humanity ever has the chance to examine it some day, the controversy about its real meaning will require a volume at least as extensive as the one dedicated to the universe itself.

If the hypothesis of a closed universe is true, then the self-deception of humanity is absolute. The subjective sensation of freedom that we have as we act in the world is nothing more than a pathetic, arrogant fiction. The human animal would, in the end, be as responsible for the movements of its voluntary muscles as it is for the secretions of its pancreas, or for the falling rain.

The inescapable fact, however, is that the future, in contrast to the past, seems to us to be genuinely *open*, and attempts to convince ourselves of the contrary do not take root in the soil of belief. Whether or not we are adherents of determinism or of equivalent notions as a speculative hypothesis, we all – even supposed determinists – end up acting as co-authors of the plot of the unpublished chapters of our lives, and as co-managers, if not of the cosmic-universal process, at least of our collective and individual micro-destinies.

If determinism is false, as all our subjective experience leads us to believe, then self-deception is not absolute and universal – humanity's ignorance of itself does not reach such a pass! It is a contingent attribute of beings who are fallible, and limited in the art of self-knowledge.

The asymmetry in human perception of time helps us to understand an important class of self-deceptions. The past is given but pliable, the present ephemeral, and the future uncertain. Self-deception may be the denial of the past or of the present – the squaring, in memory or perception, of the circle we experienced. This is the case, for example, of the victim of anorexia who sees herself as obese in spite of her emaciated image in the mirror, or of the addict who sincerely denies the existence of his problem. But it also projects itself over the future, asserting what will not happen, and manipulating the shape of the circle to be squared.

The road to the Indies in self-deception about the future – the compass in the hands of the internal hypocrite – is the logical indeterminacy of statements made in the present about future events. Through the logical breach opened by what we can't know of and still may happen, there comes into existence a numerous family of self-deceptions.

Suppose, for the sake of argument, that it were possible to travel in time. Imagine someone who, having offered himself as a human guinea-pig in a pioneer experiment for such a thing, was transported to the afternoon of 10 February 2006, and by coincidence (the technology is new and doesn't yet allow for the time and place the person is despatched to to be given exactly) ended up witnessing a tragic occurrence which you are deeply interested in: on that day, you will have a car accident at kilometre 137 of the road from Rio de Janeiro to Santos, will go into a coma and die immediately after. The traveller comes back to the present and tells the scientists all he has seen. Those responsible for the project deliberate and finally decide to seek you out and apprise you of the sad news. Once the shock is over, you will take two solemn decisions: to avoid that road and never again to touch a car.

The plot is hatched. For, notice: you are still not safe. It may be that the *pre-vision* of the traveller has already taken into account everything that would happen after you were warned. A plausible story could run like this: as the years pass, you began to have serious doubts about all that. First, the guinea-pig traveller had a psychotic attack and never recovered his sanity, that is if he ever had any. But the final straw was when the 'Time travel' project was interrupted, months later, surrounded by allegations of scientific fraud and financial irregularities. What with all this, and after the fervour of the original decision has lapsed, you imperceptibly started relaxing your attention and making concessions. To make a long story short: when the fatal afternoon came there you were, in a friend's car, happy and oblivious on your way to Carnival at the seaside. It was written in the stars – do I need to finish the story?

Another, equally plausible possibility is that, in spite of all the confusion surrounding the project, you decided to act with the greatest prudence and managed to spend Carnival 2006 on board a ship in Japan. The traveller's story about your death was true at the moment it was told, you gambled on it, and, precisely because of this, succeeded in doing what no one had ever done – objectively change the future. The only problem is that your salvation leaves us to deal with a real logical brain-teaser.[13]

On 11 February 2006, the prophetic story of the time-traveller will have shown itself to be, once and for all, either true or false. If you died as foreseen, he told the truth. But, if you escaped your fate, then he had lied, in the sense that his story turned out to be contrary to the truth. The first question is to know if the traveller's pre-vision refers to one possible future amongst an indefinite number of other futures, or if it describes something that, whether you want it to or not, cannot fail to happen. But the logical sting of the question is the character of the traveller's original story: was it true or false?

It's difficult to say. If you really *died* in the accident, the story was true before and after the tragedy – the determinist gives a smile, and logic heaves a sigh of relief. The traveller was always right, even though you twice made mistakes: first, in thinking you were capable of changing destiny when you were not, and, second, in having allowed yourself to slip towards silencing the warning-bells in your memory. But if you didn't die in that accident, the story was rigorously true at the moment of its telling, and until the eve of the fateful day, but turned out to be false when the time came – the determinist grumbles and logic blows the whistle.[14]

What is true in the world when it is looked at from the beginning may not be in the world seen in retrospect, from the end. Having had privileged cognitive access to your life's epilogue, you didn't like what you read. Everything that was written was true, and you had the wisdom to trust in it. That was how you managed to cut some sentences out, correcting others and improving the ending. The traveller was not lying: the proof of that is that his pre-vision was the stepping-stone to making it false! The original story was simultaneously true and false. It was rendered false *because* it was true. The truth lied.

4. Scenes from a Negotiated Awakening

The pre-vision of the time-traveller is a limit-case in the family of true assertions about the future. But we don't have to go so far. The paradox of the death foretold puts into relief and depicts a whole spectrum of situations in which the existence of some cognitive competence to know the future accurately alters our knowledge and, therefore, makes room for corrective actions that negate the original forecast. Unlike prophecies that are self-fulfilling – those that may be improbable at the beginning, but end up becoming true to the extent that they make us believe in them and act as though they were going to happen – this is a class of predictions that are self-negating, that is, it is exactly their condition of *ex ante* accuracy that opens the way for them becoming *ex post* wrong.

The logical indeterminacy of beliefs and statements about what still has to happen is a trapeze that invites us to incredible and silent feats. From the not always successful effort to wake up at the desired time, to pledges of eternal love sworn in the heat of passion, it's from this logical seed that an exuberant fauna and flora of self-deceptions germinate. Some prosaic examples of occurrences of this type, plucked in the garden of ordinary life and in the inno-cent tumult of the passions, help to clarify the mechanisms whereby we square the circle.

Sleep is a habit. When it is well rooted, going to sleep and waking up are almost automatic. The internal clock obeys the external one. But when routine is broken and the sleep habit derails, the conscious will has to be mobilised. The act of getting to sleep now depends on the correct pro-pitiatory behaviour, and the act of waking now demands the opposite – not surrender to the body's spontaneous impulses, but affirmation of the sovereign will over the enticing seductiveness of sleep.

Consider my own case. When I have external engage-ments (giving classes, participating in some event, or meet-ing someone early in the morning), I rarely succumb to the temptation of sleeping beyond the appointed hour. Others protect me from myself. But, when the engagement is internal – when it is only the strictly personal intention to make better use of the day – I have to take more drastic measures. It's then that the struggle begins.

If the alarm-clock is by the side of the bed, within reach, I'm perfectly capable of switching it off while practically asleep. Experience recommends that I put it at a certain distance from the bed, so that I am forced to get up and take a few steps to turn it off. When this works, the next step is to the wash-basin, cold water on my face, and then the victory will have been consolidated. However, it so happens that this scheme doesn't always work. There are days, and, sometimes, whole periods when the undercurrent of sleep carries the day and takes me half-undressed back to bed. Sleep's victory, on these occasions, invariably passes through a rapid and murky negotiation. It is astonishing how many noxious weeds and siren voices can surface, in a matter of seconds, in the mind of a drowsy, lethargic person.

The first round is all imploring. I ask, even beg myself: 'Just a little more, fifteen minutes, half an hour at most!' The second stage is the instant profusion of good reasons. Not that I invoke them all at the same time, or on each occasion. There's a whole subtle art in choreographing this dance, but they are all there, ready to come on stage. And don't they know how to do it! After all, 'what's fifteen minutes?', 'you shouldn't interrupt deep sleep', 'don't be so puritanical!', 'the brain works better when it's had a rest', 'I can work later tonight', 'I drank too much yesterday', 'just let's finish that dream', 'I really do need a holiday' . . . When the right reason hits home, the contract is ready: 'OK, done, but not a minute more!'

Once the right to another mini-sleep has been won, the pleasure is more intense. When I wake up again (the clock is a long way from the bed), more than two hours have gone by! Resigned, I come to the conclusion that the morning's lost. Oh well, in for a penny, in for a pound . . .

The previous night, then, there was the intention to get up early. The following afternoon, there comes the remorse at having failed to get up and the comforting certainty – in reality, no certainty at all – that tomorrow will be different. Laziness is a slippery slope, and we go down it slowly, step by step, backwards most of the way. The slow rate of progress – its incremental nature – belongs to the mechanism whereby we subtly neutralise for ourselves the guilt and the bad conscience caused by the encroaching habit. When we realise, for some reason, how much distance has been covered, it has already taken root. To get rid of it now is a hard task that requires, apart from perseverance, an authoritarian act of will that is the opposite of the propitiatory action of involuntary emotional and mental processes. The solemn promises and categorical resolutions that usually go with such decisions betray the lack of firmness that almost always threatens them.

The logical indeterminacy of beliefs and statements about the future affects the whole world of promising. Who can guarantee beforehand that a promise will be kept? The simple fact that a promise *had to be made* is symptomatic – it shows that there are doubts about whether it will be carried out. Consider, for example, the repeated promises I make to myself every time the seductiveness of sleep beckons to me in the morning. If they were uniformly false, they wouldn't delude me for

LIES WE LIVE BY

long. Whether I slept the whole morning or not, I wouldn't give them the least credit. But things are not always that way. The great alibi for self-deception is that often – but without me being able to know beforehand or say why – the promise of sleeping only for another fifteen minutes is genuinely kept. The alarm-clock sounded, sleep asserted itself and the promise of just an extra mini-doze opened up: am I telling the truth or lying?

In half an hour at most everything will be plain. If I wake up at the promised hour and begin my day, I will have managed the best of both worlds: I have satisfied all the reasons – legitimate or not – not to play at being a puritan, I have used the morning well, and, as an additional bonus, I have gone one step up virtue's ladder. The promise was true. But, if I don't wake up, and end up wrapped in the soft sheets of 'fifteen minutes, half an hour at most', the promise will have shown itself to be false. Was I lying?

The basic point on which self-deception rests here is a near relation to the paradox of death foretold: the promise was reasonably true *at the moment it was made*, even if the later course of events has taken it upon itself to make it false. The *ex ante* truth of what was promised is the condition *sine qua non* for its *ex post* falsity.

There is no room for doubt about the sincerity of the original promise, and the genuine nature of my intention to fulfil it. If I knew it to be false, I wouldn't believe in it, and I wouldn't let myself go back to bed. The promise has turned out to be false because it was true, that is, it had all the appearance of truth about it, and it was taken to be true. It was precisely because I told the truth when I made the promise that I trusted it and went into reverse

144

THE LOGIC OF SELF-DECEPTION

gear back to sleep, slithering one step down the slope of laziness. The truth has lied.

Truth that lies is an innocent party who is guilty. *Innocent* because true – or at least not totally implausible – at the moment it is proffered; and *guilty* because it turns out to be false when the moment comes. This does not excuse it, however, from differing degrees of guilty innocence. The accomplice of the internal hypocrite is the hearer's generous disposition to believe. All credulity, of course, has limits. If I resolve that from now on I'm going to sleep four hours at most each night, the promise will be greeted with gales of laughter by the internal audience. 'Tell us another!' What is more intriguing in the occasional trap of the fifteen minutes' sleep is the regenerative power – rising from the ashes like a phoenix – of the propensity for sincerely believing in the truth that knows how to lie.

The *ex ante* uncertainty of the result helps a great deal, it's true; the spontaneous ease of believing in what corresponds to our desires, also. The body's urge to return to sleep, as is natural, feeds and drugs the mind.

But the inductive weight of the experience accumulated in the memory, over years of intimate familiarity with murky negotiations of this kind, should even up the balance and recommend the greatest of caution in the face of similar contracts. When the moment comes, however, induction sleeps the sleep of the just, and lets the moment for firm action pass by. When induction reawakens, at the end of the morning, all that remains for it is to put one more example into its already formidable collection. The triumph of self-deception is not only that it makes one forget. The squaring of the circle is the innocent and guilty art of forgetting – even if it's only for those few moments

145

that count – that we do forget. Forgetting is the key to remembering.

5. *The Delights and Pitfalls of Passionate Love*

The guilty innocence of self-deception becomes guiltier, but no less innocent for all that, in cases where the squaring of the circle is part of the plot of an interpersonal deceit. There are various possible combinations from the logical point of view. The limit-case is that of interpersonal deceit based on the double coincidence of reciprocal, criss-cross self-deception. It's extremely difficult, in situations of this kind, to know who is deceiving whom. On the one side is self-deception M with its formidable arsenal of appetising, mendacious truths. On the other is the perfect target: self-deception W with its insatiable appetite for delicious lies that sincerely believe in what they say. M is inversely symmetrical to W: the meeting of hunger with the desire to eat, and vice-versa.

Any form of eager appetite is ideal material for self-deception to feed on. Privation, whether real or imaginary, usually brings about a strong, blinding desire for what we are missing. Idealising what we haven't got is a propensity almost inherent to human nature. The sweetest songs of liberty are sung in prison. Exile makes one's country seem all the more wonderful. The poor don't laugh at the wealth of the rich. 'To those who sweat for their daily bread', observed Keynes long before the instituting of generous unemployment benefits in Europe, 'leisure is a longed-for sweet – until they get it.'[15] The girl from Ipanema, tall and tanned and young and lovely, is always the one who passes by, not the one who lingers and stays.

The voracity and the focus of human appetites admit of extraordinary diversity. What leads one person to acts of folly may leave another indifferent. Once we are past the threshold of the most elementary biological pressures – an area less well-defined than might seem at first sight – the demands of our imagination know no frontiers. There are two powerful centres of interest, however, on which tend to converge a great deal of human expectation and action: the appetite for *sex and love* in private life and the appetite for *power, wealth and prominence* in public life. Around these two vectors gravitate robust passions within any society's dynamic. It is not surprising, therefore, that they are also, each in its own way, privileged spaces for the involuntary fixing of beliefs and the operation of self-deceptive promises.

The ancients were not mistaken when they represented Cupid – the winged deity of love's ties and embraces – as an archer with excellent aim but eyes blindfolded. Love is blind. Passionate lovers who dare to love unreservedly tend to become blinded by love. They live here as though they were somewhere else, with a reduced perception of reality and of themselves, possessed by the sublime, inexpressible moment they are living through. It is as if they were *outside themselves* – intoxicated by Wagnerian potions, hypnotised by the fascination of Circe and spellbound by charms like those that, according to the legend, sent Lucretius mad.[16] People in love lose sleep, dance in the rain, and hear the music of the spheres. Everything seems to shine and beckon to them, or wants to see them weep, mad with love for one another. United in the radiant dawn of victorious love, nothing bad can reach them – except their own self-deceptions.

Love between the sexes, when it explodes, is the nothing that is everything. The lovers seem moved by a secret impulse that genuinely makes them idealise one another and find as much beauty as they can – and more – in each other. When the snake bites and the blood is on fire, the avalanche of uncontrolled emotions uproots everything in its path, and sweeps it onwards. Lovers beg, implore, swear eternal love. They declaim their unconditional belief in one another in prose and verse. The intimate certainty that they will never again love like this is overwhelming. The breaking loose of the wild particle of the sexual urge takes on the violence of a tropical storm. Bacchus feasts, Venus glows. Caresses are a benediction, kissing a prayer, and copulation communion. It would be a sin to deny what is written – for this *had to be*. There are moments that redeem our existence.

The only problem, of course, is that lovers' ecstasy (from the Greek *ékstasis*: 'outside oneself') doesn't last for ever. Passionate love is mortal – eternal *as long as* it lasts, infinite *as long as* it shines. On the morning after some weeks or months of passionate sex, the sun of certainty no longer shines, and the shadows of doubt begin to thicken. The liberating tyranny begins to oppress, the unconstrained hope begins to feel suffocating, and the glowing beauty loses its spark. The illusion that began the journey with such fire pauses to take breath and finds itself exhausted. All that is left to the lovers is the bitter road of a scarred disillusionment and the return to the bruised awareness of a dull and empty routine. The memory of the miracle, however, doesn't give in. The breaking loose of that tiny, wild particle might be a will-o'-the-wisp, but the radiation it emits sets off some astonishing changes.

Lovers' promises deceive but don't lie. The best way of deceiving someone else is to be self-deceived. The lover M and his loved-one W are a perfect pair – the call of passion is stronger than they are. Both of them believe sincerely in each other, and in themselves. It's a case of supply and demand. M's deceiving is convincing because he, self-deceived, deceives without having to deceive: he says the truth, and 'the truth is his gift for deluding' (Caetano Veloso). W, to do him justice, even betrays a little doubt – 'Yes, but afterwards? What will become of the two of us? Your love is so fleeting and treacherous!' (the woman's voice in 'Tabuleiro da baiana', by Ari Barroso).[17] The will to believe, however, overwhelms fear: 'In love, it is the heart that rules' (idem).

But if M and W could, from the start, see the end: how would they see the beginning of the affair? Where is truth, where are lies? In love in its infancy, or in love breaking down? In the flames as they burst forth, or in the dying embers? Passion seen from its start and from its end are not the same thing. Consider the passionate young person who swears eternal love, or the unhappily married man who promises, in the heat of a bed, an early divorce and marriage soon after. Are they lying? As for the actual fulfilment of what was promised, only time will tell. But how can we doubt the genuineness of the intention and the truth-value of the promise, at the moment it is made? The paradoxical logic of impassioned swearing is caught by Shakespeare in the play within a play staged in *Hamlet*. To the queen's promise of eternal love and fidelity, the king implacably replies:

I do believe you think what now you speak;
But what we do determine, oft we break.
Purpose is but the slave to memory,
Of violent birth but poor validity,
Which now, the fruit unripe, sticks on the tree,
But fall unshaken when they mellow be.
Most necessary 'tis that we forget
To pay ourselves what to ourselves is debt.
What to ourselves in passion we propose,
The passion ending, doth the purpose lose.
(Act III, Scene 2, ll. 181–90)

The fall of the ripe fruit to the ground – the true purpose that turns false – is the squaring of the circle: the lover's drunken binge, followed by his coming to his senses; the guilty innocence that catches itself at it, but returns to itself, reborn from the ashes. There are truths that lie. Madness, true, but not without method. Shakespeare's sonnet scorns logic but is faithful to life: 'When my love swears that she is made of truth / I do believe her, though I know she lies' (Sonnet 138).

The heart that we actually have is not always the one we think we have. Our prosaic and urgent motivations – like, for example, intense sexual desire for someone – are cunning at the art of making themselves pass for noble sentiments and lofty aims, mostly in our own eyes. It would perhaps be an exaggeration to say that the reliability of what is promised is in inverse proportion to the degree of emphasis and fervour in the promise. But faced with insistent flights of enthusiasm like 'I swear to you, this time it's really serious', 'you must believe in me', or 'I know I'm going to fall in love with you' it's difficult to avoid the suspicion that something is rotten in the kingdom of passionate love.[18]

The miracle, as always, is the waking anaesthesia of the double forgetting. To the stubborn pulsation of the lover in full ascent there corresponds a frail, affable remorse – the hangover doesn't last long, and the weight of inductive logic is like that of a feather in the eye of a hurricane. The reborn phoenix is ready to take off. Virginal, like a child, it's as if this were the first time. In the art of passionate love, the consummate master of self-deceived promises is the one who thinks, in the silence of his own mind: 'When the love I feel swears to me that it's all true, I do believe in what it says, and woe to him who suspects falsehood!'

6. The Hypnosis of a Good Cause

The universe parallel to passionate love in private life is the passion for power and prominence in public life. In politics and in the business world, as in religion, art or in any other hierarchically organised area of endeavour, the demands of practical existence impose their own laws. As in love, the beginning can be capricious, but the first step is fatal. The arrow leaves the bow, and its tip hits the mark: ambition is as blind and accurate in its aim as Cupid. From its passing sting arises the insistent itching that irritates, excites, upsets the equilibrium, and fires the imagination: 'Why not me?'

Many think they are called, but few are chosen. The struggle in the competitive arena of the quest for votes, allies, preferences and applause is a tough business. Lack of energy, just as much as an unsuitable combination of heat and light, can be fatal. Aiming high, fighting hard, not giving up, carrying on regardless, persevering and going one step further, are actions that demand not only gigantic doses of motivation but also – something that is less well known – all kinds of feats, somersaults and acrobatics in the field of belief.

The number one requisite of the ambitious person in any area of activity is *belief in himself*. It's not enough to pretend. Social hypocrisy can only deliver the goods when what needs to be satisfied is the pattern of behaviour identified by La Rochefoucauld when he said that, 'In order to succeed in the world people do their utmost to appear successful'.[19] Up to that point, deceit is a simple matter: the practices of self-praise and the more or less subtle showing off of one's own merits are what the Greeks called 'playing your own flute' – in English, 'blowing your own trumpet'. The sophisticated poseur knows he cannot overdo it, and is even refined enough to feign a certain timidity as he shows off.

But convincing oneself – at the beginning and all along the way – that it is worth gambling a good deal on a given strategy to rise socially and achieve positions of leadership is another story. To lull the inner ear, and keep the internal audience engrossed, the music has to come from inside. It needs to seduce and sincerely convince us that we know what we want and deserve what we are striving to attain – that we are justified, in our own eyes, in harbouring such ambitions. Few people, it seems, suffer from a lack of appetite or good reasons when it comes to the real perspective of power. But if our will is, for some motive, unconvinced or not legitimate in our own eyes, the balloon will not inflate. Ambition can't take off.

The quest for and the exercise of power obey a strange principle. No leader (or aspirant to the position) inspires more confidence in his followers, actual or potential, than the confidence he has in himself. If I don't bet on myself, who will? If I don't think a lot of myself, and if I'm not absolutely convinced of what I believe in, how can I hope that others will respect me or believe what I say? Doubting oneself is, for the leader, doubly harmful: it not only cools his own enthusiasm and undermines his inspiration; it also inspires mistrust and injects followers with despondency. For the man of action fired by ambition, revealing lack of self-confidence is like letting your impotence show in public. But there is nothing to fear. Cocksure belief and certainties as thick as the hairs on the back of a wild boar are, for him, as natural as blinking and sweating.

The spontaneous and gently biased character of belief-formation in the mind of the committed leader appears clearly in cases of disputes about polemical issues.

Honesty and cold reason recommend that we should make an effort to give an equal hearing to the best arguments *against* the causes we're espousing. In the austere republic of the quest for objective knowledge, convictions are pariahs and unshakeable certainties have no citizenship rights. The corollary of this is that any belief and any attachment to causes, of whatever nature, should be tentative and open to revision. 'The surest proof of animal-stupidity', remarked Montaigne, dumbfounded by the fanaticism and the religious wars of his time, 'is ardent obstinacy of opinion'.[20]

Logic applauds and is grateful, without much enthusiasm, of course, but a delicate question remains: how far can one get, with all this cognitive rectitude, in the implacable and highly competitive arena of public life? Thinking *against* oneself – ruthlessly seeking what complicates the life of our most cherished and protected beliefs – may be a valuable tonic from the point of view of knowledge, but it is a lethal poison when it invades the fortress of belief. Thinking *in one's own favour* – cherishing and reaffirming the beliefs that give us so much strength because we have them – has the opposite effect. If the warmth of well-rooted certainties is the enemy of clear thinking, there is no better ally or more effective fuel for action. Caught between the conflicting imperatives of knowledge and action, the committed leader has no hesitation. Our causes are above all suspicion, and the internal hypocrite is always at the ready. Self-deception is having a good conscience while squaring the circle.

One of the most effective mechanisms for fixing the beliefs favourable to our aims and ambitions is the spontaneous selectivity of our attention and memory. The results obtained by experimental psychology in systematic tests reproduce in a controlled environment what anyone can observe for himself.

From abortion to the death sentence, from free sterilisation to euthanasia, choose a controversial issue and find a group of people with firm positions about it. Give, then, to each member of the group, two arguments *in favour* of the cause at issue, and two *against*, making, in each case, one of these arguments quite plausible, and the other so implausible as to be almost absurd. After a short interval, ask: which arguments do these people spontaneously recall?

The hypnosis of the good cause is blind, but has a good aim. It doesn't matter what side of the polemic they are on, the basic pattern of assimilating and memorising is the same: people markedly tend to remember the plausible arguments that support their position, and the absurd ones opposed to it. All this, of course, with the greatest ease and good faith in the world.[21]

The hypnosis of the good cause, whichever it may be, produces a kind of protective blindness in the individual. In the case of economic policy, as Alfred Marshall once observed, it has the gift of 'enabling people to see just those parts of economic truth which fitted in with their policy, and to remain honestly blind to those which did not'.[22] The honesty and good faith of the blind spot are the password for self-deception and the essential conditions for it to work.

The empirical retail world of small causes, however, is only a minor spectacle in comparison with what happens in the dialectical wholesale market of revolutionary passions. There is no place for amateurs in the epic drama of world-historical development. The intimate, unassailable faith that the truth has been found and is on our side works miracles. In the radiant glow of its dawn everything falls into place – the monstrous mistakes and aberrations of the past vanish away. Whole epochs become clear. Millennia of historical experience converge obediently in the synthesis of a single formula. The sacrifices of those who suffered for us to get where we are take on meaning. Nothing was in vain. The future, now, is within our grasp. When there is plenty of powder, all that is needed is the spark to set off the explosion.

The individual is the nothing that is everything. The revolutionary lives outside himself, possessed by a truth that transcends him. He is the spokesman of Providence on earth, like Cromwell; he is the incorruptible incarnation of the General Will, like Robespierre; he is the advanced instrument that History makes use of to move forwards in its dialectical progress, like Lenin. The urgency of his certainties is stronger than he is. His eyes shine, an unrestrained fervour electrifies his voice, the body speaks and the heart thinks. The magical, contagious confidence that inspires him carries multitudes with it. Like Dostoevsky's gambler, he plays for the highest stakes, and gambles everything on the conviction that the final victory has the irresistible force of destiny. No sacrifice is too great. 'If you think of revolution,' says Lenin, 'dream of revolution, sleep with revolution for thirty years, you are bound to achieve a revolution.'[23]

One of the most recurrent features of revolutionary self-deception is the recourse to higher authorities to sanction actions and decisions that are less exalted. The omelette of revolution requires spiritual eggs. The invitation made to the philosopher Cicero, in Shakespeare's *Julius Caesar*, to join the conspirators, lending the grey hairs of his wisdom and the veneer of his virtue to Caesar's assassination, is emblematic. Gods and dead prophets, however, are more pliable: 'the authority of the dead is anxiety-free and definitive.' Cromwell overthrew the British monarchy brandishing the Bible; a revolutionary ayatollah will find all he needs in the Koran; the Japanese 'Supreme Truth' sect got the spiritual authority to attack the Tokyo underground with poisonous gas from Buddhist quietism. Robespierre the incorruptible implanted terror and operated the guillotine while plucking quotations from the moral weave of Rousseau's work, while Lenin, as we will presently see, availed himself of the concept of *Aufhebung* for a memorably erudite exercise in squaring the circle.[24]

In his Swiss exile, in the months that preceded the Russian Revolution, Lenin went deeply into the secrets of Hegelian logic, and reached the following conclusion (registered in writing in his posthumously published philosophical notebooks): 'It is impossible completely to understand Marx's *Capital*, and especially its first chapter, without having thoroughly studied and understood *the whole* of Hegel's *Logic*. Hence', the Bolshevik leader concluded with impeccable logic, 'half a century later none of the Marxists understood Marx.'[25]

When he returned to Russia, then, during the gestation of the revolutionary crisis that opened the doors of power to him, Lenin could bask in the delicious sunlight of an inner, invigorating certainty – he was the first Marxist truly to understand Marx! More than that: as Hegel's *Logic* continues to defy the efforts that several generations of logic experts have lavished on it, it's probable that Lenin was not only the first, but also the last living being to decipher the hieroglyphs of the 'Bible of the working class'. After all, as Nietzsche said, possibly with Hegel in mind, 'every profound thinker is more afraid of being understood than of being misunderstood'.[26]

Every revolution is a promise of a future. That is why revolutionary passions, like passionate love, have a special vocation for self-deception. The spark, of course, needs the opposing stone to be struck – it is lit by the impact. The backdrop of this spectacle of fire and fury is a crisis of disillusionment with the old regime. Where despair mounts, the desperate search for salvation also grows. On one side is the arsenal of tempting truths that are not yet lies, but already guarantee salvation; on the other, lies the atavistic hunger for appetising promises that genuinely believe in the salvation they offer. It's a perfect match.

It's the meeting of appetite for power with the (literal) hunger for food. If the one didn't exist, the other would create it.

The innocence of revolutionary promises has the moving purity of a virgin's voluptuous fantasies. The experience of a long period in opposition – often in hiding, in prison or exile – tends to produce vigorous illusions about the possibilities of transforming the world by means of political action. More than a question of will, the promised paradise is the product of the most rigorous dialectical deductions from historical development or (as Lenin said about Marxism) of a 'complete scientific sobriety in the analysis of the objective state of affairs'.

In the distance, the obstacles fade away and the mirage shines forth. The ability to underestimate uncertainties and difficulties in the creation of the new order reaches the climax of a Pangloss-like belief that 'humanity only sets itself problems that it is able to solve'. Once power has been won, the solutions will fall like ripe fruit. 'Communism', Lenin said, 'equals Bolshevik power plus electrification.'[27] How beautiful the future is in the revolutionary dawn!

The only problem, of course, is that the brave new world dreamed of in the long night of the old regime usually has little (or nothing) to do with the nightmare born from its womb. One doesn't have to be blind, or a hired advocate of reaction, as the enemies of any self-respecting revolution are invariably called, to understand the warning given by Engels – with his impeccable revolutionary pedigree – in a letter written towards the end of his life: 'People who boast that they made a revolution always see the day after that they had no idea what they were doing, that the revolution made does not in the least resemble the one they would like to make.' Is this reactionary rhetoric, as Albert Hirschman has claimed? The experience and logic of self-deception suggest that it is not.[28]

That was what Lenin himself, it appears, began to realise at the moment when, once the euphoria of success was over, he found himself at the head of a victorious revolution. 'It is much easier to seize power in a revolutionary epoch,' he admitted, 'than to know how to use this power properly.'[29] The great pity is that the Bolshevik leader didn't take advantage of the peace and seclusion of his Swiss exile to think the matter over. But the real tragedy is that Lenin's heirs, leaders of the stature of Stalin, Vishinsky and Lisenko, never revealed any doubts about what to do with the power they wielded. The revolution carried out in the name of economic rationality and the end of the State as a form of political dominance resulted in its opposite: a grotesque economic madhouse overseen by one of the most brutal machines of political oppression of the modern age. The *ex ante* dream was the seed of the *ex post* nightmare.

7. *Strength of Belief as a Truth Criterion*

Dreaming and believing in one's dreams are the spice of life. There's nothing wrong, in principle, in laying large bets in private or public life, running risks in love, in politics, in business, in art or whatever it may be. Exploratory behaviour – daring to do new things, try what's never been tried before, thinking the unthinkable – is the source of all change and advance, of the individual and collective ambition to live better. Living defensively, without hope or adventure, doesn't lead to disaster, it's true, but it also leads nowhere. Worse than that: it leads to the nothingness of embittered and inactive resignation that is death in life – the absurd and bored nihilism of 'a future corpse that breeds'.

The problem lies, not in dreaming and gambling, but in the quality of the dream and the nature of the bet. The best of all worlds would be to combine the *practical ideal* of the courage of our convictions, when it comes to acting, with the *epistemological ideal* of the greatest coolness and ability to revise our own convictions, when it comes to thinking. In a way, this is what Goethe proposes: 'There is a kind of enthusiastic reflection that is of the greatest value, so long as man does not let himself be carried away by it.'[30] A virtuous squaring of the circle: a measured passion.

The difficulty lies in living up to this simultaneous demand for surrender and self-control: recognising that nothing great can be done in this world without enthusiasm and passion, but not allowing, just because this happens to be true, that the passion and fire of enthusiasm become truth-criteria in our understanding of the world. In public life, this double danger is well described by Yeats: 'The best lack all conviction, while the worst are full of passionate intensity.'[31] For the individual, the risk is clear: measured and analysed passions fade away and die, while inordinate, uncontrolled ones carry one away and knock down everything down in their path.

What we are and do may have little in common with what we think we are or are doing. Someone moved by a powerful passion, whatever it may be, is living through a moment of the greatest strength and fragility. His certainties shine out, but they also blind him. His self-confidence gives him new strength, but also tends to stifle clarity of thought. That same self-confidence that moves mountains in public life, and waters stony ground in private existence, is the passport to self-deception – truths that lie, utopian nightmares, the betrayal of confidence. Believing is the ally of instinct. While man, with his cunning, is on his way there, nature, with its innocence, is on the way back. That's why our desires and goals have an ingratiating talent for justifying themselves in our eyes, inspiring us with the intimate, reassuring and immovable certainties that never fail to give them support.

There is no necessary reason why exploratory behaviour has to involve some kind of self-deception. Human relationships are what they are: love between the sexes hates moderation, and political passion fights shy of doubt. It's the exacerbated belief that the truth has been found – that the certainties and convictions that drive us forward have the cognitive value of a divine revelation or a mathematical theorem – that betrays the presence of some spontaneous and tortuous process of self-deception. The fatal step from the logical point of view, though it is absolutely normal from a psychological perspective, is to mistake heat for light. It is to turn the strength and glow of a belief – its intensity – into a truth-criterion.

The squaring of the circle is insidious and follows a well-defined pattern. Doubting is painful. If the certainty that overtakes me is so intimate, vehement and overwhelming, then it must be true. If my enthusiasm for the cause is so intense and the convictions that move me onwards are so strong, then they cannot be false. Everything in me conspires to attribute to the cause I espouse and to the convictions that surround it, the legitimacy and rationality of inescapable truths. There's never any lack of authority for this kind of assurance. My promises and analyses, however crazy they may seem to the unsuspecting or the uninitiated, are the product of a higher inspiration, of a profound dialectic, or of the most complete scientific rigour. Make no mistake: anyone who knew what I know and felt what I feel would inevitably reach the same conclusions.

It would, it's true, be an exaggeration to suppose that the stronger a belief, the less the probability of its being true. But the involvement of powerful emotions in the process of belief-formation is more than enough reason to proceed with all possible caution. No care should be spared. The intense glow dazzles and heat is the enemy of light. Beliefs saturated with desire may be true, false or indeterminate. But the simple fact that they are saturated with desire is a sign that we have an enormous interest – and virtually no impartiality – in determining their truth-value. The back door is open for the guilty innocence of consequences that make a brutal mockery of our intentions.

It is true that the strength of belief works miracles. But that does not make it a truth-criterion, just as the willingness to resist, and put up with any kind of persecution in the name of an ideal, reveals bravery, of course, but tells us nothing about the validity of the cause in question from an ethical point of view.

The confusion, however, is as common as it is seductive, and our capacity for resisting it is variable and limited. The lies we tell ourselves don't have their credentials stamped on their forehead. The analysis of the subtle paths of self-deception helps clarify the enigma of the suffering we so often cause ourselves and others – the metamorphosis of sincere promises into obscene betrayals in private existence, and the absurd transformation of infectious certainties into monstrous errors in public life.

The principle of complementarity in quantum physics says that 'a great truth is a statement whose opposite is also a great truth'. The poet Hölderlin says that 'man is a god when he dreams, a beggar when he reflects'.[32] From the point of view of self-deception, however, the opposite of this great truth is no less true: man is a beggar when he dreams, but has something divine about him when he reflects.

4

MORAL PARTIALITY AND HUMAN SOCIABILITY

1. The Frontiers of Impartiality: the Individual and the Species

Partiality is inherent to the human condition. The bias of being who we are is already inscribed in the constitution of our sensory organs. Look, for instance, at sight. It's not easy to see what we are in fact seeing. The objects that surround us never show themselves as they are, but according to the point of view and the particular position we occupy. Everything adjusts itself to our look, without asking permission. To the eyes of a pedestrian attentive to what he is really seeing in front of him, the light on the lamppost at night is bigger than the full moon. The firefly just in front of your nose shines brighter than the most majestic star in the heavens. Copacabana beach easily fits into an aeroplane window. The innocent evidence of the senses makes every human being a moving centre of the universe.[1] If the retina can take in the infinite horizon and everything in between, why should we feel humbled by the vastness of the cosmos?

The natural tendency of the senses is to inflate what is close to us and reduce what is distant. In practice, of course, we know that things are not that way. The naked sensory perception – free of inferences, censors and logic inspectors – is not the same as the experienced perception. In the most varied ways, and almost without us realising it, we are always correcting in our mind the exaggerated partiality and the illusory disproportion of the sense-data in their crude state. The habit of matching and comparing information from the senses, on the one hand, and the experience and knowledge acquired throughout life, on the other, works its way into the perceptual act, and attenuates, at least in part, the natural inflation of the senses. Under the modulating light of consciousness, the lamppost is scaled down to size, the firefly's light is dulled, and the plane that is carrying us, seen from the beach in reverse perspective, is a speck in the sky. If the solar system is no more than a point in the infinite universe, how can we not feel absurdly tiny, faced by the vastness of the cosmos?

The sense organs that link us to the world are part of a whole. The bias of being who we are – the indelible mark of our individuality – is not limited, of course, to the make-up of our perceptual apparatus. The partiality inherent in the human condition continues, by other means, and varying in its degree of permeability to our will and conscious reasoning, in the body's functioning and in the dynamics of our mental processes.

Our body's metabolism – the myriad biological functions that are principally monitored and ruled by the hypothalamus – is a self-regulatory system, cut off from our conscious will and completely partial in the automatic way it supplies the needs and demands defined by the cells, organs and tissues under its jurisdiction. Unlike the perceptual apparatus, the self-centred and iron logic of the internal workings of the human body allow of no interference from the mental deliberations associated with the cerebral cortex.

In the process of digestion, for example, the food passes through a complex chain of metabolic operations until it becomes suitable for distribution and due assimilation by the rest of the organism. From the mouth on out, admittedly, the individual can refuse the satisfaction of the body's demands by making a prolonged fast or going on hunger strike. From the throat down, however, the organism is sovereign and knows how to look after itself. St. Teresa of Ávila is no different from Genghis Khan. Everything happens within the strictest, most prejudiced and self-centred sense of priorities. What the body fails to acknowledge as belonging to itself is fated to remain unsatisfied. An intrusive micro-organism or an invading parasite that aims to live off someone else's digestion will have to get round the defensive system and the niggardly zeal of the host organism in some way. The partiality of the hypothalamus and other organs responsible for the body's sophisticated internal homeostasis can be cheated, or it can work badly, but it cannot be dissuaded or diverted from its ends.[2]

Our minds' internal functioning seems to reflect, to a large extent, the modus operandi of the perceptual apparatus and the metabolic system. To the natural partiality of the senses and the body there corresponds, on the psychological level, the spontaneous partiality of our mental life: our emotions, desires, beliefs and interests. All that has to do with our person, in a direct or even an imagined way,

166

tends to acquire a subjective magnitude and weight that only make sense – that is, if they make any at all – from the particular point of view and the unique position we occupy in the world. What is mental is essentially bound up with what is perceptual and organic, even though, happily, as we shall see, it is also, at least in principle, more open to the correction of mistakes, excesses and abuses.

Every person is of vital importance to himself. Around each human being, however humble or self-negating he may be, there is a concentric circle of which he is the centre. It's only starting from his subjective self – from his personal gamut of experiences, and from his capacity for imaginatively removing himself into another's situation and interior life – that he can assess and judge the experience of others. Everything I think and feel, from my palate to my vaguest desires, has an internal relationship with my own subjective life that excludes all possibility of direct apprehension by another person, however close he may be. It provides the only parameter and yardstick in my attempt to conceive of and judge what others think and feel from their own internal perspectives. However much we may apply ourselves, and perfect the art of de-centring and self-abandonment, in the attempt to transcend the circle of individuality within which we make our way through life, we will never succeed in becoming another for ourselves.

The attitude of each one of us to his own existence is inevitably dominated by the fact that it is not just any life, but ours. *Some* partiality in relation to ourselves is, in the end, a condition for survival and reproduction – an exigency of nature. Suppose, for the sake of argument, a person who not only *doesn't* imagine himself more important than he is, but truly thinks himself as important (or unimportant) as any other human being; someone so neuter, impartial and free of bias with regard to himself, as to be able to feel for others exactly as he feels for himself. What would it mean to eradicate completely from our mind any trace of bias towards ourselves? What would a radical effort to strip ourselves of our subjective partiality bring about?

It only needs a moment's reflection to see that this would produce an absurd, unsustainable situation. For a being thus constituted, his own sensation of hunger would have exactly the same appeal as that of any other individual's hunger; any pain he might feel would hurt as much as an equivalent pain in another person's body; the idea of his own death would have, in his own eyes, the same gravity and interest as that of some unknown person. Contrary to Machado de Assis' dictum – 'One puts up patiently with someone else's stomach-ache' – , sensitivity to others' suffering would contaminate his whole existence. When he got out of the cage of his individuality, he would fall into an abyss of despair and shattering fragmentation: truly loving his neighbour as himself, he would destroy himself. Martyr or monster? Saint or madman? One thing is certain: if someone like this (or remotely similar) did come to exist, he would not last long. As Nietzsche reminds us: 'In reality there has only been one Christian, and he died on the Cross'.[3]

There is a proper perspective for everything. What is true of the individual deprived of his individuality holds true, one can argue, for the human species divested of its humanity. The exercise of reflective distancing with regard to his position in the world makes the human animal try to see himself from a neutral, detached point of view, that is, one as removed as possible from the natural partiality and the particular bias defined by his pre-reflective condition.

One option is to remove oneself into the skin and the eyes of species other than our own. 'If cattle or horses or lions had hands and could draw, and could sculpture like men,' observes the poet and pre-Socratic philosopher Xenophanes, 'then the horses would draw their gods like horses, and cattle like cattle; and they each would shape bodies of gods in the likeness, each kind, of their own' (fragment 15). Seeing from outside cools belief. Imagining oneself in the centre of things is a natural fantasy for beings on the margin; but if the centre is everywhere, it is nowhere. As it pictures and conceives what surpasses it, the human species continually finds the indelible mark of its humanity – immanence injects itself into transcendence. 'My idea of God', confesses the Spanish thinker Miguel de Unamuno, 'is different each time that I conceive it.'[4] The human animal's partiality with regard to humanity does not even spare our idea of perfection.

Another, more radical option is to transport oneself outside in terms of space and far away in terms of the emotions, provisionally suspending the complicity that unites and moves us in the presence of what is human. Seen from outside and from afar – from the impassive and immutable viewpoint of the universe – the preoccupations, projects and ambitions that move us seem to lose their urgency and meaning. There was no need to wait for the Copernican revolution, Galileo's telescopes or the space race for men to realise how absurd life is when seen from the outside, deprived of the particular bias of those living it. The variations on this cosmic perspective in the history of ideas – always a favourite among sceptics, moralists or simple melancholics of all times and theoretical affiliations – seem as numerous as the stars in the heavens. In the footsteps of Lucian, the satirical poet of the second century AD, the Renaissance philosopher Erasmus invites us to a sojourn on the moon:

> If you could look down from the moon, as Menippus [the hero of Lucian's satirical dialogue *Icaromenippus*] once did, on the countless horde of mortals, you'd think you saw a swarm of flies or gnats quarrelling amongst themselves, fighting, plotting, stealing, playing, making love, being born, growing old and dying. It's hard to believe how much trouble and tragedy this tiny little creature can stir up, short-lived as he is, for sometimes a brief war or an outbreak of plague can carry off and destroy many thousands at once.[5]

Just as, on the individual level, radical de-centring leads the person to a state of indifference and self-destruction, so, on the collective level, a parallel move leads to an unsustainable position. The human animal's aspiration to know himself from afar and from outside – like a separate animal, or as another species might see him – ends up in mystification and nihilism. Deprived of the partial subjectivity of those living it, life *sub specie aeternitatis* is not life, but a violent commotion with no ulterior purpose: 'but a motion of limbs', in Hobbes's words.[6] The human drama seen from a remote point in emotional space, by a spectator armed with critical distance and absolute analytical coldness, loses its dramatic quality and begins to look like a bad amateur farce, banal and absurd – 'full of sound and fury, signifying nothing'.

When he comes out of his shell, looks around and then goes back to his own self, the human being comes to his senses. The pre-reflective experience we have of being who we are is negated by the reflective detachment that leads us to suspend our natural partiality for ourselves and enquire into who we are and what we represent in the general order of things. The human animal examines himself from far off, looks through a telescope at his little stage, incites the plot to confess its secrets, dissects and tortures the insect-protagonist, but at no time does he definitively transcend himself or stop being who he is. As he journeys on, shadowed by the very distance he generates from himself, the human animal finds that he is diminished and terrified by his own shadow. He can discover every sort of contradiction in himself, depending on how he looks at himself: central but insignificant, essential but accidental, necessary but contingent, eminent but forlorn.

In practice, of course, the mystification and nihilism associated with the radically external perspective are no more than a passing inebriation – or moment of sobriety! The cosmic point of view reveals itself to be as unsustainable in the natural make-up of the mind as is the idea of an individual divested of his own individuality. However forceful and convincing the appeal of that dark vision may seem to be while we breathe the cold and rarefied air of emotional detachment, our spontaneous partiality – the specially affectionate consideration we harbour for ourselves as a species – wins out in the end.

The triumph of partiality, it's worth noting, is so complete that it spreads into the enemy camp. The nihilist who goes out of his way to propagate his profound disbelief, and share his total indifference to the ways of the world, is implicitly denying what he is affirming. After all, we might ask, why should a person for whom in fact nothing matters, and 'it makes no difference whether you think or not', go to the effort of putting forward such an opinion, and trying to persuade anyone of such a thing, or anything else? There are less troublesome and more effective ways of warding off boredom.

2. *The Emotional Centre of the Universe*

Impartiality has its limits. A part will never see, be or entirely understand the whole it belongs to. A being gifted with senses that faithfully translated the true magnitude and proportion of things would lose its sense of direction and disappear in its own insignificance. An organism that didn't rigorously discriminate between what belongs to itself and what to others, would be invaded by worms and swallowed up like a corpse. An individual that felt for others with the same intensity he feels for himself would go mad in the clamour of an infernal cacophony of appetites and impulses. A species that radically lost its belief in itself would collapse under the crushing weight of the futility of any effort and the pointlessness of existence.

It's one thing, however, to fix the boundaries of impartiality. It's quite another to penetrate into the vast and lushly overgrown continent of our spontaneous partiality with regard to the things that have to do with us. There exist limits to impartiality, as we have seen, and we cannot transcend them. But, when it comes to the natural partiality we tend to have for ourselves, *what are the limits*? How far can our subtle, insinuating preference for ourselves go? How does the bias of being who we are affect our personal strategies for living and our life together in society?

In the realm of sensibility, as in the perceptual apparatus, nearness works miracles. A simple example, easily generalised and close to common experience, helps to illustrate the point.

Modern means of communication bring us every day, often at the very time they are happening, terrible scenes of calamity and human suffering. Suppose, along these lines, an air disaster of gigantic proportions: a huge jet that crashed just after takeoff in the suburbs of Calcutta, causing hundreds of deaths. The images of the accident instantly invade the living rooms of the planet.

How do we react to the tragedy? The immediate sensation is one of horror and sincere sympathy for lives cut short, for the suffering of relatives and the absurd horror of the crash. It's possible that some viewers' thoughts might stray to the risks of flying, while others may be comforted as it occurs to them that they never expose themselves to such risks. The news programme goes on, the images follow on one another's heels, the attention wanders. Minutes later, in animated conversation at the dinner table, who still remembers or feels anything about the day's awful tragedy? In a few hours everything will be conveniently forgotten.

Now suppose a small airborne mishap that did not even

reach the local news. The left engine of the plane we are travelling in has a sudden failure in mid-flight, and it has to make an emergency landing at the nearest airport. Panic. 'Fear is extreme ignorance at an acute moment of great tension.'[7] Some passengers disguise their fear, others shrink into their seats; the more excitable ones completely lose their composure, and the children on board scream in terror. It's a terrible fright, but the landing is successful and happily there are no victims. There is applause and general relief. In a few hours everybody is back in their homes and offices, telling their family and friends the details of the adventure they've just been through.

How do we react to what has happened? The panic and uncertainty are left behind ('I got off this time . . .'). The effects of the trauma, it's true, will depend on each person's susceptibilities. But the emotional consequences of our little adventure, which after all was nothing more than a mishap accompanied by some turbulence, will in every case go far beyond the effect produced in us by the scenes of the tragic death of hundreds of victims in the Indian disaster.

Objectively, in retrospect, it was no more than a near accident without injuries; subjectively, however, the effects of this lived experience tend to persist with us, casting their shadow over us for a considerable time. It may be that some will be unable to sleep that night, or may get drunk, or have nightmares; it may be that others will – for a time or for ever – abandon planes as a means of transport. That was what I did.

Two weights, two systems of measurement. Put the two events in the scales: on the one hand, the irreparable loss of hundreds of lives and the relatives' suffering; on the other, the fright and the momentary discomfort caused by a forced landing with no casualties. There is a huge disproportion between the two events. It's no accident that only one of them reached the news.

However, we can also note that, in the spontaneous measurement of our emotions, the impact of the second event outweighs the first, taking on a gravity out of proportion, just as the firefly just in front of my nose blots out the largest star in the sky. The weight of proximity upsets the scales, and gives our subjective side a violent push. The effect of the peculiar position we occupy in the world dictates the pitch and reverberation of our feelings, without asking our permission. The innocent witness of the passions tends to make each human heart the emotional centre of the universe.

The disparity between the two measures stands out clearly when we try to determine the *terms of exchange* between the two events. Suppose that neither of them has happened yet, and that there exists the possibility of choosing *which one* will become a reality in the future, thus avoiding the occurrence of the other. If we were to judge solely on the basis of its subjective impact on us, the occurrence of the Indian disaster would clearly be preferable to our small airborne mishap. It is a shocking imbalance. We still have not reached the extreme, self-destructive point of Hume's provocative formula – "'Tis not contrary to reason to prefer the destruction of the whole world to the scratching of my finger'[8] – but it would, without a doubt, be a monstrous choice. It would be an absurdity worthy of a mad psychopath, a new-born child desperate with hunger, or a Roman emperor who cuts slaves' heads off to relieve his boredom.

Happily things are not as bad as that. The verdict of any moderately reflective judgement is more than enough, in a case like this, to annul the absurd partiality of self-love and reveal that the prevention of passing terror and discomfort, whoever it may happen to, can never justify the death of hundreds of unknown victims on the other side of the world. With the moderating counterweight of moral judgement, the force of proximity is overcome, and the scales respond to the corrective action of the conscious will. It would even be a privilege, some might conclude with a certain pleasure, to be able to suffer the hardships of a near-accident in exchange for preventing a terrible disaster. Our fleeting and prosaic incident would take on another, more dignified dimension (and, who knows, the headlines . . .).

The problem of partiality, however, still remains. It shows its claws again to the extent that we begin to alter, even slightly, the parameters of the original situation. Imagine that the choice is now between an air disaster in India identical to the one we saw on the television news, and the occurrence of engine failure in the plane we're flying in, but with a single difference: there exists a small probability that the forced landing might cause one or two deaths and some serious injuries to some of the passengers on the flight. What would it be realistic to expect?

There are several possibilities. If the choice is made in the light of the known fact that, in spite of the trauma, no one close (even one of us) suffered irreparable injuries, there's no reason not to opt for the lesser evil, that is, the smaller number of dead. But if it has to be made *ex ante* and in ignorance of the identity of the victims, our judgement teeters in the balance. How many of us would *in reality* be ready to accept the small risk of a large loss to prevent the certain death of hundreds of strangers? Any hypothetical reply, within the comfort of the pages of a book, is suspect. The only certainty is that if that same possibility of choice were given to the passengers on that Indian flight, there would be no doubt. Nothing could be more certain than that. We too, in their position, would not hesitate.

The natural partiality of human emotions seems, on occasion, to rise to such virulence that it even shocks and offends the scruples of the person with the feelings. When this happens, the spontaneous preference of the person for himself is apt to grow into a passion capable of invading and flooding the most sacred recesses of inner decorum. The understandable repulsion and horror of feeling, even if only obliquely and in the half-light, what we do in fact feel, seem to lie behind some of the strangest short-circuits and black-outs our minds are capable of. An intimate episode experienced by Machado de Assis's hero-narrator in *Dom Casmurro* illustrates the point well.

The young Bentinho is obsessed by his desire to marry Capitu, but cannot fulfil his passion: he has been promised by his venerated mother, from birth, to the seminary and to a religious life. An attempt to be open with her, to solicit her maternal understanding in the matter, turns into a humiliating fiasco. Cowardice silences him, and the future seminarian gives in. One day, however, his mother falls ill. Bentinho's heart glimpses a twisted ray of hope. Instead of praying and begging for his mother's speedy recovery, as his duty as a son demands, he harbours the fantasy that, with his mother dead and buried, the road to his beloved's arms would be open. There'd be no need to act; just stand on the sidelines and wait. In time, of course, his mother gets slowly better, and Bentinho repents having dared to contemplate something so wicked. Consumed by remorse, he proposes to expiate the guilt with a typical gesture of the most impeccable self-deception, the fruit of pure innocence allied with pure malice:

> So, moved by remorse, once more I used the old expedient of spiritual promises, and asked God to pardon me and save my mother's life, and I would say two thousand paternosters. [. . .] The crisis I found myself in, no less than my habits and my faith, explains everything. It was two thousand more; and where had the old ones gone? I paid neither the latter nor the former, but if such promises come from pure, true souls, they are like fiduciary money – even though the debtor does not redeem them, they are worth their face value.[9]

It is not always easy to feel what we are in fact feeling. There are some things that the underground man doesn't tell his intimates, and others he doesn't even reveal to himself; it is possible that, the more just and honest an individual is, the more such things he will have. From time to time, however, they surface and defy whoever hears them. The person then becomes aware of what he was feeling inside him, though he did not dare to acknowledge.

Bentinho disguises his feelings from his mother, failing in his resolve to open his heart to her once and for all. What he does not, finally, manage, is to disguise from himself what he feels for her. When his mother falls ill and the opportune moment appears, the sacrilegious monster takes the place of the candidate for holy orders. The untamed, scheming voice of an obscene partiality temporarily stifles the minuet of decorum and tramples underfoot the voice of conscience and impartial judgement. Pusillanimity is his protection against matricide. Once, however, he has recovered a certain inner composure, and with his mother better, remorse takes over, and the status quo of self-deception is restored. The mortal hatred of his mother and of everything that separates him from Capitu again disappear from the reach of his conscious attention. Bentinho, contrite, goes to the seminary as the obedient son he always was: a model youth, up to his eyes in debt where the 'paternosters' are concerned, but incapable of hurting or disappointing his mother.

The *internal hypocrite* is the younger – more elusive and more cunning – brother of the *social hypocrite*. The natural desire for others to think well of us, and favour us in some way, frequently prevents us from telling others what we are thinking and feeling. Bertrand Russell, for example, in a letter to a confidant, suggested sending the following message to possible future biographers: 'I did not respect respectable people, and when I pretended to do so it was humbug. I lied and practised hypocrisy, because if I had not I should not have been allowed to do my work; but there is no reason to continue the hypocrisy after I am dead'.[10] The picture, of course, would not be complete without the other half. After all, one wonders, what would his collaborators and ex-lovers think of the respectable philosopher, but thought better to hide from him as well? This is the social hypocrite in action.

The external masquerade, though, is only the public, overt face of the inner masquerade. If the desire to occupy and hold on to a place of honour in the minds of those around us means that we must acquire a certain aptitude and training in the art of dissimulation, the same can be said of the natural desire that anyone has to think well – or at least not too badly – of himself. Inner decorum and self-esteem frequently demand that we do not reveal *to ourselves* everything that we in fact are thinking and feeling. The individual suppresses from the arena of conscious experience his astonishing – and sometimes frankly terrifying – spontaneous partiality for himself. The innocence of the operation is fundamental to it.

Some people, it seems, have a special gift for this. 'Lively natures lie only for a moment,' Nietzsche suggests, 'immediately afterwards they lie to themselves and are convinced and honest.' Others, less favoured, do what they can with the scarce means at their disposal. Young Bentinho, as we have seen, signed a concordat with the Christian deity in the desperate attempt to save his mother and save himself from what at bottom he felt for her. The poet Fernando Pessoa puts his finger on the nerve of the matter: 'No one knows what he really feels: it is possible to feel relief at the death of someone we love, and think we are feeling pain because that is what one should feel on these occasions; the majority of people feel conventionally, though with all human sincerity.'[11] The lie we silently tell ourselves will only convince if it is sincere. This is the internal hypocrite in action.

3. *Social Dissimulation and Moral Partiality*

Human subjectivity contains two parallel, symmetrical forces. On one side is our resistance to a *radically impartial* – neutral, free and external – vision of ourselves: nobody can step beyond the circle of his individuality, and really be another for himself. It is possible to remove oneself somewhat, to try to find an external point of view, and approach our partiality critically, but there are logical and psychological limits to the attempt to look at oneself from the outside.

At the other extreme, meanwhile, we find a tough, rooted resistance to what strikes us as an *excessive partiality* for ourselves: nobody can live for long with a repugnant image of himself, and we are always trying to correct, at least to some degree, the disproportionate bias of our spontaneous sensitivity for everything that touches us and affects us closely. If impartiality taken to its limits hurts and suffocates the human animal, excessive partiality towards ourselves, when it becomes explicit and is consciously recognised, offends, insults and shames our humanity.

Nobody is born with one, but some kind of moral faculty, perhaps analogous to our innate competence in the use of language, is part of the basic equipment of man for life in society. This capacity is manifest, amongst other things, in the sense of shame, modesty and respect for others, and in the exercise of some form of discernment between right and wrong in situations that involve moral choice. A person entirely without moral aptitude, whatever the code of conduct in question may be, would be someone as far removed from the possibility of human sociability as a being for whom the notion of linguistic communication itself – not merely a specific natural language – was completely foreign.

Even where the particular moral codes of each human group are concerned, it turns out that the ethical agreement about *right* and *wrong*, *just* and *unjust*, and *good* and *evil* seems to be more uniform and inclusive than might at first sight appear. The pattern of socially accepted and recognised behaviour is clearly revealed, as Bishop Joseph Butler observes, 'in what every man we meet tries to make it appear that he is'.[12] The validity of the code in force is even endorsed – and with more show, some might say – by those who fail to conform to it. 'Hypocrisy is a homage paid by vice to virtue'.

The fact is that, no matter how diversified and heterogeneous we conceive the psycho-cultural experience of humanity to have been in the long historical process since the acquisition of language, it's difficult to imagine a society in which individuals don't prefer being respected to being despised by those they live with, and don't prefer feeling pride to shame at being who they are. Even a member of an ultra-traditional community – someone, let's say, who doesn't even think of himself as an individual as he blindly obeys the norms and taboos of his tribe – is not freed from having to worry, from time to time, about his image and reputation in the eyes of others. He alone will be able to feel in an individual, private way, in the silence of his own mind, the secret terror that the other members of the tribe might discover his deliberate or inadvertent transgression of the norm.

The existence of some discrepancy between reality and

appearance – the social practice of dissimulation – is inseparable from social life. Not just hypocrisy, but courtesy and a certain sense of duty take us in that direction. It seems not unrealistic to suppose that, when there is an option open to us, our greatest ambition would be not only to conquer in some way, but also to deserve, the respect, sympathy and approval of others. Who would not wish to win in the great lottery of life with goodness for a ticket? In practice, as we know, the options are limited and this is not the general rule. In the absence of less costly alternatives, there are those who prefer to be respected and praised for what they *are not*, to being held in less regard for what they *are*. A thief successful in burglary or fraud parades his riches to the bedazzlement of those around him, with the same pride and presumption as a nouveau riche with a perfectly honest business.

The extent of the gap between what we are, on the one hand, and what we like to look as if we were, on the other, can be judged by two simple conjectures. Who would continue to act as he presently does if he enjoyed total, unrestricted impunity? What if, by accident, he found a ring, as in the Platonic myth, which allowed the person that found it to become invisible when it suited him, and so have the benefit of absolute immunity from any type of external sanction? 'To be good means to do no wrong; and also, not to want to do wrong,' says Democritus, the pre-Socratic philosopher.[13] A really good man, according to this definition, would be the one who, even in the possession of such a ring, did not in the least way modify his conduct in his own interests. Hands up, anyone?

The other conjecture suggestive of the extent of social

dissimulation is the hypothesis of a *shock of interpersonal transparency*. Imagine what would happen if each one of us came to know, owing to a shock of this kind, *everything* the people we relate with were thinking and feeling. It's easy to foresee that social co-existence would suffer an upheaval of unimaginable proportions – the immediate impact of the shock would be devastating.

But what about later on? It's not easy to say. 'Truth in society', suggests the American economist Frank Knight, 'is like strychnine in the individual body: medicinal in special conditions and minute doses; otherwise and in general, a deadly poison.'[14] In the transparency shock, however, the poison would not need to kill. It could be metabolised and gradually assimilated into a new form of sociability. Perhaps the only thing sure is that, once we are over the first seismic shock, our whole family, emotional and social life would have to be reconstructed on an entirely different basis.

Social dissimulation is the art of managing the impression one makes. The phenomenon has an enormously wide spectrum. In the simplest cases, as for example that of someone who pretends to be interested in what someone else is saying, the effect is almost harmless. In more serious ones, like that of a corrupt magistrate or a false friend, tremendous harm can be done. In such cases, the person dissimulating shelters and screens himself behind a veil of socially accepted morality, so as to cover up actions that give the lie to what he appears to be. The moral standard is flouted, and the social actor may emerge unharmed from the story, but there is no doubt about the nature of the action. Professionals in the art of imposture – characters stylised in their devilish cunning, like

Iago, Mephistopheles, and Don Juan – know what they are doing.

But the thing that really complicates matters in the plots of our common existence is not social dissimulation. If the borderline between *good faith* and *bad faith*, between what's *farcical* and what's *serious*, between being *right* or being *wrong*, were always clear and unmistakable; if *good* and *evil* were always in opposing, well-defined camps, with both those dissimulating and their victims always aware of the nature of their good or bad intentions, the world would not be what it is.

The origin of evil in human society cannot be reduced to a single cause. Real, dissimulating cynicism does exist, who can deny it? But so do self-deception and sincere rationalisation. The true mystery lies not in the cold, calculating dissimulation of the social actor, but in the passion, elevated and tragic, generous and self-destructive, overwhelming and blind, of characters like Othello, Faust and Dona Elvira.

One needs to take care – and I say this first and foremost to myself – to avoid extreme positions. It would surely be going too far to believe, as some adepts of Romantic philosophy do, that no one practises evil in a deliberate, cynical way. Thomas Carlyle, for example, says this:

All battle is misunderstanding; did the parties know one another, the battle would cease. No man at bottom means injustice; it is always for some obscure distorted image of a right that he contends; an obscure image diffracted, exaggerated, in the wonderfulest way, by natural dimness and selfishness; getting ten-fold more diffracted by exasperation of contest, till at length it becomes all but irrecognisable; yet still the image of a right. Could a man own to himself that the thing he fought for was wrong, contrary to fairness and the law of reason, he would own also that it thereby stood condemned and hopeless; he could fight for it no longer.[15]

The flaw in this point of view is that it advances an absolute and unnecessary generalisation of an important truth. It's obvious, on the one hand, that not every case of social dissimulation has the object of covering up the conscious practice of evil; but it would be unrealistic to suppose that this latter never happens, that is, that at least *one part of it* doesn't have precisely this aim. A possibility that cannot be ruled out is that evil may be the result, at least in a few cases, of the desire for a perverse *goal*, as for example in the case of a sadistic pleasure in someone else's suffering.

Another group of cases, certainly much more frequent, are those in which evil is practised in a conscious, calculated way, not as a desired end, but as a means to obtain other ends; as the easiest short-cut to the apparent good one wants to achieve (wealth, power, sex, fame, etc.). The extent of the practice of social dissimulation suggests that there are at least some occasions when, even if a person knew perfectly well how much evil and suffering he was causing, this would still not stop him perpetrating the deed.

But what really does surprise one in human social existence – and from this point of view the Romantic position seems to be essentially right – is the frequency of situations in which not only is evil *not* the aim directly aimed for, but it also *does not appear* to the individual concerned to be the evil it is. If we look to history for examples, that's what we find in the horrific atrocities committed in the name of political, ideological or religious faith. 'Philip II and Isabella the Catholic', it has been rightly said, 'inflicted more suffering in obedience to their consciences than Nero and Domitian in obedience to their lusts'.[16]

The sincere good conscience of some of the greatest oppressors and terrorists in human history is the most enigmatic and appalling chapter in the annals of self-deception. If evil were not so often intimately and strangely linked to the vision of good, it seems reasonable to suppose that the plots of our social existence would be less ambiguous and dangerous, but they would also lose something of what gives them an aura of mystery: something of the interest and wonder that man arouses in man.

The thing that complicates human relationships in practical existence – what above all obscures the boundaries in social interaction – is the fact that our moral equipment has some specific features that often make it unreliable, not to say fickle and treacherous, and this particularly in moments and situations when reliability is most needed. It's these features, I will argue, that basically explain the need for impersonal rules of conduct, exterior to the subjectivity of particular individuals, in social interaction. The first step in the argument is to identify the inherent vulnerability of our moral equipment.

The relationship that each individual has with himself is of a different nature from the one he has with others. The image of our own face in the mirror and the recorded sound of our voice produce a curious sensation of familiarity and strangeness in us. However much we try to surprise ourselves and see ourselves as others presumably see us, we cannot do so. Something elusive and indefinable –

an instantaneous interference associated with our own presence – gets in the way and undermines the neutrality of the meeting. An analogous process takes place, curiously, when we try to tickle ourselves. The same brain that sets off the muscular movement that we are about to do – moving the hand to the chosen place – disseminates instantly through the nervous system the message concerning what is being done.[17] The result is that the fingers faithfully obey orders, but the aim of tickling is foiled.

The problem of the difficulty of looking at oneself appears in an acute form in the field of moral judgement. When what is at stake are actions and concerns remote from the network of our emotions and interests; when all that we have to do is approve or condemn a given conduct, while the onus of carrying it out rests on other shoulders, each of us is a competent judge, with an appropriate notion of what's right and wrong. It's as easy as being charitable with someone else's money, demanding less corruption in politics, despising state-run trade unions, loving nature, being shocked by the dreadful state of primary education, getting patriotic goose-pimples when the national anthem is played, or getting furious at the loud music played by one's neighbour. The list is interminable. The opinion and letter pages of the papers and magazines provide acres of examples.

But when it's a case of appreciating the real dimensions, and seeing the true import of something closely regarding *ourselves*; when what's at issue is the establishment of a balanced perspective between our interests and those of people around us, and making sure that our actions reflect this balance in practice, our talent for discernment and moral judgement tends to become seriously weakened. Proximity in time and space, on the one hand, and nearness in terms of our emotions and interests, on the other, powerfully interfere with the functioning of the moral faculties. Human competence to see and judge with a minimum of disinterestedness and impartiality seems to fall exponentially, the nearer we get to everything that closely affects and concerns us. Thus the ancient proverb, which in its original formulation comes from Aristotle's *Politics*, that *no one is a good judge in his own cause*.[18]

The heart of the problem is that our natural partiality for ourselves is not simply restricted to the perceptual apparatus, the metabolic system or the spontaneous ebb and flow of the emotions. Partiality has a voracious appetite. It perseveres and insinuates itself into the core of our moral equipment and often gets its way, that is, it succeeds in deflecting or distorting its corrective influence. Moved by our partial, fond affection for ourselves, the underlying current of the bias of being who we are disfigures beyond repair the functioning of the moderating conscience. The excessive partiality of the individual where he himself is concerned no longer offends and appals him, since he somehow takes it upon himself to cover its tracks and obliterate all sign of it from his mind.

When this happens, it's as if the moral capacity – the faculty that in theory should protect us from our excessive preference for ourselves – has been hijacked by that same partiality and submitted to its logic and its power. The voice of moral conscience dies out at the suitable moment, or even takes the other, ruling side. Instead of moderating the demands of our natural impulses and feelings, the moral equipment becomes their secret ally, and ends up being placed at the service of their legitimisation. Worse still, the internal make-up of our mind seems to conspire to increase our propensity to lose the talent for moral judgement just when that talent is most needed. The more intense the appeal of the emotions or of the cause that moves us, the greater also seems to be the probability that this hijack – followed by passive complicity or active collaboration – will take place.

4. Moral Partiality: Examples and Discussion

The distortions brought about by judging in our own cause are linked to a double asymmetry. The view each of us has of himself is not the one others have of him. The individual's inner view of his own character and conduct in ordinary life differs from the essentially external perspective of those he interacts with. But it is not only that. The reverse is also true. The view that others have of themselves, from their respective inner viewpoints, is not the one that we have of them. The asymmetry doesn't merely hold *from them to us*; it also holds *from us to them*. Every individual has an inner viewpoint, and our possibilities of apprehending it are inevitably limited and external.

The moral effects of this double situational asymmetry, fed of course by the naturally special consideration we have for ourselves, are everywhere. A simple example, but one which helps to bring the concrete side of the question into relief, is what happens in that extraordinary laboratory of social interaction and psychology: the traffic system.

A survey of opinion carried out in the homeland of the motor-car revealed an intriguing fact: *nine out of every ten* American drivers think they drive better than the average. It is, of course, a statistical impossibility. It's probable that many of those who say they are below average are in fact above it, since at least they don't overestimate their skill at the wheel. The fact is that the individual opinion of drivers, based on the inner view they have of their capacities, does not correspond to the external, general perception of those who interact with them on the roads. Can they be lying? I don't think so. The answers – sincere in spite of being false for the majority – perfectly reflect the maxim formulated by La Rochefoucauld when he noted how acutely 'Each one of us finds in others the very faults others find in us.'[19]

Another fertile soil for the flourishing of moral partiality is the attribution of praise and blame in group activities. Here, bias in judgement seems to obey a systematic, bifocal refraction, so subtle as to become almost imperceptible to the person experiencing it.

The responsibility for success, however fleeting it may be, is usually hotly disputed. There is an inflationary growth of parents and ancestors, to the nth generation. After all, in good conscience, who thinks that his merits and contribution are properly recognised? Who, in the silent tribunal of his own soul, thinks he's got what he deserves, gets more than he gives? But when things begin to go wrong – when the government plan, the partnership, the team or the political movement show evident signs of going under – recriminations and mutual accusations of blame aren't long in coming. Failure is an orphan. Reasons, excuses, unforeseen events, and culprits of all kinds and origins occur to us, in profusion – and help us out. Human ingenuity for getting out of a tight corner by rationalising mistakes, weaknesses, defeats and omissions seems inexhaustible.

It's undeniable that there are exceptions. When the storms set in and the inner sky really darkens over, moral inflation can turn into a violent *deflation*. A depressive state of mind removes that modicum of goodwill, esteem and respect for himself that make anyone's self-awareness something agreeable. The depressed person lives like a pariah in the gutter of his subjective life ('There isn't a beggar I don't envy, just for not being me'). Happily, however, in the vast majority of cases this is a temporary scenario. One day the weather improves, enjoyment in being who one is is reborn, and the subtle bias of partiality begins to move, as its nature demands, in the inflationary direction. In normal conditions of temperature and pressure, as Adam Smith says, 'we are all naturally disposed to over-rate the excellencies of our own characters'.[20]

Moral inflation flourishes at a distance – while the virtues we attribute to ourselves are still comfortably hypothetical and abstract – but the winds of conflict and negotiation are also highly favourable to it. The tendency to a self-deceived idealisation of one's own character when one is at a safe distance – the sincere rapture of a Rousseauistic love for humanity – is well portrayed by Dr Johnson:

> To charge those favourable representations which men give of their own minds with the guilt of hypocritical falsehood, would show more severity than knowledge. The writer commonly believes himself. Almost every man's thoughts, while they are general,

are right; and most hearts are pure while temptation is away. It is easy to awaken generous sentiments in privacy; to despise death when there is no danger; to glow with benevolence when there is nothing to be given. While such ideas are formed they are felt, and self-love does not suspect the gleam of virtue to be the meteor of fantasy.[21]

In public, as in private life, the comfort of distance when the sea is calm is deceptive. Machiavelli's advice to the Prince hits the same note:

> A prince cannot rely upon what he sees during periods of calm, when the citizens need his rule, because then everyone comes running, makes promises, and each one is willing to die for him – since death is unlikely; but in times of adversity, when the state needs its citizens, then few are to be found [. . .] For one can generally say this about men [that] while you work for their good they are completely yours, offering you their blood, their property, their lives, and their sons, as I said earlier, when danger is far away; but when it comes nearer to you they turn away.[22]

It's curious to note that in some specific cases, the pin of reality may burst the balloon of self-deception, but the passage of time takes it on itself to inflate it again. The young Darwin, for example, imagined that he was above concerning himself with questions of scientific priority. When the first serious opportunity to test this belief occurred, and there was a serious threat that a rival biologist (Alfred Wallace) might anticipate him in the publication of the theory of natural selection, Darwin came to his senses. As he confided at the time, in a letter to a colleague, '[I had] fancied that I had a grand enough soul not to care; but I found myself mistaken and punished'. Years later, however, when he wrote his *Autobiography* at the peak of the prestige attained through this discovery, Darwin again underlined his indifference about questions of priority, saying that it mattered little to him whether they attributed more originality to him or to his rival.[23]

An analogous pattern can be found in the field of obstetrics. Many women who opt for natural birth without the use of anaesthetics change their mind the instant the birth-pangs become acute. After the birth, however, they again express their original preference, and in some cases go to the point of complaining about the doctor who administered the anaesthetic. . . The problem of moral partiality in this case, as we will see in the next section, has to do not with the relationship *between* different people (interpersonal), but between forces or viewpoints in conflict *within* the same person (intrapersonal).

Moral partiality is a two-way street. The counterpart of inflation of one's own self is the deflation of someone else's. This is not a necessary relationship, but it tends to happen with remarkable frequency, particularly in situations of animosity, conflict, and negotiation. A personal experience I had while writing this book – another example gathered in the Hobbesian laboratory of behaviour in traffic – helps us to visualise the risks associated with the spiral of inflation-of-the-self v. deflation-of-the-other.

I was walking absent-mindedly round the streets of my neighbourhood, ruminating on my propensity to self-deception, when suddenly a car comes hurriedly out of the garage of a block of flats and very nearly knocks me down. First comes the fright, then the cause. Who is to blame? If the driver of the car showed any signs of recognising *his* part of the blame, I would naturally be disposed to temporise and admit *my* portion of responsibility (my absent-mindedness). It so happens, though, that his expression exudes fury and indignation at my stupidity. The effect this has on me, in its turn, is like a bullet, swift and unstoppable. Anger and the overwhelming certainty that this fellow is a total idiot flood my mind. In the heat of the moment, the swearwords are nearly there, on the tip of my tongue.

But what if they had been uttered? What might have happened then? An escalation of insults might have reduced us, in a matter of seconds, to the level of two angry bulls or two ridiculous fighting-cocks, embroiled in the arena of our injured vanities.

What is the proportion between cause and effect? What do I know about him or he about me? What if *I* had been in the car and *he* on foot? How did *he* see the whole thing? And what if some expression in *my* eyes provoked his reaction, which I interpreted as one of unjustifiable arrogance? I walked back home, relieved at having come out of the incident unscathed, but unsure about everything; speculating about how many might have been hurt or ended their days in just this kind of way, not because of chance tiles falling off roofs, but in duels, vendettas, altercations in traffic, bar brawls, gang fights, momentary flare-ups, pointless arguments, a simple word, a facial expression, or a gesture taken the wrong way...

Human ambitions and concerns, seen from outside and far off, without the particular bias of the person living through them, lose their vigour and fade away in their ephemeral insignificance. But from the inner point of view of each individual – from the personal, non-transferable angle of vision defined by one's own life – nothing seems so insignificant or ephemeral that it can't arouse the most virulent passions.

The logic of conflict and of stubborn, aggressive negotiation – whatever the practical or real importance of the contention – tends to act as a catalyst, and to magnify moral partiality.[24] How can one fight a war without piously believing that one's enemy is to blame? How can one plunge into a dispute without good cause? How can one enter a controversy or a public debate without having right on one's side?

'Most men like their own writing best of all,' said Sir Thomas More.[25] Our natural talent for belittling and distorting the ideas of our opponents and rivals in the world of thought is one of the most astonishing traits of intellectual life – a notable fact, considering that we rarely realise we are accomplishing this feat, and that the distortion is almost invariably *for the worse*. The danger of inflationary escalation is next door.

Perhaps only party politics is worse. 'A true party-man', says Adam Smith, 'hates and despises candour; and, in reality, there is no vice which could so effectually disqualify him for the trade of party-man as that single virtue'. Or as Nietzsche would say later, with the vehemence characteristic of his final phase: 'This desiring *not* to see what one sees, this desiring not to see as one sees, is virtually the primary condition for all who are in any sense *party*: the party man necessarily becomes a liar.'[26] Exaggeration aside, this is a tricky point to negate. To deny it is to corroborate it. What, after all, could be better confirmation of the moral inflation to which we are naturally prone than to think of oneself as an exception?

Excessive partiality offends our moral conscience. Contemplating someone else's cruelty, that is, that type of cruelty we neither do nor are tempted to do, upsets our sensibility and leads us to an attitude of genuine disapproval. Drummond de Andrade's naturalist czar illustrates an extreme case of asymmetry in the perception of cruelty:

Once upon a time there was a naturalist czar
who hunted men.
When they told him you can also hunt butterflies
   and swallows,
he was quite amazed
and thought it barbarous.[27]

The czar's amazement is the mirror-image of the reader's. Others' cruelty, seen from outside, differs from that which we commit, seen in others' eyes. In the worst cases, the desire to think well – or at least not too badly – of oneself has the ability to remove the evil one has done from the field of conscious attention.

How far can we go in the spontaneous expulsion and suppression of things within ourselves that offend us? How far can a person go in the inner concealment and self-deception necessary to keep the mind quiet, and thus guarantee a harmonious relationship with himself? The extraordinary biblical story of King David's moral de-blocking under the accusatory gaze of the prophet Nathan (2 Samuel, 11–12) offers a perfect illustration.

Beauty caresses the eye. It's late afternoon. King David, the unifier of the twelve tribes of Israel, is reclining idly on the highest veranda of the royal palace when a beautiful woman bathing nearby comes into his field of

vision. Immediately he sends to know who she is – she's
Bathsheba, the wife of the soldier Uriah – and orders her
to be brought to him. The two make love. Bathsheba goes
back home and soon discovers that she is pregnant. David
is the only possible father: Uriah is away on service and
observing the ritual abstinence of those fighting in a holy
war. It's necessary to act. If nothing were done, the usual
punishment for a woman taken in adultery would be death
by stoning. The king's first impulse is to get out of trouble
by the convenient exit of social dissimulation. He tries to
hide the deed and prevent the royal paternity of the child
from being generally known.

David orders Joab, his most trusted general, to make
Uriah return from the war and come straight into his presence. The king then tries to persuade him to go and spend
some days at home, sleeping with his wife. It so happens,
however, that Uriah is a loyal and zealous soldier, strict in
the fulfilment of his duty. Instead of going home, which
would mean breaking with the ritual of a man fighting in
a holy war, he stays with the palace guards, and goes so
far as to upbraid the king for trying to deflect him from the
right road. The pressure grows. David, bewildered, takes
a criminal course of action. He orders Uriah to rejoin the
serving forces, and, through him, sends a letter addressed
to Joab with the following instruction: 'Set Uriah in the
forefront of the hardest fighting, and then draw back from
him, that he may be struck down, and die.'

The letter is delivered and the royal orders complied
with. When he learns of Uriah's death, David feigns sorrow
(it's what one should feel on such occasions) and exhorts
his troops not to lose heart in the holy war. The hero's
widow observes a conveniently short period of mourning,

and then straight away marries the king. The couple's first son is not long in coming. The Israelite army surrounds and takes the enemy's capital. Life returns to its normal course. Appearances have been saved and the repugnance of the crime duly obliterated. Uriah, to all intents and purposes, died as a true hero in action. Ugliness offends the eye. 'But the thing that David had done displeased the Lord.'

At first, nothing happens. Almost a year passes without David showing any sign of remorse or contrition. One day, however, everything changes. The prophet Nathan appears for a visit, and tells the king the story of a recent event in a town where there lived two men, one rich, the other poor. The rich man owned a great number of flocks and herds; the poor man owned a single sheep that he brought up with his children, as if it were a member of the family. But, when the rich man received a guest, a man who happened to be passing, he revealed himself to be the penny-pincher he in fact was. Instead of killing an animal from his own flock, he went to the poor man's house and took his only sheep to serve it to his visitor. When he hears of such a great injustice, King David, indignant, bursts out: 'As the Lord lives, the man who has done this deserves to die; and he shall restore the lamb fourfold, because he did this thing, and because he had no pity.' The prophet Nathan then replies: '*You are the man!*'

It's only after this revelation has been made that the fury and the punishment of the Lord fall on the house of David, cutting short the life of his first son with Bathsheba, and bringing about an escalation of conflict in the royal family. But it is also then that the enormity of the crime he has committed – the premeditated murder of an innocent, loyal subject – reaches his dulled conscience with the crushing effect of a flash of lightning. The blacking out of guilt and memory had given peace to the king's subjective palace, but the prophet's ploy lit up the blind spot in his conscience. The king comes to his senses.

The prophet does not accuse the king directly. He sharpens and whets David's sense of justice with the parable of the two men, only to turn the knife in the king's hand and force him to cut his own flesh. Nathan corners David in front of David himself. He lures the monster, arouses him, subtly removes the mask and then *lifts up the mirror*. The injustice that David had no difficulty in finding in someone else, to the point of condemning him with absurd severity, he was not capable of seeing in himself, in spite of the gigantic disproportion between the gravity of the two acts. If the self-deception of the boy David led him to confront and defeat Goliath (see p. 50,) the self-deception of King David made him banish the murder of Uriah from his active memory. But the repugnant vision of his own crime reflected in the mirror of conscience – by the prophet's trick – bursts the dike holding back the memory and the repressed guilt. The *cordon sanitaire* of self-deceived forgetting is broken and the past breaks through. David unmasks David. The blind spot can now see.

5. The Intertemporal Siren Song

The bias of moral partiality affects the perception the individual has of himself, and his interaction with others. When it is linked to the exercise of political authority, the result is *abuse of power*: blind and systematic in cases like the naturalist czar, and blind and momentary as in the case of King David.

But the problems of judging in one's own cause are not restricted to external and interpersonal relationships. 'Every human being is a small society.'[28] The art of hearing, negotiating and managing the conflicting impulses and drives in our breasts involves the exercise of an internal – intrapersonal – authority that exposes us to a real minefield of ambushes, rebellions and possibilities for self-imposed damage. Intrapersonal moral partiality affects the perception of value in time and the relationship between different forces in the internal microcosm that constitutes the individual.

The proximity of things in space – their greater or lesser distance from the particular position we occupy in the world – influences our visual perception of size and proportion. A window takes in the street and the building opposite. An analogous effect can be found, *mutatis mutandis*, in the human experience of the temporal dimension. The nearness of events in time – their greater or lesser distance in relation to the lived present – influences our sensibility and, in varying degrees, our sense of value.

A day is a day, no matter what. But our subjective experience of time does not easily submit to the conventions of the clock and the calendar. The distance between today and tomorrow naturally seems to us greater than an identical interval of time ten months hence. The greater the time separating us, the greater the discrepancy: the distance between today and a fortnight's time seems greater than the interval of a month, but in ten years' time. In the same way, the anticipation of a routine visit to the dentist *early next morning* hurts more in the imagination than a much more painful visit, after a long absence, but still a few months off.

If the choice is between, say, a fortnight's holiday in Bahia three years hence or a month four years hence, there's no reason *not* to wait: the second option will win. But, if the choice is between a fortnight's holiday starting this weekend or a whole month but *only a year from now*, the tendency to wait teeters in the balance. How much wait is worth an additional fortnight in Bahia? From a neutral point of view, *sub specie aeternitatis*, they are two strictly identical choice situations. In the first of them, the choice is easy. In the second, however, how many would really prefer to wait?[29]

Interpersonal conflict puts the first person and the others into opposition: it's a case of *me* against *you*, or *us* against *them*. *Intrapersonal* conflict, however, is internal to the first person and happens essentially in the intertemporal dimension. It's a case, then, of *me now* against *me later* (the same goes for *us*). It is the product of the perennial tension between the present and the future in our deliberations: between what would be best from the tactical or local point of view, on the one hand, and from the strategic or wider viewpoint, on the other. Smoking a cigarette or eating a sweet, for instance, are tactical decisions; stopping smoking and dieting are strategic. Studying (or not) for tomorrow's exam is a tactical choice; to start a course in higher education is part of a life plan. Flirting is tactical; marriage strategic.

Strategic decisions, like tactical ones, are taken in the present. The difference is that they have the long run as their horizon, and aim at the realisation of remote objectives. 'Man', said Paul Valéry, 'is the heir and the hostage of time – the animal whose principal home is in the past or in the future.'[30] It was this ability to retain the past and act in the present, but having the future in mind, that removed us from the condition of healthy, hand-to-mouth primates.

The problem, however, is that our faculty of arbitrating wisely between the urgent needs of the lived present and the aims of an imagined future is often prejudiced by our natural propensity to give much less relative weight to the future, that is, to give disproportionate value to what is nearest to us in time. The problem of temporal myopia in human existence is magnificently portrayed by the Greek poetic tradition concerning the dangers faced by sailors when they heard the sirens' song.

Who is so steadfast that nothing can seduce him? The sirens' song's origins can be traced back to Greek mythology and literature. The versions of the fable and the details of the story vary from author to author, but the essentials of the plot are common to all of them.

The sirens were super-human creatures: nymphs of an extraordinary beauty and sensual magnetism. They lived alone on a Mediterranean island, but they had the gift of attracting sailors, thanks to the irresistibly seductive power of their singing. Attracted by this divine music, ships came close to the island, hit the submerged reefs along the coast and were wrecked. Then the sirens pitilessly devoured the crew. The coastline of the island was a vast marine cemetery in which were piled up the innumerable ships and skeletons swallowed up by this sublime singing, since the beginning of time.

The primrose path of dalliance leads to bitter ruin. How are we to survive the sirens' song? Many have tried, but few have escaped. Greek literature records *two* successful solutions. One of them was the way out found, in the heat of the moment, by Orpheus, the incomparable genius of music and poetry in Greek mythology. When the ship he was travelling in accidentally came within the reach of the sirens' influence, he managed to avoid letting the crew lose their heads by singing an even sweeter and more sublime song than the one coming from the island. The crew, with only one exception, were so taken with Orpheus's song that they paid no attention at all to the sirens' song. The ship went through the danger zone unharmed. The thrilling beauty of the Orphic music dimmed the warm promise of the sirens' song.

The other solution was the one found and adopted by Ulysses in Homer's poem. Unlike Orpheus, the hero of the *Odyssey* was not gifted with super-human artistic talent. Singing his way out of trouble was not an option for him. His main weapon to defeat the sirens was not a brilliant sleight of hand or talented improvisation. It was the open and courageous recognition of his own weakness and fallibility – the acceptance of his inescapable human limitations.

Ulysses knew that, when the time came, he and his men would not have the strength and firmness of purpose to resist the seductive appeal of the sirens. That is why, when the ship he captained began to get close to the island, he commanded every member of the crew to stop their ears with wax, and ordered them to tie him to the central mast. He also warned that, if by any chance he demanded, with gestures and shouts, that they should loose his bonds, what they should do is to tie him even more tightly to the mast. And that was what happened. When the moment came, Ulysses was seduced by the sirens and did everything to convince the crew to leave him free to go to them.

His subordinates, however, managed to refuse his urgent requests and faithfully obeyed the order not to loose him, under any pretext, until they were far enough from the danger zone. Ulysses, it's true, almost went mad with desire. But the sirens, despairing at having been defeated by a mere mortal, drowned themselves in frustration.

Orpheus escaped from the sirens as a divine being; Ulysses as a mortal. As he came near to the time and space of the sirens, the choice facing the Homeric hero was clear: the apparent good, with the false promise of immediate gratification, or the permanent good of his life's project – to continue his journey, return to Ithaca and regain Penelope. The most surprising thing is that Ulysses didn't fill his own ears with wax – he *wanted to hear*. He knew he would be unable to resist, but insisted on letting himself be seduced and maddened with desire by something he knew was lethal.

Knowing is not enough. Ulysses did not shrink from the experience of desperately desiring something that would cause shipwreck and certain death. He did not escape from the suicidal partiality of his desire for the over-whelming promise of immediate pleasure, at whatever cost or sacrifice to himself. What saved Ulysses was not the awareness of the deathly deceit of the singing, but the wisdom never to overestimate his capacity to resist the sirens' power of seduction. Tying himself to the ship's mast, he temporarily gave up his freedom of choice in the present so as to save future life and liberty. Mortal, but able to respect his own limitations, he knew how to deal rationally with his dizzying temporal short-sightedness, inventing an ingenious stratagem to protect himself from it.

What happens to the music and the singing – nothing

more than physical vibrations in the surrounding air –
in the inner experience of the person hearing them and
charmed by them? Ulysses' real victory was over himself
– over and above the suicidal opportunism and deranged
deafness he succeeded in hearing and recognising in his
own soul.

The struggle between Ulysses and the sirens dramatises
and gives epic proportions to a conflict that permeates our
prosaic odyssey through life. As David Hume puts it, 'there
is no quality in human nature, which causes more fatal
errors in our conduct, than that which leads us to prefer
whatever is present to the distant and remote, and makes
us desire objects more according to their situation than
their intrinsic value'.[31] How many forms can the sirens'
song take, in the context of any person's life?

It's the 'one for the road' of songs and advertisements;
it's the extra pint of soup for which the prisoner in a Nazi
concentration camp was tempted to exchange his soul and
his loyalty; it's the addiction to opium that led Coleridge to
the unusual decision to employ a servant with the specific
task of physically standing in his way every time he went to
the chemist's to get the drug; it's the habit and pleasure of
smoking cigars that Freud never succeeded in overcoming,
in spite of decades of self-analysis and the awareness of its
harmful effects, which later included cancer of the mouth;
it is the acquisitive abandon of Johnny Hodges (Duke
Ellington's saxophonist), who impulsively spent all the
money that fell into his hands, and thus preferred to get
paid in daily quotas; it's the insidious sleepiness that makes
a driver drop off at the wheel; it's the smoker who pays, on
the same day, for cigarettes and for cures for the habit;
it's the fat woman who goes to the cake-shop next door

and the slimming clinic . . . the list is endless. The prosaic versions of the sirens' song are like the legendary glass of Guinness, that had the knack of filling up and tempting one again, every time it was emptied. 'Every man makes his own shipwreck.'[32]

The conflict underlying all these situations opposes two characters who compete for power in everyone's intrapersonal parliament. The first is the *me-now*: an enthusiastic young man, often intoxicated with desire, and always ready to enjoy whatever the moment offers; generous no doubt, but with limited vision and a strong tendency to discount the future heavily. Immediate good is his raison d'être.

On the other side, on the benches of the moderate, conscientious coalition – reactionary and repressive, according to the opposition – sits his eternal, austere opponent, the *me-later*: a wary adult, often soured by worries, with one eye always on his own health and his savings account, his mind always on his professional future, cautious when in the midst of doubts, but able to see further than the *me-now*, even though at the expense of heavily discounting the present. Distant good is his sole concern.

The *me-now* has an intense awareness of his fleeting subjective self, and tends to face life, not as a whole, but as a sequence of isolated moments of opportunity, without a common thread giving them coherence or unity. The *me-later*, in its turn, tries to fix an appropriate critical distance from itself, and face life, if not as a whole and from beginning to end, at least as a reasonably structured and coherent sequence of strategic options. The *me-later* is, at bottom, the *me-now* seen from outside and from a distance, in the light of its own past, but with all momentary passions silenced and from a point of view somewhere in the future.

The art of living with oneself is linked to the search for some kind of stable balance between these two forces. Excesses can come from either side. The *me-now* without the chastening perspective of the *me-later*, is, at worst, an impulsive, feather-headed primate – food for sirens. But the *me-later* without the dreamy disposition of the *me-now* is nothing but a calculating, predictable automaton – a being deaf to any call that might threaten its future existence in pain-free comfort. The robot and the monkey need one another.

It is also reasonable to suppose that the strength of each relative to the other will tend to alter as life progresses, with the *me-later* winning more seats in the inner parliament as the fires and fevers of youth's long intoxication are left behind. The problem, though, is that the balance of power between these two factions is not always kept within minimal standards of equity and justice. Abuse of power and exploitation are not the exclusive prerogatives of interpersonal relationships. They may also be present, to some extent, in the intrapersonal microcosm.

Abuse of power on the part of the *me-now* – and some careful or desperate measures to avoid it – appears with clarity in the case of Ulysses and the prosaic examples listed above. What cannot be underestimated, however, is the persuasive cunning of the *me-now* when it's a matter of giving legitimacy to its strong preference for the apparent good of immediate gratification. 'Give me chastity and continence', as the young St Augustine famously prayed, 'but not yet.' The American philosopher William James sets out a brilliant sequence of rigged ballots in the dispute for intrapersonal power:

> How many excuses does the drunkard find when each new temptation comes! It is a new brand of liquor which the interest of intellectual culture in such matters obliges him to test; moreover it is poured out and it is a sin to waste it; or others are drinking and it would be churlishness to refuse; or it is but to enable him to sleep; or just to get through this job of work; or it isn't drinking, it is because he feels so cold; or it is Christmas day; or it is a means of stimulating him to make a more powerful resolution in favour of abstinence than any he has hitherto made; or it is just this once, and once doesn't count, etc., etc., *ad libitum* – it is, in fact, anything you like except being a drunkard.[33]

It is obvious that the interest of this passage transcends the nominal values – the details and the particular colouring – of the situation described. The dark aspect of the problem is the fact that the abuses of power by one of the parties – in this case, the *me-now* – do not leave the other indifferent. A plausible reaction may be some kind of authoritarian move on the part of the *me-later*, imposing, for example, a state of emergency, based on acts of force like complete abstinence or clinical internment. The next step in the escalation of the conflict would be a possible reaction on the part of the *me-now*, furious at the absurd intolerance and oppressive violence of the faction in power. A clandestine, terrorist action of the *me-now* could, finally, produce further and even more aggressive acts of strength from the *me-later*, leading the spiral of violence to culminate (in the worst scenario) in the mutual and irreversible destruction of both contenders.

Interpersonal *exploitation*, like abuse of power, is a two-way street. The basic difference is that here it is not a recurrent relationship of inordinate abuse of power, as in the example of escalation just described, but a process whereby decisions taken (or merely avoided) in a certain phase of our lives more or less permanently harm the perspectives and conditions of existence in a later phase of life.

The period of youth and the beginning of adult life is inevitably the setting for this dispute – it is logically impossible for an older person to take decisions that can affect, for better or worse, the future of the young man he once was. But the dispute between the *me-now* and the *me-later* for ascendancy over a young man's mind can have as a result either *a*) the exploitation of the old man he will one day be by the young man he is or *b*) the exploitation of the young man he is now by the old man he imagines he will become one day.

In the first case – certainly the commoner – it's the young man who exploits the old man. The *me-now* takes advantage of his natural affinity with youthful impetuosity, love of risk, and irresponsibility to dominate the decision process and the young man's life-style, condemning the *me-later* party to exile. Under the influence of the temporal short-sightedness of the *me-now*, this young man begins to discount his future at an exorbitant rate in the choices he makes. His life doesn't necessarily have to revolve around sex, drugs, surfing and pop music, to the exclusion of everything else. The crucial thing is for the young man held in thrall by the *me-now* to make huge bets, take out loans, mortgage his inheritance and give IOUs without thinking of the consequences, always with the comfortable notion that the bills won't have to be paid now, or in the immediate future, but only much later, in a remote and hypothetical future, and that they will be debited to the account of an older man who, though he bears the same name, has no relationship with him at all.

One day, however, assuming that the sirens didn't get all they want before that, the bills begin to arrive. The *me-now* no longer has the freshness and bloom of better days, and has lost some crucial seats in the inner parliament to the *me-later*. The older gentleman (or lady) begins to feel the weight of years and little by little begins to realise the sad fact that he has been ruthlessly exploited, with no opportunity to defend himself, by the young man he once was – a daydreaming spendthrift, generous with his own future as if it belonged to someone else, and who on top of that has spent all he had and more in the older man's name, and on his account. The wild, unfinished dream of youthful night gives way to the repentant insomnia of old age. Why not have just another drink to forget and remember?

The problem, however, is that the (perfectly justified) fear that the young man tyrannised by the *me-now* might exploit the old man he will one day become can lead to a clumsy attempt at a pre-emptive move. Invert the poles of the relationship. There is a risk of excess, too, the other way around. The road of moderation is not free of the threat of overdoing it, when it takes us too far in that direction. The shadow of an imagined future can oppress and stifle the present as we are living it.

The other basic modality of intrapersonal exploitation

is the one in which the old man exploits the young one in advance. The young man's *me-later* rules over his decision-making process and his way of life, banishing the fiery *me-now* to a Siberian exile. Under the protection of the temporal long-sightedness of the *me-later*, this pseudo-youth takes on a steely discipline that makes him put an exorbitant discount rate on the present. Again, his life doesn't necessarily have to revolve around study, vitamins, computers and jogging, to the exclusion of everything else. The crucial thing is that this pseudo-youth tyrannised by the *me-later* should never bet, should save whenever he can, should work out the best marginal rates of return on each minute of the day, and never let the apparent good of something immediately desired take precedence over the lasting good of what is desirable in the cold light of his life's plan. All is done so that the older gentleman (or lady) he will one day be can enjoy a safe, comfortable situation and a calm sleep.

The way through is narrow. The pseudo-youth avoids crashing into Scylla, the savage monster of immediate, thoughtless desire, but is swallowed by the boring sameness of Charybdis, the obsessive whirlpool of caution and existential defensiveness. He goes through the odyssey of his life under the shadow of a menacing, tyrannical future, as if he were an anonymous member of the crew of the ship that is himself – with the compass always in his hands, and his ears stuffed. He does, it's true, protect his imagined old age, but at the exorbitant price of losing his youth.

Tyrannised by the authority of the *me-later*, this pseudo-youth is a Kantian automaton in the service of duty. He 'works without happiness for a decrepit world',[34] but one in which his old-age pension is guaranteed. He lives like an old man without being one. When he reaches his real old age, he will perhaps realise that he has unnecessarily wasted the best years of his life; that he was brutally exploited by a stingy young man with no imagination – a mean-minded little tyrant who did all this, what's more, under the pretext that he was protecting him. What can the future of a colourless past be, a winter without spring or summer? The controlled and anaemic dreaming of youth's night doesn't take the old man's sleep away, but he never dreams and never had anything to dream about. 'I made of myself what I did not know, and what I could have made of myself I didn't.' Sitting on the edge of his bed in a morning suffused with self-deception, he silently asks: is there time?

6. *Moral Partiality and Impersonal Rules*

The bias of moral partiality accounts for a good part of the damage and suffering that we cause one another in society, and to ourselves. From King David to the anonymous crew-member in Orpheus's ship who yielded to the sirens, no mortal is immune to the problem. And amongst those who sincerely imagine themselves to be exceptions are no doubt some of the worst cases of moral inflation. 'The fool is right in his own eyes'(Proverbs 12:15), says Solomon (David's second son with Bathsheba). How are we to find a way out?

Ulysses tied himself to the mast; humanity has tied itself to moral rules. The important point is that human society, through an extremely gradual, tentative and cumulative learning process, has found a general method of preventing and containing the worst effects of the spontaneous partiality that skews our moral equipment.

The essence of this method consists in the creation and adoption of *impersonal rules* – a formal code of *laws* accompanied by the threat of punishment, and an informal collection of *norms* of conduct – whose principal function is to standardise the exercise of moral judgement in certain situations of our social interaction, so as to make it as objective – that is, as independent of personal bias – as possible.[35] The necessity of these impersonal rules for the perfecting of standards within social life – above all, preventing society from drifting into an escalation of conflict and oppression – is intimately linked to the threefold bias (perceptual, emotional and moral) that makes us what we are.

How does the device of impersonal rules operate in practice? The traffic system lab again helps to bring the question down to earth. The moral partiality of the large majority of drivers, as we saw earlier (p.191), induces them to overestimate their skill at the wheel. As he steers his car or bus along streets and motorways, each motorist is free to think of himself as a potential Ayrton Senna – he is the flying centre of the universe, and his urge to get going and arrive as soon as possible at his destination is unquestionable. Nothing could be more natural, therefore, than that he should think himself perfectly justified, and with a right to judge whether he should respect the traffic regulations in any given situation. After all, doesn't everyone know what he is doing? Who doesn't think himself skilled and able enough?

It so happens, however, that if each driver – or a

reasonable number of them – sets himself up as having the right to be the judge in his own case, and to decide whether or not he is going to heed a particular rule, the collective result of those individual decisions would be a traffic system that would not only be unpredictable and anarchic, but unnecessarily dangerous and violent. It is a perfect example of the *fallacy of composition*. The attempt of each of the parts to do what is best for himself produces a situation that is worse for all of them. Each person's trust in others and in the general respect for the rules collapses. The actions of individual drivers are combined in such a way in the crucible of the traffic system that everyone ends up in a much worse situation than they would be if they had acted otherwise. The whole negates, prevents and literally smashes the moral inflation of the parts. It is a fools' – hellish – paradise.

The formal traffic regulations and the system of penalties and punishments that back it up are there to protect everyone that uses the roads from each other, it's true, but principally to protect them from themselves. Their basic function is to establish clearly and precisely the bound-aries between what is *forbidden* and what *permitted*, and between what is *compulsory* and what *optional*. However skilled, experienced and sensible each one of us may be in fact or in their own fancy – just out of driving-school or Formula One champion, crook or monk – no one is an exception; the rule is impersonal, and applies to everyone, without distinction.

Faced by a particular option or choice, like going through a red light or not, putting one's seatbelt on or not, or having another drink before leaving, the impersonal rule is there to neutralise the bias of being who we are; to prevent and avoid the moral partiality of other road-users and our natural preference for ourselves from bringing us into situations where human lives are put in danger. Each road-user is free to exercise his own skill, choose his route and live his fantasies within the limits of the law. But if he decides to trespass, or disregard compulsory rules, he needs to be pulled up and reminded who he is. The flying centre of the universe, seen from outside and far off, is merely an insignificant part of it.

This traffic model can be extrapolated, with appropriate changes, into other areas of social interaction. Consider, for example, the incident described earlier (pp.194–5) in which I was nearly run over. If the driver of the car that very nearly hit me looks at me with a peeved expression, I can do the same thing. If I go on to swear and he pays me back in the same coinage, no law has been violated. The norms of civil behaviour have been broken – it's not the kind of thing that I and (possibly) he would do in front of our children – but the raw nerve of justice has not been touched. A style of sociable living has been scratched, but its grammar is still in place.

Suppose, though, that I really *was* run over, and suffered a fractured leg. The driver pretended it had nothing to do with him, didn't take me to casualty, made no amends, and got no punishment. There were no witnesses, I couldn't even get the evidence to make a formal accusation. My resentment at the harm caused hits the ceiling. I decide to take justice into my own hands: I bribe the night porter in the apartment block and early one morning smash all the windows and the dashboard of the accursed car that ran me over. I come back home feeling some relief at having avenged the damage and the injustice I was the victim of, even though with the feeling that it wasn't much beside my fractured leg.

It so happens, however, that now the sensitive nerve of justice has been hit, and one of the grammatical rules of life in society has been breached. It turns out that the owner of the car was a public prosecutor; he extracts the criminal's identity from the porter, takes me to court and I am sentenced to compensate him for the material damage caused.

Now my options are: pay up or prison. To the expense and the pain of the fracture are now added the bill and the shame of the sentence. I've not only paid as victim, but as felon. The original crime has not been paid for; only the reprisal was punished. The prosecutor is delighted. Where's the justice in that?

No one should be a judge in his own cause. The injustice I was a victim of – running someone over followed by criminal negligence – is real. If there had been a witness, the driver would certainly have been punished. My resentment has every justification behind it. But between that, and thinking that this gives me the right to pass my own verdict and carry out the punishment, lies the distance that separates us from a Hobbesian conflagration, or, in other words, from an unstoppable escalation of interpersonal bitterness and conflict. The spontaneous bias of our moral equipment makes any whims one might entertain in that direction foolish and prohibitive.

The point is that, if the rules of justice allowed any route for citizens to settle their differences and mutual resentments by themselves – however just and deserving they may seem in their own eyes – the consequences would be uncontrollable. The strong probability is that, in no time at all, the logic of *an eye for an eye, a tooth for a tooth*, fed, of course, by the highly inflammable fuel of moral inflation/deflation, would take us to the edge of a general conflagration. All that would be needed would be a spark of misunderstanding – a wounded ego or the suspicion of a threat – to set off a domino effect of hidden attacks, lynchings and retaliations.

The impersonal rules formalised by the law remove from the ordinary citizen's sphere of competence the possibility of judging, especially when they themselves are involved, if and when a given conduct is forbidden or permitted, compulsory or optional. It defines the reach of the possible (what is licit) and of the necessary (what is imposed) in human social life, and, in this way, protects us, at least to some degree, from everyone's partiality for himself.[36] With the exception of the extremes of criminal medical pathology, the transgressor has some notion of what he is doing, so much so that he hides the act and feels shame when he is caught. The seed of the guilt that is imputed to him, when he is caught and sentenced, is already planted in his own mind.

In the case of *informal norms* of conduct, as, for example the principles of veracity (not lying) and of punctuality (not being late), the boundaries are not as strict and well-marked as in the legal sphere, but the function of the impersonal rules is essentially the same. The norms are definite standards of judgement, based on some kind of intersubjective agreement between citizens, that help to prevent and neutralise, to some degree, the natural bias of our subjectivity when it's a case of judging what would be right and appropriate to do in the particular situation we find ourselves in.

If people began, for example, to calculate the advantages of lying or telling the truth every time they opened their mouths, interpersonal communication would become a labyrinthine, bewildering pandemonium. One doesn't do everything one says one does, and one doesn't talk about everything one does do; but the assumption of veracity in the overall majority of verbal exchanges is an indispensable condition of human communication and sociability.

The liar fears opprobrium, takes care that the internal consistency of his story is preserved in all its ramifications, and feels ashamed when he is caught. While the formal law has a powerful back-up in the threat of set penalties (fines and prison), the equivalent mechanism in the case of the informal norms is the threat of emotional loss and social disapproval – the contempt of people we value, and coolness from those we esteem. The sanctions imposed on those who transgress the norm have a doubly negative effect on them. Their reputation suffers in the minds of those around them, and their self-image suffers in the reflection of their own conscience.

The extent of the power of impersonal rules in human society can be judged by what happens when it is absent. The laws and norms of a given society don't have an existence separate from, that is, above and beyond the individuals who compose it. What the experience of some critical episodes of collective hardship suggests, however, is that the perception of the circumstances in which we live and of the behaviour of those around us can sharply alter the degree to which citizens adhere to impersonal rules of social existence. Thucydides' striking story of the moral regression experienced by Athens at the end of the age of Pericles, under the impact of the epidemic that afflicted the city during the Peloponnesian war, gives a detailed portrait of just such an episode:

There were other and worse forms of lawlessness which the plague introduced at Athens. Men who had hitherto concealed their indulgence in pleasure now grew bolder. For, seeing the sudden change – how the rich died in a moment, and those who had nothing immediately inherited their property – they reflected that life and riches were alike transitory, and they resolved to enjoy themselves while they could, and to think only of pleasure. Who would be willing to sacrifice himself to the law of honour when he knew not whether he would ever live to be held in honour? The pleasure of the moment and any sort of thing which conducted to it took the place both of honour and expediency. No fear of god or law of man deterred a criminal. Those who saw all perishing alike, thought that the worship or neglect of the gods made no difference. For offences against human law no punishment was to be feared; no one would live long enough to be called to account. Already a far heavier sentence had been passed and was hanging over a man's head; before that fell, why should he not take a little pleasure?[37]

The radical uncertainty about what the next day would bring and the dramatic reduction in life expectancy brought on by the plague opened the way, according to Thucydides, for another equally contagious epidemic – the collapse of the authority of impersonal rules in the mind and practical existence of Athenians. In terms of the intertemporal and intrapersonal conflict discussed in the previous section, it's as if the circumstances produced by the plague (a burst of hyperinflation can have an analogous effect) had provoked a triumphant, collective revolt of the *me-now* against the formal and informal restrictions on its predominance that the *me-later* had gradually set up over time, under the aegis of less frightening visions of the future.

In analogous fashion, the power of the external context and of practical circumstances over individuals' degree of adherence to the impersonal rules appears in a vivid and suggestive form in relation to the experience of the European conquistadors and colonists who ventured into the Latin American tropics during the colonial period. As Diderot brilliantly describes it, basing himself on the testimonies and accounts of travellers who were able to observe the phenomenon directly:

> Beyond the Equator a man is neither English, Dutch, French, Spanish, nor Portuguese. He retains only those principles and prejudices of his native country which justify or excuse his conduct. He crawls when he is weak; he is violent when strong; he is in a hurry to acquire, in a hurry to enjoy, and capable of every crime which will lead him most quickly to his goals. He is a domestic tiger returning to the forest; the thirst for blood takes hold of him once more. This is how all the Europeans, every one of them, indistinctly, have appeared in the countries of the New World. There they have assumed a common frenzy – the thirst for gold.

The veneer of the European's civic morality, Diderot suggests, wears away under the impact of the change of hemisphere. The authority of impersonal rules obeyed by the *me-later* in the country of origin is weakened and undermined by the excesses of lust and greed put into action by the *me-now* in the tropical colonies. *Ultra aequinoxialem non peccari* – 'There is no sin beyond the Equator'[38] – is the seventeenth-century Latin motto that best sums up the atmosphere of dissipation, opportunism and anarchic selfishness created by the European colonial adventure in the tropics.

It seems fair to assume that Thucydides' story of the effects of the plague in the Athenian *pólis* and Diderot's version of tropical licentiousness lay it on thick in their contrast between two patterns of social interaction so as to heighten their differences as much as possible – the *before v. after* in Athens and the *here v. there* of the European colonist. The important thing here, however, is not to pass judgement on the degree of historical-descriptive realism of the pictures they paint, but to identify and analyse what extreme situations like these reveal about the relations between moral partiality and impersonal rules.

The inflationary bias of moral self-representation in normal and peaceful times, when danger, pressure and temptation are far removed, has been discussed above(pp.192–3). Situations of adversity (the Athenian *pólis*) or permissiveness (the colonial tropics) force one to put one's cards on the table, and show up the element of bluff in the images we have of ourselves.

It is pleasant to imagine that we are able to resist the sirens' song, when it's only a remote prospect in time or distant in space. As much as the singing itself, it is the seduction of that self-deception that has littered the sirens' rocks with bones and dead bodies. What cannot be underestimated is the difficulty of foreseeing, however uncertainly, *who we will be* and *how we will react* when the pressure of external circumstances and the heat of the moment conspire to take us to the unknown threshold of our limitations. The balance of power between the *me-now* and the *me-later* in the parliament of the individual mind is subject to sudden reversals.

The weakening of the authority of impersonal rules, as in the exemplary laboratory of road traffic, tends to produce a situation typical of the fallacy of composition in social existence – a setting in which the whole resulting from a myriad of individual actions and reactions seems to take on a life of its own and ends up falling like a plague on the short-sighted cunning of each of the parts.

From the point of view of each one of them, the consequences of their own intermittent violations of the rules seem infinitesimally small and of no great consequence considering not only the immediate benefits that such violations produce, but also the greater importance of the transgressions committed by others. The harmful results of the lie we tell, the law we break, or the promise we fail to keep naturally seem lesser and less harmful in our eyes than in the eyes of those who are, directly or indirectly, affected by our actions.

Each person's example, in its turn, acts as a justification and a pretext for everyone to imitate. However, when he sees that wickedness and greed dominate general behaviour, the individual finally concludes that 'the manner in which we live, and that in which we ought to live, are things so wide asunder, that he who quits the one to betake himself to the other is more likely to destroy than to save himself; since anyone who would act up to a perfect standard of goodness in everything, must be ruined among so many who are not good.'[39] After all, who would want to be the fall-guy, the martyr, or some absurd Quixote, victim of his own integrity? The naive and underpaid crusader amongst a gang of knaves and rogues? Nobody, surely enough, can afford the luxury or run the risk of doing on his own account what might in theory be best for everybody, on the condition that everyone – or at least a large enough proportion of people – does the same.

The problem, though, is that, if the isolated effect of small, intermittent violations is not that important, the aggregate and cumulative effect of the combination of these violations in the general stew-pot tends to be very great. The kind of expectations we have of others – the confidence that we think we are justified in placing in one another in our emotional and professional lives – is an asset of immeasurable value in practical existence. The gradual wearing down of that asset by a large number of withdrawals from the general stock of interpersonal trust dramatically reduces the range of opportunities for advantageous co-operation, whether it be in the private realm of love and friendship, or in the public arena of politics and collective action, or in the realm of market transactions.[40]

When short-term opportunism is seen to be the rule of the game, then it's everyone for himself. But as they try to grab their own advantage or immediate pleasure, and as they break and ignore the impersonal laws and norms of civilised society whenever it suits them, the parts unwittingly create a collective monster that they didn't foresee – a hostile social whole, in which they fail to recognise their collective existence, and that falls on their lives with the innocent inevitability of a natural disaster.

Each part's sincere and generalised feeling, as it looks both at itself and at what surrounds it, is that it *has nothing to do with* the evil it sees. The evil it finds outside itself, however, is at bottom no more than the cumulative effect of a myriad of deviant actions, each of them tiny compared to the social whole, but together and in the fullness of time powerful enough to erode the stock of interpersonal trust and to establish a context of acute uncertainty, hardship and violence that, even if it doesn't completely ruin human relationships in practical and emotional life, certainly harms and considerably impoverishes them.

The double plague in Athens described by Thucydides and the human tropical jungle in colonial times portrayed by Diderot are extreme episodes in a numerous family of similar cases. For each one of the parts separately, short-term opportunism is the best way forward, since everybody is at it. But for all of them together, in the shared space of their public and private life in society, the cumulative result of this choice is terrible. Even if each person might be in an even worse situation if he were the only one to abandon his calculating self-centredness, all together would certainly be better off if they could find a collective way out. In the words of Solon, the great Athenian law-giver and poet responsible for the constitutional reforms that created the foundations of the first democratic experiment in the history of humanity: 'True, you are singly each a crafty soul / But all together make one empty fool.'[41]

7. Civic Ethics, Freedom and Personal Ethics

The individual is a contradictory whole. Irresolvable tensions and opposing forces disturb the microcosm of our subjective life. They determine states of consciousness that are more or less shifting and accessible to the surface level of the mind, and finally, get translated, or not, into choices and actions in the world. Our impartiality with regard to ourselves has insurmountable logical and psychological frontiers, but the vast ocean of partiality seems to acknowledge no limits. Human capacity to judge objectively tends to weaken exponentially as we get closer to the centre of all that moves and affects us – just when a serene and impartial discernment would be of the greatest importance. Worse: the veil of self-deception often hides from our view of ourselves just those traits and failings that strike the eye when what is at issue is the character and conduct of those around us. The blind spot in the inward-looking eye is the obverse of the acuteness of our vision when we look out.

The moral equipment of the human animal is what it is. To imagine that it might be radically improved or regenerated, whether by means of sermons, intensive training courses and inspired exhortations, or by political engineering and new modes of production, is to embrace fantasies that may provide short-lived consolation but have no validity. If well-intentioned speeches, leaps forward or violent breaks with the past could produce the doubtful miracle of a 'moral regeneration of man', then the promise of a 'new man' – whatever the 'new human nature' that we want to put into him – would have occurred innumerable times in the course of history.

Reality, however, has been hard on this kind of wishful thinking. The centuries go by, revolutionary mirages make a noisy appearance on the scene and soon retire to oblivion in the unfathomable stream of history, and old human nature, with all its undeniable potential and shortcomings, gives no sign of being impressed by the spectacle. What the experience of our own century suggests is that, if there is any risk of an abrupt discontinuity in the field of morality, it lies much more on the side of degeneration – as the unspeakable insanity of the Nazi and Soviet concentration camps shows – than in any supposed regeneration of our ethical standards of social conduct.

None of this means, of course, that we should adopt a fatalist or resigned position with regard to the world *as it is*. The virtual elimination of some of the human animal's ancestral practices – habits and customs like cannibalism, incest, lynching for adultery and enslavement for debt, by military defeat or physical intimidation, just to mention the most obvious examples – shows that progress in fundamental matters *is* possible, even if it is restricted to specific areas and with no absolute guarantee against backsliding.

Substantial advances like these are landmarks of our capacity for social living. They are conquests of the collective, co-operative effort of humanity to construct a more harmonious grammar for our common existence: intersubjective agreements that have shown themselves to be perfectly compatible with the hard substratum – nervous, emotional and mental – of the human animal.

It's quite probable that habits and customs that are normal today – especially in the realm of labour relationships, the status of economic goals as cultural values, the use of natural resources and the treatment of children and the old – may in the future be seen as practices as unjustifiable from the moral point of view as some of the worst excesses committed by our ancestors in the past. I find it hard to imagine that the gap between the world *as it is* and *as it can and ought to be* shows any signs of disappearing or being dramatically reduced in the foreseeable future. What we can do, however, and we certainly should not underestimate the importance of this, is to try to make sure it is progressively narrowed in critical areas of our social life, and does not become even wider than it is.

In the perfect society, endowed with a faultless and uniformly heeded grammar of rules for social existence, there would be nothing to change. Any conceivable change could only be to a situation worse than that already prevailing, or, at best, as good. Obviously, nothing could guarantee that individuals were completely happy or that they always achieved their objectives. The basic difference is that they would find conditions and opportunities as good as possible – beginning with an adequate initial provision of health and basic education – to develop their talents and projects in life.

In the perfect society, the fundamental problems of human existence and achievement would go on being exactly what they always were; but individuals could no longer blame 'the system', 'social injustice', or 'the others' for their mistakes, frustrations and failures. Think how many comforting rationalisations would go up in smoke! And how many sophisticated new 'reasons', hitherto unthought of, would instantly spring up in their place!

The idea of perfection is obviously a human fiction. Its great merit – as in the case of all utopias – is to act as a contrast, to inspire and allow one to throw into relief the extent of the gap between *what is* and *what can be*: the distance that separates us from our potential. More than a dream, the ideal is a weapon that we can use to show up an unjust, corrupt and oppressive world.

In practice, of course, nothing that is human comes near perfection, beginning with utopian thought itself. A risk that can never be eliminated – and the last century is full of lessons of this sort – is that of trying to better things and ending up making them worse than they are. 'The road to hell is paved with good intentions', as St Bernard first said.[42] The problem is that opposition to change and resignation also get there. If taking action is often dangerous, not taking action can be fatal too.

The art of living together in society is linked to the art of living with oneself within oneself. The impersonal rules of civic ethics are a necessary evil. They exist not to save us, but to protect us from each other and from ourselves. 'Could anything show a more shameful lack of culture', as Plato asks in the *Republic* (405 *b*), 'than to have so little justice in oneself that one must get it from others, who thus become masters and judges over one?'

Much more serious and terrible than this, it could be argued, would be a situation in which, even though citizens recognised the need to get justice from outside, it was denied them or perverted by a neglectful and/or corrupt judiciary. The ground zero of civic ethics, however, would be a situation in which citizens felt so convinced and certain that they had all the justice they needed inside themselves, that they begin to judge and settle their disputes on their own account, that is, without the need to incur the Platonic shame of having to have recourse to any kind of external arbiter to solve their conflicts and disagreements.

The aim of the impersonal rules of civic ethics should be not to confine the individual or to force him to fit into a life project that is not his, but rather to facilitate the full and free expression of his individuality. If the demands of civic ethics reduce the scope for freedom of choice to some degree, they, at the same time, allow an enormous expansion of that same freedom, by the widening of the space available for permanent experimentation in the personal and social art of living. Experience shows that a progressive weakening of civic ethics can become as corrosive and destructive of individual freedom – undermining the confidence that we feel justified in placing in each other in our practical and emotional lives – as its totalitarian over-expansion.

The great challenge is to find an equilibrium between the demands of civic ethics and those of personal ethics – a grammar of social existence that in some way will find the right balance between the two requirements of society at its best: freedom and justice. It is only by grounding itself in a legitimate civic ethics, well-rooted and properly framed, that an aggressive personal ethics – free, bold and pluralist – will be able to prosper and flourish.

The ideal is to try to preserve, on the one hand, the greatest possible freedom for the active exercise of individual autonomy in the quest for personal values; but also to guarantee respect for the impersonal rules that reduce damage and unjustifiable friction in interpersonal relations to a minimum.

The grammar of justice is a set of moral rules – formal laws and informal norms – that define the parameters and set out the frontiers of what is prohibited or permitted, and what is obligatory or optional in human interaction. The goal is a collectively sanctioned intersubjective agreement that, without restricting any more than is strictly necessary the sphere of individual autonomy in the search for and definition of life projects, would be capable of preventing and containing in a clear and neutral fashion the disputes and conflicts that inevitably permeate human interaction in a pluralist, complex society.

The risks and threats, as always, lie in excesses on either side. If a faulty social existence, on the one hand, sacrifices autonomy – condemning, for example, a good number of the individuals of a given society to a childhood of material and educational privation that permanently damages their future – a badly managed autonomy, on the other, may harm social existence, leading us, for example, to incur the fallacy of composition in social interaction and to self-destructive behaviour patterns, under the call of the sirens. The way through is narrow. No solution is definitive. Every victory is partial, every advance brings new challenges and every conquest may still be followed by a relapse. The avoidance of evil is a great help, but it does not satisfy the human desire to find the good. We must sail on. With our ears open, eyes on the compass, and the mast to hand.

NOTES

1. THE NATURE AND VALUE
OF SELF-DECEPTION

1. The idea of the biological uniformity of living beings goes back to Aristotle's *Historia animalium*: 'The life of animals, then, may be divided into two acts – procreation and feeding; for on these two acts all their interests and life concentrate [. . .] whatever is in conformity with nature is pleasant, and all animals pursue pleasure in keeping with their nature' (589*a*). On the history of this idea, and its adoption as a basic principle in modern biology, see: Larson, *Reason and Experience* (pp. 20–30); Jacob, *Logique du vivant* (pp. 98–100), and note 10 to this chapter. Darwin's admiration for Aristotle's contribution appears clearly in a letter of 1882 to the author of a recently published book on the subject: 'From quotations which I had seen, I had a high notion of Aristotle's merits, but I had not the most remote notion what a wonderful man he was. Linnaeus and Cuvier have been my two gods [. . .] but they were mere schoolboys to old Aristotle' (*Life and Letters of Charles Darwin*, vol. 3, p. 252).

2. Except when indicated, all the examples of deceit in the

natural world in this and in the following section are from the systematic account given by Rue in *By the Grace of Guile* (pp. 108–24). On the strategies of deception and its prevention, both inter and intraspecies, see also Krebs and Dawkins: 'Animal Signals: Mind-reading and Manipulation', and the entry 'Communication' in *The Oxford Companion to Animal Behaviour* (pp. 78–91).

3. The experiment on the bees' preference for orchids is from Krebs and Dawkins, 'Animal Signals' (p. 385).

4. The example of the sunfish is also discussed by Wright, *Moral Animal*, pp. 79–80. It is interesting to note, as was originally pointed out by John Maynard Smith, that the competition between the two reproduction strategies naturally leads to a situation of 'evolutionary equilibrium'. The greater the number of exploiters in relation to those being exploited, the harder life will be for the former. If the relative population of precocious fish grows too fast, they will have difficulty in finding normal males to deceive and places to procreate; the proportion of precocious fish in the population will therefore tend to find its equilibrium at about a fifth of the total population. For an analogous situation in human societies, pitting 'wiseguys' against 'mugs' (New York), 'malandros' against 'otários' (Brazil), or 'furbi' against 'fessi' (Sicily), see: Mandeville, *Fable of the Bees* vol. 1, p. 48, and Elster, *The Cement of Society*, pp. 269–70. As the Victorian political economist Macdonell noted: 'roguery can only be profitable when honesty is general' (*Survey of Political Economy*, p. 59).

5. It's worth pointing out that even Cartesian reductionism does not conclusively deny animal subjectivity, merely leaving it out of consideration in explaining behaviour. Replying to the objections of the Cambridge neo-Platonist Henry More, Descartes said: 'But there is no prejudice to which we are all more accustomed from our earliest years than the belief that dumb animals think [. . .] I am not disturbed by the astuteness and cunning of dogs and foxes, or all the things which animals do for the sake of food, sex and fear; I claim that I can easily

explain the origin of all of them from the constitution of their organs. But though I regard it as established that we cannot prove there is any thought in animals, I do not think it thereby proved that there is not, since the human mind does not reach into their hearts.' (*Philosophical Letters*, p. 243). Concerned with the ethical implications of this agnostic position, the philosopher Mary Midgley comments: 'If a torturer excused her activities by claiming ignorance of pain on the grounds that nobody knows about the subjective sensation of others, she would not convince any human audience. An audience of scientists need not aim at providing an exception to this rule' (quoted in Masson and McCarthy, *When Elephants Weep*, p. 49). Stephen Clark makes an eloquent defence of animal rights from an Aristotelian ethical perspective in his *The Moral Status of Animals*. For a careful survey of philosophical thinking and recent scientific research on animal subjectivity, see Walker, *Animal Thought*.

6. An account of the different modalities and functions of animal language, and of recent experiments with training and teaching in the laboratory can be found in the entry 'Language' in the *Oxford Companion to Animal Behaviour* (pp. 90–91 and 332–36). For a detailed and careful review of the 'hidden food problem' and the attempts to teach language to apes, see Walker, *Animal Thought* (pp. 352–81).

7. The pranks and wiles of Chantek the orang-utan are described in Rue, *By the Grace of Guile* (p. 124).

8. Emerson, 'Nature' (*Works*, p. 830); Schopenhauer, *The World as Will*, vol. 2, p. 581. On the stoic and atomist views of nature, see: Sambursky, *The Physical World of the Greeks* (Chapters 5–7) and Glacken, *Traces on the Rhodian Shore* (Chapters 1 and 2). The contrast between Democritus and Heraclitus is based on Seneca, 'On Tranquillity of Mind' (p. 65), and Montaigne 'On Democritus and Heraclitus' (*Essays*, pp. 337–40). The attitudes and the concept of nature in Rousseau and Baudelaire are clearly set out in works like *Les Rêveries du Promeneur Solitaire* (Walks 2, 5 and 7), and *Le Peintre de la Vie Moderne* (esp. Chapter 11).

The posthumous works 'Nature' by J.S. Mill, and *Dialogues concerning Natural Religion*, by Hume, offer critical reflections on the wide diversity of totalising concepts of nature in the history of philosophy. On the meanings of the word Nature (Greek: *phýsis*; Latin: *natura*) in the history of ideas, see: Lewis, 'Nature' (*Studies in Words*, pp. 24–74); Williams, 'Nature'(*Keywords*, pp. 184–89); and the appendix, 'Some Meanings of "Nature"', in which Lovejoy analyses and illustrates no less than 66 different meanings associated with the term (*Primitivism*, vol. 1, pp. 447–56).

9. The examples of radical anthropomorphism cited in the text are taken from Masson and McCarthy, *When Elephants Weep*, a discussion of the emotional life of animals. For a discussion of the problem of attributing mental states to other living beings, from the point of view of Wittgensteinian language philosophy, see Manser, 'Pain and Private Language'.

10. Darwin, 'M Notebook' (*Early Writings*, p. 21). Further on in the same notebook, Darwin notes: 'Our descent, then, is the origin of our evil passions!! – The Devil under the form of Baboon is our grandfather!' (p. 29). Why Locke? Presumably because of Locke's associationist theory, which in the young Darwin's eyes represented an outstanding contribution to the scientific study of mental phenomena. The principle of continuity originally appears in Aristotle's biological treatises: 'Nature proceeds little by little from things lifeless to animal life in such a way that it is impossible to determine the exact line of demarcation, nor on which side thereof an intermediate form should lie.' (*Historia Animalium* 588 *b*); on the Aristotelian notion of continuity in the natural world, see Lovejoy, *The Great Chain of Being* (esp. pp. 56ff.). Darwin's fondness for the maxim *Natura non facit saltum* can be seen in the simple fact that he quotes it four times, in Latin, in the *Origin of Species* (pp. 194, 206, 460 and 471). This was the principal point contested by T.H. Huxley in his important review of the *Origin*, which appeared soon after publication (*Darwiniana*, p. 77); for a contemporary view of the question, see Dawkins, 'Universal Darwinism', esp. pp. 412–18.

11. This interpretation of the biblical myth of the Fall and of the divine 'lie' follows the suggestion of the Italian psychoanalyst Luigi Zoja, in *Growth and Guilt* (pp. 142–46).

12. Montaigne, 'An Apologie of Raymond Sebond' (*Essays* [tr. Florio], p. 224); Locke, *Essay concerning Human Understanding*, Book 3, Chapter 9, ¶23, pp. 489–90. In the second part of my *Beliefs in Action*, I tried to analyse the problem of misunderstanding in the transmission of ideas and messages, giving a taxonomy of the most important patterns of distortion.

13. The experiment with the rats' hypothalamus is described in Young, *Philosophy and the Brain* (pp. 178–80). The idea of meddling with the natural reaction of plants to the changing seasons by genetic manipulation is based on techniques developed by researchers at the University of Wisconsin – Madison (see *The Economist*, 13 January 1996, p. 80).

14. Piaget, *The Moral Judgement of the Child*, pp. 114–16. In the Preface to 'De Cive', Hobbes compared a perverse man to a vigorous child: 'Unless you give children all they ask for, they are peevish and cry, aye, and strike their parents; and all this they have from nature [. . .] a wicked man is almost the same thing with a child grown strong or sturdy or a man of a childish disposition.' (*De Cive*, Preface, p. 3). Commenting on this passage in his article on Hobbes' philosophy in the *Encyclopédie*, Diderot observes: 'Imagine a six-week-old child with the imbecility of mind appropriate to its age and the strength of passions of a man of forty. He will manifestly strike down his father, ravish his mother and strangle his nurse. No one who approaches him will be secure' (*Political Writings*, pp. 28–29).

15. Indirect evidence of the universality of deceit in human relationships can be found in language itself. The lexicon of trickery has hundreds of words, designating the vast range of the linguistic and non-linguistic repertoire of deceitfulness in ordinary life. Just as, so they say, the language of the Eskimos has a very rich vocabulary to denote different kinds of snow, English for rain, Hebrew for sin, and Portuguese for

inflation – just so, every natural human language seems to have a profusion of terms and expressions for all the subtleties and varieties of deceit.

16. Machado de Assis, *Dom Casmurro*, Chapter XLI, p. 80; on interpersonal lying, sees also note 6 to Chapter 3.

17. On the psychic phenomenon of hallucination, see *The Oxford Companion to the Mind* (pp. 299–300 and 648). Several episodes of visual, auditory and tactile hallucination are described by Oliver Sacks in *The Man who Mistook his Wife for a Hat*. A clear example of hallucination in literature is Macbeth's vision of the imaginary dagger while he is planning to kill Duncan: 'I have thee not, and yet I see thee still./ Art thou not, fatal vision, sensible/ To feeling, as to sight? or art thou but/ A dagger of the mind, a false creation,/ Proceeding from the heat-oppressed brain?/ I see thee yet, in form as palpable/ As this which now I draw'. (*Macbeth*, Act II, Scene 1, ll. 35–41).

18. The source for the examples of the 'phantom limb' and the phenomenon of 'kidnapping of the neural circuits' is the work of the neurologist V. Ramachandran, of the University of California – San Diego, reported in *The Economist*, 27 April 1996, pp. 87–88. On self-deception in relation to one's own body, see also: *The Oxford Companion to the Mind* (pp. 200–01); Damasio, *Descartes' Error* (pp. 87–90 and 184–85) and Sacks, *The Man who Mistook his Wife for a Hat* (pp. 82–86).

19. Novalis, 'Fragmentblatt' (*Pólen*,p.43).

20. Machado de Assis, *Dom Casmurro*, Chapters XXX and XL, pp. 55 and 78. Why does daydreaming not satisfy the demand for fantasy? In 'The Mind as a Consuming Organ' the American economist Thomas Schelling suggests that the undisciplined imagination and, in particular, the tendency to inflationary escalation in daydreaming are factors that lead consumers to prefer externally produced narrative fiction (*Multiple Self,* pp. 178 and 190).

21. The relationship between children's games and literary creation is analysed by Freud in the lecture 'Creative writers

and Day-dreaming': 'Couldn't we perhaps say that when
he plays, every child behaves like a creative writer, since
he creates a world of his own, or, better, he adjusts the
elements of his world in ways that please him better? [. . .]
the opposite of play is not what is serious, but what is real
[. . .] The creative writer does the same thing as the child who
plays. He creates a fantasy world which he takes very seriously,
that is, in which he invests a great deal of emotion, while
keeping a clear separation between this world and reality'
(pp. 101–02).

22. Horace, *Satires and Epistles* (Book 2, Epistle 2, ll. 128–40,
pp. 186–87). Pollux, one of Zeus and Leda's offspring, was
taken by his father to the gods' dwelling-place, but refused
to accept immortality while his mortal brother, Castor, stayed
in the lower world of the dead; the solution found by Zeus
was to allow each of them to spend alternate days in the
company of the gods. On Horace's spectator, and variations
on the same theme, see: Montaigne, 'Apology for Raymond
Sebond' (*Essays*, p. 552); Erasmus, *The Praise of Folly* (¶38,
pp. 121–22); Fontenelle, *Nouveaux Dialogues* (p. 226) and
Nietzsche, *Daybreak* (¶509, p. 206).

23. Diderot, 'The Paradox of the Actor' (p. 121). It is interesting
to compare Diderot's observation with that of the modern
Brazilian dramatist Nelson Rodrigues: 'Fiction, if it is to
purge, needs to be horrific. The characters are wicked, so
that we will not be so. They perpetrate the evil that we all
carry unacknowledged within us. Watching Anna Karenina,
or Emma Bovary, betray their husbands, many women in
real life will refuse to do likewise. In *Crime and Punishment*,
Raskolnikov kills an old woman; at that very moment, the
social resentment fermenting inside each of us will be reduced
and assuaged. He killed for us all. And, in the theatre, more
three-dimensional, more direct, and which has a much more
immediate impact, this phenomenon of transference is still
more operative. In order to save the audience, we have to
fill the stage with murderers, adulterers, madmen: a gang of
monsters, in short. They are our monsters, from which we

can perhaps free ourselves, so that we can recreate them later on' (quoted in Ruy Castro, *O anjo pornográfico* [The pornographic angel], p. 273). The two dramatists clearly differ on what happens once we are outside the theatre: while for the Frenchman the spectator comes out exactly the same as when he went in, for the Brazilian he comes out purged, and, at least for the time being, different from when he went in. But the two seem completely in agreement on what happens during the performance: that is, on the mechanisms of transference and fictional transport by which the spectator comes out of himself and subjectively identifies with the character in the plot. The purgative function of the theatre and of narrative fiction is discussed by Dodds when he analyses the appeal of Dionysiac rituals in the Greek world (*The Greeks and the Irrational*, pp. 76–77) and in the Introduction to his edition of Euripides' *Bacchae* (p. xlv).

24. Wallace Stevens, 'Adagia' (*Opus Posthumous*, p. 189).
25. Plato, *Protagoras*, 323 *b*. The context and some of the implications of this statement are discussed in Chapter 2 of my book *Vícios privados, benefícios públicos?* [Private vices, public benefits?].
26. The hypothesis of an 'arms race', in which the escalation of the deliberate practice of deception gives way to spontaneous occurrence of self-deception, was formulated in the mid-seventies, by the American biologists Robert Trivers and Richard Alexander. For a review of the theory, see: Wright, *The Moral Animal* (pp. 263–86) and Rue, *By the Grace of Guile* (esp. pp. 146–47). The basic idea is that self-deception is, at bottom, a continuation of interpersonal deception by other means: i.e. that it is a functional evolutionary strategy for the survival and reproduction of the individual's genes. The main flaw of this hypothesis, as several of the following examples suggest, is that it does not explain self-deception which is entirely for one's own, internal consumption, just as it also appears not to take into account the high frequency of cases in which self-deception is actually prejudicial to the individual's supposed biological interests.

27. Hitler's and Goebbels' declarations can be found in Joachim Fest's brilliant study of the psychology of the Nazi leaders (*The Face of the Third Reich*, p. 143). Summing up the German horror, Fest concludes: 'The course of the [Nuremberg] trials confirmed what has already been hinted: they [the Nazi leaders] did not even feel sworn to an idea, so that everything – violence, war and genocide – finally assumed the character of an error, a terrible misunderstanding, from whose consequences they wanted to slink away with a shrug of the shoulders. [. . .] The preconditions of totalitarian rule in a country are to be sought at a deeper level, for they are the result of man's faulty understanding of himself' (pp. 455–56). On the Furtwängler affair, see Michael Tanner's remarkable review of B. Wessling's biography of the German conductor (*Times Literary Supplement*, 4 October 1985, p. 1087).

28. Álvaro de Campos, 'Tabacaria (The tobacconist's)' (Fernando Pessoa, *Obra poética*, p. 365). [Álvaro de Campos is one of several 'heteronyms' – roughly, personifications of sides of his poetic personality – created by the Portuguese poet Fernando Pessoa (1888–1935) – tr.]. Amongst other similar examples we could recall are those of the nocturnal soliloquy of the half-awake Richard III (Act V, Scene 3), and the reckoning Wilhelm Meister makes of his life: 'At the end of *Wilhelm Meister's Apprenticeship*, Wilhelm looks back at his life and his eyes remain fixed in shock at the tangle of mistakes and diversions, like those of a child unable to grow up. All his experiences seem a useless mesh of gestures, words, actions, decisions. His whole existence seems a single, unpardonable mistake: something to be denied and thrown out in a single move' (Citati, *Goethe*, p. 55).

29. Álvaro de Campos, 'Apostila' [Postscript] (Fernando Pessoa, *Obra Poética*, p. 367). Other similar examples are Nietzsche's distress as he confesses to a friend – 'If I don't discover the alchemist's device for making gold even out of this crap, I'm lost' (letter to Franz Overbeck, 25 December 1882); and Baudelaire's entreaty in the prose-poem 'À une heure du matin': 'O my Lord and God, grant me the grace to produce

a few lines of poetry which will convince me that I am not one of the dregs of mankind, and not inferior to those I despise' (*The Poems in Prose*, p. 69).

30. Hume, *Second Enquiry*, p. 264; Adam Smith, *The Wealth of Nations*, p. 126. On uncertainty over choice of profession, see also Marshall's comments in the *Principles*, pp. 460–62. Mephistopheles' comment on originality appears in Goethe's *Faust*, Part Two, p. 98.

31. These lines and the problem they allude to are discussed by Arrow in *The Limits of Organization*: 'Rationality and foresight are indeed capable of creating delay and doubt; so, too, are conscience, respect for others, the sense of vague respect to distant and unforeseen consequences that we may worry about. The True Believer is much more effective in social action, but whether it is in the right direction may be another question' (p. 29). For two diametrically opposed views of this same problem see Dostoevsky, *Notes from the Underground*, p. 26; and Butler, 'Upon Self-deceit' (*Analogy of Religion*, p. 477).

32. Ovid, *Metamorphoses*, Book 7, ll. 20–21: 'Video meliora, proboque, / Deteriora sequor' (these same lines are quoted in Bacon, *The Advancement of Learning*, p. 140; Spinoza, *Ethics*, p. 200, and Locke, *Essay concerning Human Understanding*, p. 254). The original source of Ovid's lines is Medea's speech: 'I know indeed what evil I intend to do / But stronger than all my afterthoughts is my fury / Fury that brings up on mortals the greatest evils' (Euripedes, *Medea*, ll. 1078–80). On the problem of *akrasía* ('weakness of will') in classical thought, see Dodds, *The Greeks and the Irrational* (pp. 178–206); Guthrie, *The Sophists* (pp. 250–60), and Nussbaum, *The Therapy of Desire* (pp. 439–83). For an analytical treatment of the problem, see, in a philosophical context: Charlton, *Weakness of Will* and, in economics, Ainslie, *Picoeconomics*. The line quoted in the middle of the paragraph is one of Blake's *Proverbs of Hell* (*Complete Poems*, p. 183).

33. Cromwell's words are taken from the *Penguin Dictionary of English History*, p. 110. The Scottish Enlightenment historian

Adam Ferguson adds: 'If Cromwell said, that a man never mounts higher than when he knows not whither he is going; it may with more reason be affirmed of communities, that they admit of the greatest revolutions where no change is intended, and that the most refined politicians do not always know whither they are leading the state by their projects.' (*Essay on the History of Civil Society*, p. 187). On the motivating role of illusory beliefs see: James, *The Varieties of Religious Experience* (esp. pp. 78–126) and Russell, *Power* (Chapter 10).

34. Gauguin's journey to Tahiti in 1891 was made possible by financial help from friends. His decision to emigrate was taken after several failed attempts to develop his art in Paris and in the French provinces. Justifying himself in a letter to his ex-wife, he said: 'I am a great artist and I am sure of it. Because I am sure, I have borne so much pain in order that I can carry on in my chosen way. If it was different I would regard myself as a scoundrel, something I am for many people, by the way. Still, no matter! What worries me the most is not so much the poverty as the constant hindrances for my art which I cannot practise as I feel and as I could without the poverty which binds my hands' (quoted in Amann, *Gauguin*, p. 13). The moral dilemma of the generic situation faced by Gauguin is analysed by Williams in 'Moral Luck', and discussed by Nagel in 'Moral Luck' and 'Williams: One Thought too Many'. An original characterisation of the problem appears in Russell, *The Conquest of Happiness*, (p. 168).

35. Wittgenstein, *Culture and Value*, p. 50 e. The sentence quoted at the beginning of the paragraph is from Goethe, *Maxims and Reflections*, ¶282.

36. Anonymous, cited in Bernstein, *Against the Gods*, p. 202.

37. Keynes, *The General Theory of Employment*, pp. 161–62. The expression 'animal spirits' has a long intellectual history, which goes back to Plato's dialogue *Timaeus* (see Sherrington, *Man on his Nature*, p. 44). There are frequent references in Descartes and La Mettrie to 'esprits animaux' as a link between the physical and the mental. Malebranche,

in particular, credits to the abundance of these same 'esprits animaux' the secret confidence optimists have in their own strength and the fact that 'they think they will encounter no opposition to their intentions that they will be unable to overcome' (*The Search after Truth*, p. 403). On the decisive role of luck in the success of innovative enterprises, see Frank Knight, 'Freedom as Fact and Criterion' (*Freedom and Reform*, p. 13). In a passage that clearly echoes the Keynesian theme of non-economic motivation in the decision to invest, Nisbett and Ross observe: 'The social benefits of individually erroneous subjective probabilities may be great even when the individuals pay a high price for the error. We probably would have few novelists, actors or scientists if all potential aspirants to these careers took action based on a normatively justifiable probability of success. We might also have few new products, new medical procedures, new political movements, or new scientific theories' (quoted in Elster, *Sour Grapes*, p. 159). A recent article in *The Economist* expresses the point well: 'Most successful firms become that way because at some point in their troubled evolution they simply refuse to quit, and press on against the odds. Unfortunately, many unsuccessful firms share this very trait. One of the hardest tasks facing managers, therefore, is rating their chances accurately. And most economists, if left to their own devices, would be far too prone to give up (or, in their parlance, "make tradeoffs"). Fortunately, however, nobody has yet suggested that economists actually be allowed to manage anything' ('Economists as Gurus', 14 June 1997, p. 67).

38. Levi, *The Drowned and the Saved*, pp. 118–19. On the wave of suicides after the liberation, Levi says: 'I believe that it is precisely due to this turning to look back at the "perilous water" that so many suicides occurred after (sometimes immediately after) the liberation. It was in any case a critical moment which coincided with a flood of rethinking and depression. By contrast, all historians of the Lager [Nazi concentration camps] – and also of the Soviet camps – agree in pointing out that cases of suicide during

LIES WE LIVE BY

imprisonment were rare' (p. 57). An analogous experience, though individual and certainly less intense than this, is recounted by de Quincey in his confessions: in his case, opium was the way out (*Confessions of an English Opium-eater*, p. 193).

39. Carlos Drummond de Andrade, 'Nascer de novo' ['Reborn'] (*A paixão medida*, [Measured passion] p. 39). The line quoted at the end of the previous paragraph is a version of an anonymous tenth-century Japanese *tanka*, translated into Spanish by Octavio Paz (*Versiones y diversiones*, p. 235).

40. On the origin of the Delphic motto 'Know thyself', see Chapter 2, note 14. The authorship of the maxim 'Nothing in excess' (*medén ágan*) is directly attributed to one of the Greek 'seven sages', the Athenian law-maker and poet Solon. Amongst his other achievements, Solon tried to establish a balance of power between the different classes and parties in society, limiting the prerogatives of magistrates vis-à-vis individuals, protecting certain rights of minorities against the majority and vice-versa, and abolishing slavery by insolvency, i.e. the common practice of offering one's own life and liberty as collateral for loans (see Zoja, *Growth and Guilt*, pp. 56–58; *Oxford Classical Dictionary*, pp. 999–1000, and Chapter 4, note 40).

41. Goethe, *Poetry and Truth* [*Dichtung und Wahrheit*], vol. 1, p. 320. Solomon's proverb was quoted by Butler in his sermon 'Upon Self-deceit' (*Analogy of Religion*, p. 474).

42. Fernando Pessoa, 'D. Sebastião, rei de Portugal' [Dom Sebastian, King of Portugal] (*Obra poética*, p. 76). A possible source for the quoted line is *Hamlet*: 'What is a man / if his chief good and market of his time / be but to sleep and feed? A beast, no more' (Act IV, Scene 4, ll. 33–35).

NOTES

2. SELF-KNOWLEDGE AND SELF-DECEPTION

1. Goethe, *Maxims and Reflections* ¶281. The notion that the advance of knowledge also expands the unknown clearly appears in Hume's observation that '[t]he most perfect philosophy of the natural kind only staves off our ignorance a little longer: as perhaps the most perfect philosophy of the moral or metaphysical kind serves only to discover larger portions of it' (*First Enquiry*, p. 31; see also his comments on the seventeenth-century scientific revolution in *The History of England*, vol. 6, p 542). In the same tradition, Thomas Kuhn asks: 'Though the bulk of scientific knowledge clearly increases with time, what are we to say about ignorance? The problems solved during the last thirty years did not exist as open questions a century ago. [. . .] Is it not possible, or perhaps even likely, that contemporary scientists know less of what there is to know about their world than scientists of the eighteenth century knew of theirs? Scientific theories, it must be remembered, attach to nature only here and there. Are the interstices between those points of attachment perhaps now larger and more numerous than ever before?' (*Essential Tension*, p. 290). This is the conclusion of the American doctor Lewis Thomas: 'The most brilliant minds of the eighteenth-century Enlightenment would be astonished if one of us revealed how little we know, and how confused the road in front of us appears. The sudden confrontation with the depth and scale of ignorance represents the most significant contribution of twentieth-century science to the human intellect' ('The Risks of Science', in *The Medusa and the Snail*, p. 80). In his methodological appendix to *Industry and Trade*, the economist Alfred Marshall compared the advance of knowledge in physics and economics and concluded that 'the certainties of physics increase in number, but its uncertainties increase much faster [. . .] Adam Smith cleared up many obscurities and uncertainties: but the area of his conscious uncertainty was far greater than that of his

245

predecessors' (p. 657); reflecting on his own career at the end of his life, Marshall declared: 'And now, at the end of nearly half a century of almost exclusive study of it [economics], I am conscious of more ignorance of it than I was at the beginning of the study' (quoted in Keynes, *Collected Writings*, vol. 10, p. 171).

2. Valéry, quoted by Quine in the article 'Anomaly' of his magnificent *Quiddities*: 'Any occult phenomenon – any clear case of telepathy, teleportation, or clairvoyance, a ghost, a flying saucer – any of these would delight the scientific mind. Scientists would withdraw in droves and glee to their drawing-boards and linear accelerators' (p. 6).

3. Wittgenstein, *On Certainty*, ¶272, p. 35 *e*. The case for common sense is put forward by G.E. Moore in 'A Defence of Common Sense' and 'Certainty' (these articles prompted Wittgenstein's notes on the topic collected in *On Certainty*). The contrast between familiarity and knowledge goes back to the Platonic myth of the cave (*Republic*, 514 *a* – 521 *b*). In modern philosophy, the question is discussed by, among many others: Adam Smith, 'History of Astronomy' (*Essays*, pp. 34–47); Hegel, *Phenomenology* (Preface, II, 3); Schopenhauer, *The World as Will* (vol. 2, p. 161); Nietzsche, *The Gay Science* (¶355); Whitehead, *Science and the Modern World* (pp. 6 and 71) and Gellner, *The Legitimation of Belief* (pp. 10–13).

4. The definitions of subjective and objective truth are taken from, respectively, Luigi Pirandello and the Spanish poet Antonio Machado.

5. For a careful reconstruction of the Greek philosophers' ideas on sight and a real 'biography of light', from ancient myths to quantum physics, see Zajonc, *Catching the Light*. On Aristotle's refutation of Empedocles' original conjecture, see Woodbridge, *Aristotle's Vision of Nature* (p. 40).

6. The context of Heraclitus' fragment (107) is discussed by Luigi Zoja in *Growth and Guilt* (pp. 85–91). In *Beliefs in Action* I tried to show some of the points of contact between Heraclitus and Bacon (pp. 162 and 226, note

4). The definition and analysis of the 'four idols' is set out by Bacon in Book 1 of the *Novum organum* (¶44, p. 18) and taken up again in *The Advancement of Learning* (pp. 126–28). Unlike the other idols, the *idola tribus* are 'inherent in human nature, and in the very tribe or race of man' (¶49, p. 23). On Bacon's philosophy of science, see Farrington, *Francis Bacon*; Broad, *Francis Bacon*, and Kuhn 'Mathematical versus Experimental Traditions in the Development of Physical Science'.

7. The sentence about 'wise interrogating' appears in *The Advancement of Learning*, p. 123. Bacon's epistemological pragmatism is a constant in his work, but it is in *Cogitata et Visa* (a Latin manuscript written in 1607 and published posthumously) that it appears in its most incisive form: 'For in nature practical results are not only the means to improve well-being but the guarantee of truth. The rule of religion, that a man should show his faith by his works, holds good in natural philosophy too. Science must also be known by works. It is by witness of works, rather than logic or even observation, that truth is revealed and established' (p. 93).

8. The primary source for Democritus' principle is Diogenes Laertius, 'Pyrrho' (9:72), vol. 2, p. 485. The contrast between genuine and spurious knowledge appears in fragment 11. The atomism and epistemology of Democritus in the context of pre-Socratic thought are discussed by: Lloyd, *Early Greek Science*, pp. 45–49; Cornford, *Before and After Socrates*, pp. 21–28; Burnet, *Early Greek Philosophy*, pp. 330–49; Bailey, *Greek Atomists*. For Democritus, of course, 'we see by virtue of the impact of images on our eyes' (Diogenes Laertius, 'Democritus' [9:45], vol. 2, p. 455). On the self-blinding legend (which is contested by Plutarch), see *The Oxford Classical Dictionary* (p. 328). It is curious to note that the idea of taking one's own eyes out appears, in another context, in the following New Testament advice: 'And if your eye causes you to sin, pluck it out; it is better for you to enter the kingdom of God with one eye than with two eyes to be

thrown into hell, where the worm does not die and the fire is not quenched' (Mark, 9:47).

9. The best exposition of the sceptical moment and the Cartesian hyperbolic doubt are the first two of the 1641 *Meditationes*. The spiralling return of doubt is contained the moment Descartes turns the weapon of scepticism against scepticism itself, forcing it to surrender to the certainty of the doubt that doubts itself. The celebrated phrase 'Cogito ergo sum' originally appeared in the compendium *Principia*, of 1644 (proposition 7), and, later, in the Latin translation of the *Discours de la Méthode*. For a careful reconstruction of Descartes' argument, and a proposal for radicalising the movement that leads to the cogito, universalising it and arguing against its claim to provide a positive foundation for knowledge, see Antonio Cícero, *O mundo desde o fim* [The world since the end] (esp. ¶¶6–8, pp. 25–45). In *Philosophical Tales* (Chapter 1), Jonathan Rée analyses the narrative and rhetorical strategies employed by Descartes in the *Meditationes*: 'It probably took Descartes an average of more than a year to compose each day's diary' (p. 20).

10. The example of a tickling sensation as an illustration of a secondary quality, and the analogy with language appear in *Le Monde* (pp. 312–14), a treatise on physics whose composition Descartes interrupted after the condemnation of Galileo by the Inquisition in 1633, and which was posthumously published in 1664. In the Cartesian view, 'philosophy as a whole is like a tree whose roots are metaphysics, whose trunk is physics, and whose branches, which issue from this trunk, are all the other sciences [viz. medicine, mechanics and morals]' (*Principles*, p. 211). In a letter to his collaborator Mersenne, soon after the publication of the *Meditationes*, Descartes confides: '[. . .] and I may tell you, between ourselves, that these six meditations contain all the foundations of my physics' (*Philosophical Letters*, p. 94). The role of the senses and of empirical evidence in Cartesian science are analysed by Larmore in 'Descartes' Empirical Epistemology'.

11. The context and the content of the series of Descartes'

contributions to analytic geometry are recounted in detail by Gaukroger in his monumental intellectual biography of the philosopher (*Descartes*, Chapters 3 and 4). On the relationship between the Cartesian concept of objectivity – based on the distinction between primary and secondary qualities – and the advance of mathematical methods in the natural sciences, see: Dijksterhuis, *The Mechanization of the World Picture* (pp. 403–18), and Burtt, *The Metaphysical Foundations of Modern Science*: 'Descartes' real criterion [for identifying the primary qualities] is not permanence but the possibility of mathematical handling' (p. 117).

12. Damasio, *Descartes' Error*, pp. 224–25. Damasio's work on the role of the emotions in the working of the brain and decision-making gives a neurological basis to Hume's thesis that 'reason is, and ought only to be the slave of the passions, and can never pretend to any other office than to serve and obey them'; reason separated from the emotions is monstrous in its indifference to human values: ''Tis not contrary to reason to prefer the destruction of the whole world to the scratching of my finger. 'Tis not contrary to reason to chuse my total ruin, to prevent the least uneasiness of an Indian or person wholly unknown to me' (Hume, *Treatise*, pp. 415–16).

13. Nagel's seminal article in which he sets out his argument about the limits of the scientific concept of objectivity and the inaccessibility of mental reality was published in 1974, with the suggestive title 'What is it like to be a Bat?'. In *The View from Nowhere*, Nagel develops this, brilliantly exploring the tension between each individual's inner point of view, on the one hand, and the objective external view ('from no particular perspective'), on the other, as it appears in the central problems of philosophy: the relationship between the mind and the brain, epistemology, free will and ethics. A great challenge, in this perspective, is the creation and perfecting of an objective concept of the *mental*, which would in some way open up the possibility of thinking about ourselves and our subjective experience from outside, i.e. in a distanced and objective fashion, but inevitably different from the one

prevalent in the scientific approach to the external world. In his philosophy primer, *What does it all Mean?*, Nagel provides an excellent means of entry to those looking for a first contact with his thought, or, more generally, with Anglo-American analytical philosophy.

14. The authorship of the Delphic inscription is attributed to the Greek 'seven sages': a group of law-givers, statesmen and thinkers from all over Greece who lived in the period from 620–550 BC, and who were admired for their good sense and practical wisdom, above all in the creation of laws (Solon of Athens, Thales of Miletus, Pittacus of Mitylene, Cleobulus of Lindus, Chilon of Sparta, Myson of Chen and Bias of Priene). Socrates himself says: '[. . .] each [of the seven sages] is the author of some brief, memorable sayings. And not only that, but they joined together to make an offering to Apollo at his temple in Delphi of the fruits of their wisdom, and inscribed there those familiar maxims "Know thyself" and "Nothing in excess" [. . .] that was the form of expression of the wisdom of former times, a Laconian brevity' (Plato, *Protagoras*, 343 b-c). The temple of Apollo at Delphi was not only the centre of Greek religious life; it was also considered to be the centre of the world, with a spherical stone marking the central point of the circular disc surrounded by ocean that was the Earth (see *The Oxford Classical Dictionary*, pp. 322–23). Amongst the pre-Socratic philosophers, it was perhaps Heraclitus who came closest to the Socratic point of view when he argued that real wisdom does not consist in the accumulation of concrete knowledge (i.e. of techniques and information), but in the soul's awakening from the sleep of its subjectivity to a rational apprehension – one that is common to all men – of the order that holds sway in the world; it is the belief that all knowledge is born from self-knowledge that probably explains the intriguing fragment 101: 'I sought for myself' (see Cornford, *Principium sapientiae*, pp. 112–17).

15. Guthrie, *Socrates*, p. 151. The controversy about the authorship of the *First Alcibiades* dialogue is an old one. Though several specialists refuse to attribute it to Plato (e.g. Taylor,

Plato, pp. 522–26), the consensus prevails that it consistently reflects the thinking of the Academy and must have been written, if not by the master himself, then by some member of his circle, or a disciple. On the theme of Socratic self-knowledge, see: Guthrie, *Socrates*, (pp. 147–53), Taylor, *Plato* (pp. 53–57); Cornford, *Before and After Socrates* (pp. 29–53); Dodds, *The Greeks and the Irrational* (pp. 179–95); Popper, *The Open Society and its Enemies* (vol. 1, p. 190), and Zoja, *Growth and Guilt* (pp. 85–91)

16. The metaphor of the 'irritating gadfly' appears in the *Apologia* (31 *a*). On the Socratic art of maieutics (*Theaetetus*) and its relationship with the Platonic theory of innate, universal Ideas (*Menon*), see: Guthrie, *Socrates* (pp. 122–29) and Cornford, *Plato's Theory of Knowledge* (esp. pp. 27–29).

17. In Greek mythology, according to Hesiod's genealogy, Typhon is a hundred-headed monster-dragon, that would have wreaked enormous damage on humanity had Zeus not defeated it with his thunderbolts and imprisoned it in Tartarus. In the passage quoted, as the *Phaedrus'* English translator points out, Socrates plays with the morphological and phonetic similarity between the Greek word for the monster and the words for 'to shade' (as in drawing), 'vanity', and 'imposture' (Hackforth, *Phaedrus*, p. 2, note 2; see note 31).

18. If Democritus, according to the legend, blinded himself so as to think better, Socrates seemed to want to go further and remove his own body: 'As long as we possess the body, and our soul is contaminated by such an evil, we'll surely never adequately gain what we desire – and that, we say, is truth. Because the body affords us countless distractions [. . .] it fills us up with lusts and desires, with fears and fantasies of every kind, and with any amount of trash, so that really and truly we are, as the saying goes, never able to think of anything because of it. Thus, it's nothing but the body and its desires that bring war and factions and fighting; because it's over the gaining of wealth that all wars take place, and we are compelled to gain wealth because of the body, enslaved as we are to its service; so for all these reasons it leaves us no

leisure for philosophy. And the worst of it all is that if we do get any leisure from it, and turn to some inquiry, once again it intrudes everywhere on our researches, setting up a clamour and disturbance, and striking terror, so that the truth can't be discerned because of it' (Plato, *Phaedo*, 66 b-d). The neo-Platonist Plotinus, according to his biographer and principal disciple Porphyry, 'seemed ashamed of being in his own body [. . .] So deeply rooted was this feeling that he could never be induced to tell of his ancestry, his parentage, or his birthplace' (*Enneads*, p. 1).

19. The American philosopher Paul Churchland contests the cognitive authority of the subject over what happens in his own mind, by appealing to our experience of dreams. 'Suppose', he suggests, 'you are dreaming that you have a splitting headache, or that you are in excruciating pain from being tortured. When you awaken suddenly, do you not realize, in a wave of relief, that you were not really the victim of a headache, or of excruciating pain, despite the conviction that attends every dream?' (*Matter and Consciousness*, p. 78) But might not the sensation of relief, contrary to what Churchland supposes, be clear evidence of the reality of the subjective experience of pain *at the moment it was being felt* by the subject? If the experience were not real, there would be no reason to feel relief on awakening.

20. Sartre, *Baudelaire*, p. 76.

21. Wittgenstein, *Culture and Value*, p. 34 (for the context of this statement, see note 31); Nietzsche, *Daybreak*, ¶ 116, p. 72 and *The Genealogy of Morals* ¶1, p. 15. See also ¶357 of *The Gay Science*: 'What we call consciousness constitutes only one state of our spiritual and psychic world (perhaps a pathological state) and not by any means the whole of it' (p. 305). It was after hearing Eduard Hitschmann read some passages from the *Genealogy* at a meeting of the Vienna Psychoanalytic Society in 1908 that Freud said of Nietzsche: 'He had a more penetrating knowledge of himself than any other man who ever lived or was likely to live' (minutes of the Vienna Psychoanalytic Society [1908] quoted

by Jones, *The Life and Work of Freud*, vol. 2, p. 385; Tanner, *Nietzsche*, p. 70; Kaufmann, introduction to *Ecce Homo*, p. 203; and Hayman, *Nietzsche*, p. 1). To say the least, Freud's reasons/excuses, given at various moments in his life, for not having read and studied the collected works of Nietzsche that he acquired when he was still young, are strange: first (1900) it was 'indolence'; later (1908) the assertion that he was not prepared to be side-tracked from his important work by 'an excess of interest'(!); and, finally (1931) 'Hence I have rejected the study of Nietzsche although – no, because – it was plain that I would find insights in him very similar to psychoanalytic ones' (Gay, *Freud*, p. 58). The paradox is clear: if Freud never bothered to read and study Nietzsche's ideas – and this in spite of repeated suggestions (e.g. from Jung) that he should – how could it be 'plain' to him that he would find his own discoveries there?

22. Montaigne, 'On the Inconstancy of our Actions' (*Essays*, p. 377). The centrality of self-knowledge for Montaigne appears in full when he says: 'I study myself more than any other subject. That is my metaphysics; that is my physics [. . .] I would rather be an expert on me than on Cicero. Were I a good pupil there is enough, I find, in my own experience to make me wise' (pp. 1217–18). The quotation from Diderot in the previous paragraph is from 'The Paradox of the Actor' (p. 45).

23. On the techniques of electrodermal conductivity and its application, see: Damasio, *Descartes' Error* (pp. 238–43) and *The Oxford Companion to Mind* (pp. 213–14). The source for the experiment referred to in the text is Wright, *The Moral Animal* (pp. 270–71).

24. The shortcomings of ordinary language for conveying sub-tleties and expressing the complexity of our emotional and mental states are brilliantly analysed by Nietzsche: 'Language and the prejudices upon which language is based are a mani-fold hindrance to us when we want to explain inner processes and drives: because of the fact, for example, that words really exist only for *superlative* degrees of these processes and drives;

and where words are lacking, we are accustomed to abandon exact observation because exact thinking there becomes painful [. . .] Anger, hatred, love, pity, desire, knowledge, joy, pain – all are names for extreme states: the milder, middle degrees, not to speak of the lower degrees which are continually in play, elude us, and yet it is they which weave the web of our character and destiny [. . .] *We are none of us* that which we appear to be in accordance with the states for which alone we have consciousness and words' (*Daybreak*, ¶115, pp. 71–72). The same question is dealt with, but from a physicalist point of view, critical, therefore, of the conceptual and linguistic network of 'folk psychology', by Churchland, in *Matter and Consciousness* (pp. 56–61 and 79).

25. Calvin, *Institutio Christianae Religionis* (quoted in Rue, *By the Grace of Guile*, p. 45). The image of the mind as labyrinth appears in Nietzsche: 'If we desired and dared an architecture corresponding to the nature of our soul [. . .] our model would have to be the labyrinth!' (*Daybreak*, ¶169, p. 104).

26. Epictetus, *Encheiridion*, ¶33 (*Epictetus*, vol. 2, p. 519). And what if someone knew us better and more intimately than we know ourselves? Erasmus replies: 'And who would carry on doing business or having dealings with an old man if his vast experience of affairs was still matched by a vigorous and keen judgement?' (*The Praise of Folly*, ¶13, p. 79).

27. The logical short-circuit in the negative form of this question is a variant of the well-known liar paradox. Consider the statement: 'I am lying.' If it is false, that means that I am not lying, which contradicts the statement made. But if it is true, then the statement is false – when I said I was lying I said the truth and so was not lying. The statement is true if it's false and false if it's true! What is said implicitly denies what's being said.

28. 'Somos nuestra memoria, / somos ese quimérico museo de formas inconstantes, / ese montón de espejos rotos', Borges, 'Cambridge' (from *Elogio de la sombra*), *Obra poética*, p. 316.

29. Dostoevsky, *Notes from the Underground*, p. 45. Similar

reflections to those of the underground man appear in the passages from Erasmus, Fontenelle, Goethe and Nietzsche cited in note 40, below. See also Dr. Johnson's comment on Pope's correspondence: 'very few can boast of hearts which they dare lay open to themselves, and of which, by whatever accident exposed, they do not shun a distinct and continued view; and, certainly, what we hide from ourselves we do not show our friends' (*Lives of the English Poets*, vol. 2, p. 206).

30. Darwin, 'M notebook' (*Early Writings*, p. 20). For a systematic commentary on the 'metaphysical notebooks' of the young Darwin and his preoccupation with unconscious mental processes, see Gruber, *Darwin on Man* (esp. pp. 233–34 and 239).

31. Darwin describes his 'golden rule' in his *Autobiography*, p. 123. Wittgenstein's advice was directed to his ex-student, the American philosopher Norman Malcolm, in a letter of 16 November 1944 (Malcolm, *Wittgenstein*, p. 94). The relevance of self-knowledge in Wittgenstein's philosophy is pointed out by Monk: 'What gets in the way of genuine understanding is often not one's lack of intelligence, but the presence of one's pride. [. . .] The self-scrutiny demanded by such dismantling of one's pride is necessary, not only to be a decent person, but also to write decent philosophy. "If anyone is unwilling to descend into himself, because this is too painful, he will remain superficial in his writing" [quoted in Rhees, *Recollections*, p. 174]' (*Wittgenstein*, p. 366). It is curious to note that Rhees also mentions, in his memoirs of the philosopher, the time when Wittgenstein came to ask him for the loan of his copy of Plato's *Phaedrus*, to find the passage about the monster Typhon (see note 17), saying that he had the same kind of doubt that Socrates had about himself (*Recollections*, p. 175). On the relationship between ethics and scientific knowledge, see also Iris Murdoch, *The Sovereignty of Good* (p. 89), and Bambrough, *Moral Scepticism* (Chapter 7).

32. The episode of Boyle's 'discovery' of the formula for making gold is described in detail by Maurice Cranston in his

biography of Locke: 'Boyle carried to the grave the hope that he had at last found how to multiply gold by combining a certain form of red earth with mercury. He sent the formula separately to Locke, whom he made one of the executors of his will, and to Newton, imposing on each of them an oath of secrecy.' Newton, however, did not keep the secret and wrote to Locke, 'warning [him] against wasting his time with Boyle's receipt' (Cranston, *Locke*, pp. 353 and 361).

33. The dream of squaring the circle goes back to Greek geometry and consisted in the search for a regular square or polygon that would have exactly the same area as a circle. One of the last philosophers to 'prove' and heatedly defend the success of his operation – thus ruining his reputation as a scientist – was Hobbes, in Chapter 20 of *De Corpore* (see Rogow, *Hobbes*, pp. 195–201; Peters, *Hobbes*, pp. 39–40, and Russell, *History of Western Philosophy*, p. 532). It's worth saying that even in the seventeenth century the idea of squaring the circle was already cited as a notorious example of a pointless quest (e.g. Spinoza, *On the Improvement of the Understanding*, p. 24, and Fontenelle, *Nouveaux dialogues des morts*, p. 316).

34. The interpretation of fossil evidence as 'primitive art' is part of the *a priori* biological anti-evolutionism defended by Hegel, and which he set against the idea of the evolution and perfectibility that, according to him, distinguished the historical from the merely natural world: '[. . .] every product of the spirit, the very worst of its imaginings, the capriciousness of its most arbitrary moods, a mere word, are all better evidence of God's being than any single [natural] object' (see Hegel, *Philosophy of History*, p. 54, and *Philosophy of Nature*, vol. 1, p. 209, and vol. 3, pp. 18–23). For comments on Hegel's use of fossil evidence and his biological anti-evolutionism, see: Findlay, *Hegel* (p. 272); Petry, *Hegel's Philosophy of Nature* (vol. 3, p. 230); Lukács, *Young Hegel* (p. 543) and Taylor, *Hegel and Modern Society* (p. 28 n).

35. The story of the burning of heretics in Lisbon during the Inquisition is based on Russell, 'Ideas that have Harmed Mankind', p. 161. The Roman precedents for the public

torture of condemned men – Julius Caesar was even thought 'mad' for refusing to follow this practice – are discussed by Montaigne in 'On Cruelty' (*Essays*, p. 485). The source for Himmler's nickname is Gerald Fleming's monograph on the decision-making process involved in the Nazi programmes for euthanasia and racial extermination, *Hitler und die Endlösung*, reviewed by Hugh Trevor-Roper in the *Times Literary Supplement* (28 January 1983, pp. 75–76).

36. The original title of Brecht's poem is 'Fahrend in einem bequemen Wagen'. The English translation is from Michael Hamburger, in 'Brecht and his Successors' (*Art as Second Nature*, p. 115).

37. On this point, see the passages from Dr. Johnson and Machiavelli quoted in Chapter 4 (pp. 192–93).

38. Guimarães Rosa, 'O espelho' [The Mirror] (*Primeiras estórias* [*The Third Bank of the River and Other Stories*], (p. 72).

39. The context of the work and the passage inserted by Stalin in his official biography are from Deutscher, *Stalin*, vol. 2, p. 555. The paradox inherent in any open or implicit denial of vanity is pointed out by Nietzsche in *Human All Too Human*, vol. 2, ¶38 (p. 224).

40. Erasmus, *The Praise of Folly*, ¶22, p. 94, and Goethe, *Poems*, p. 205. A similar reflection appears in Fontenelle's *Nouveaux dialogues des morts*: 'Ah, don't you know yet what madness is for? It's to prevent us knowing ourselves, for seeing ourselves is a sad business indeed. And since we are always liable to know ourselves, madness must not abandon men for a single instant. [. . .] Lunatics are only madmen of another kind [. . .] those whose madness does not chime in with everyone else's' (pp. 226–27). Nietzsche, in his turn, asks: 'How much truth does a spirit *endure*, how much truth does it *dare*? More and more that became for me the real measure of value. [. . .] Every attainment, every step forward in knowledge, *follows* from courage, from hardness against oneself, from cleanliness in relation to oneself' (*Ecce Homo*, ¶3, p. 218).

41. Carlos Drummond de Andrade, 'Do homem experimentado' [Of the experienced man] (*Obras*, p. 850). As Montaigne says

in 'Of Experience': 'Even the life of Caesar is less exemplary for us than our own; a life whether imperial or plebeian is always a life affected by everything that can happen to a man. [. . .] Is a man not stupid if he remembers having been so often wrong in his judgement yet does not become deeply distrustful of it thereafter?' (*Essays*, p. 1218).

3. THE LOGIC OF SELF-DECEPTION

1. Nietzsche, *Beyond Good and Evil*, ¶141, p. 89. The hypothesis that this aphorism contains an autobiographical element is reinforced, amongst other things, by the fact that, in January 1889, a few days after his mental collapse, Nietzsche began to sign his letters 'Dionysus' and 'The Crucified' (Hollingdale, *Nietzsche*, pp. 173–75). The theme of self-deception runs throughout Nietzsche's work; one of the most incisive passages (which could serve as an epigraph to this book) appears in *The Anti-Christ*: 'I call a lie: wanting *not* to see something one does see, wanting not to see something as one sees it: whether the lie takes place before witnesses or without witnesses is of no consequence. The most common lie is the lie one tells to oneself; lying to others is relatively the exception' (¶55, p. 173). On the squaring of the circle in the history of philosophy, see note 33 of the previous chapter. The image of the squaring of the circle as a metaphor for self-deception was used by Loyal Rue in *By the Grace of Guile* (pp. 145–46).

2. It may be said in passing that that's why it is logically possible, though very rare, for someone to *lie* and *say the truth*. All that is needed is for the liar to be mistaken about what he is saying and end up accidentally hitting the target he intended to miss. A doctor, for example, can lie to a patient, hiding the diagnosis of the illness he thinks is terminal; the patient, however, recovers and defeats the disease, confuting the doctor's expectations and making him have said the truth when he lied. An art-dealer defrauds a client, selling him as genuine a sculpture that he knows to be a copy of the original;

the buyer dies and the heirs call in specialists, who authenticate the work, making the dealer's lie true.

3. 'Le meilleur moyen de persuader consiste à ne pas persuader' (Isidore Ducasse / Lautréamont, *Poésies*, p. 86). The expression 'internal hypocrite' is based on the notion of 'internal hypocrisy' coined by Bishop Joseph Butler, in the sermon 'Upon self-deceit' (p. 479).

4. De Quincey, *Confessions*, p. 214. In 1621, at the high point of his political power and prestige, Bacon was charged with having secretly accepted gifts in cash from litigants in trials in which he was the magistrate, and sent to prison by the English parliament. When he publicly admitted his guilt, Bacon tried to argue in mitigation that the presents had not influenced the verdicts, and that one should distinguish between *vitia temporis* (the vices of the time, of which he was culpable), and *vitia hominis* (the vices of the individual, of which he was not). The sentence quoted in the text is part of a speech written by the philosopher at the time of his trial, in which he manifests not only his repentance for the acts committed, but his conviction that his career in public life had been a mistake (Farrington, *Bacon*, p. 159). In his essay 'Lord Bacon', Macaulay writes a magnificent study of the relationship between philosophy and politics in the career of the Viscount of St. Albans (*Essays*, esp. pp. 379ff.). It is curious to note that, analysing the psychology of the rich and powerful ten years before his condemnation, Bacon concluded: 'they are the first that find their own griefs, though they are the last that find their own faults. Certainly men in great fortunes are strangers to themselves, and while they are in the puzzle of business they have no time to tend their health of body or mind' ('Of Great Place', *Essays*, p. 96).

5. La Rochefoucauld, *Maxims*, ¶119, p. 52.

6. Machado de Assis, *Dom Casmurro*, Chapters XLI and CXXXII, pp. 80 and 222. The problem of self-deception is a constant in Bentinho's intimate reflections: 'A certificate saying I was twenty years old might fool others, like any false document, but not me' (Chapter II, p. 6; see also the remarkable

example quoted in Chapter 4, note 9). For a detailed analysis of the moral consequences of, and the possible justifications for interpersonal lying, in public as in private life, see Sissela Bok, *Lying*.

7. Marcus Aurelius, *Meditations*, Book 9, ¶29, p. 144. This passage is commented on by Lecky in *The History of European Morals* (vol. 1, p. 251). On the 'impotence of power' in the ex-Soviet Union and the problems connected with forcing anyone (or oneself) to believe in anything, see Elster, *Sour Grapes* (Chapter 2).

8. Lempe, an ex-soldier in the Prussian army, had been Kant's personal servant for about forty years; the memorandum is dated February 1802. The whole of the Lempe affair and the moral dilemmas Kant went through on his account are related by Pastor Wasianski, who ministered to the philosopher in his old age (*The Last Days of Kant*, pp. 131–38). According to the Pastor, Kant's categorical wish to forget the matter had another enemy: 'So intense had been the uniformity of his life and habits, that the least innovation in the arrangement of articles as trifling as a penknife or a pair of scissors disturbed him; and not merely if they were pushed two or three inches out of their customary position, but even if they were laid a little awry' (p. 134). Kant's memorandum on Lempe was recalled by Wolf Lepenies, the director of the Wissenschaftskolleg, in Berlin, in the context of a discussion on how the Germans deal with the memory of the terrible Nazi past (see 'The Step-fatherland', *The Economist* 8 April 1995, p. 76). Wittgenstein's observation on love appears in *Remarks on Frazer's* Golden Bough, p. 3 e. Wittgenstein's personal notebooks contain reflections that take up this observation and give it further depth: 'A person cannot come out of his skin. I cannot give up a demand that is anchored deep inside me, in my whole life. For love is bound up with nature [. . .] What good does all my talent do me, if, at heart, I am unhappy? What help is it to me to solve philosophical problems, if I cannot settle the chief, most important thing?' (Monk, *Wittgenstein*, pp. 505–06).

9. Goethe, *Maxims and Reflections*, ¶99. This was also Nietzsche's opinion: 'Even the most rational man from time to time needs to recover nature, that is to say his illogical original relationship to all things' (*Human All Too Human*, ¶31, p. 28). In his essay 'On Tranquillity of Mind', the Stoic Seneca makes a defence of the use of alcohol to cleanse the mind of tensions and worries: 'At times we ought to drink to intoxication, not so as to drown, but merely dip ourselves in wine: for wine washes away troubles and dislodges them from the depths of the mind, and acts as a remedy to sorrow as it does to some diseases. The inventor of wine is called Liber, not from the licence which he gives to our tongues, but because he liberates the mind from the bondage of cares, and emancipates it, animates it, and renders it more daring in all its attempts. Yet moderation is wholesome both in freedom and in wine' (p. 286). The Plato of the *Laws* takes up a much more restrictive attitude to wine (645–8 and 673–4). Baudelaire's *Le Poème du haschisch* and de Quincey's *Confessions* discuss the motivations for taking drugs and their moral consequences.

10. Ruskin, *Unto this Last*, p. 73; Bailey, *Epicurus*, p. 99. The eminently psychological nature of economic goals is underlined by the American economist Irving Fisher: 'For each individual only those events which come within the purview of his experience are of direct concern. It is these events – the psychic experiences of the individual mind – which constitute ultimate income for that individual. [...] [neither all productive activity] nor the money transactions following them are of significance except as they are necessary or helpful preliminaries to psychic income – human enjoyment' (*Theory of Interest*, pp. 4–5).

11. Fernando Pessoa: the first quotation is from 'Autopsicografia' ['Autopsychography'], the second from 'Isto' ['This'] (*Obra poética*, pp. 164 and 165). The tradition of the poet as 'feigner' goes back to archaic Greek poetry. To the Homeric line, which is that 'the poets tell many lies', the poet Hesiod replies: 'We know how to tell many lies that resemble truth; but we know how to tell truth too, when we wish' (Curtius,

European Literature, p. 203). For Hume, poets were 'liars by profession' who 'always endeavour to give an air of truth to their fictions' (*Treatise*, p. 121). In the second part of my *Beliefs in Action* I tried to analyse the psychology of Baudelaire's 'hypocritical reader'. The relationship between author, actor and spectator is brilliantly analysed by Diderot in 'The Paradox of the Actor': 'The actor is weary, and you [the spectator] are sad, because he has exerted himself without feeling anything, and you have the feeling without the exertion' (*Selected Writings on Art and Literature*, p. 108); see also Furbank, *Diderot*, esp. pp. 354–56).

12. Laplace's conjecture concerning an omniscient intelligence, originally formulated at the end of the eighteenth century by the French mathematician, and father of the classical or subjective theory of probability, first appeared in his *Philosophical Essay on Probabilities*, of 1795 (p. 4), and is discussed, amongst others, by Lange, in *The History of Materialism* (Book 2, Section 2, Chapter 1), and Popper, in *The Self and its Brain* (esp. pp. 21–26). For a review of contemporary philosophical thought in the analytic tradition on the question of freedom, see the collection organised by Gary Watson, *Free Will*.

13. It's worth pointing out that the hypothesis of a journey *into the past* brings about an even more intractable paradox: it opens up the possibility of altering things that have already happened, and thus making the present into a logically absurd reality. Suppose someone goes back to the past and manages to kill his own grandfather, or stop his parents marrying. In such a case, he wouldn't have been born and so could never have gone back in time to prevent his own birth.

14. The paradox of the death foretold goes back to the paradox on fatalism formulated by Diodorus Cronus (a Greek philosopher of the school of Megara in the fourth century BC) and discussed by Aristotle in *De interpretatione*. If every proposition must be true or, if it's not true, it must be false, then it follows logically that no event is contingent, and man has no free will. The law of excluded middle implies fatalism.

What will happen in the future is as necessary and determined as what happened in the past. From the logical point of view, this can be seen if, as Quine suggests, one changes all references to time to references to dates, so that every statement is true or false once and for all and for ever, even if we are in no position to know whether it is or not. If the statement *event X happens on day Y* is either true or false, this implies that the occurrence (or non-occurrence) of X on Y is determined, independently of whether Y is, from the point of view of the author of the statement, a day in the future or the past. The rejection of logical fatalism requires an attenuation of the law of excluded middle for events that refer to the future, thus opening a space for *indeterminate* propositions; those, that is, that one day will be true or false, but that, in the present, are neither true nor false. For a detailed analysis of logical fatalism and alternatives to it, see Steven Cahn, *Fate, Logic and Time*.

15. Keynes, *Collected Writings*, vol. 9, p. 327. As Wittgenstein – who gave his own inheritance away so that others could devote themselves to creative work – said: 'It is much harder to accept poverty willingly when you have to be poor than when you might also be rich' (*Culture and Value*, p. 19 *e*). Or, as Nietzsche put it: 'The great advantage of having noble origins is that it enables one more easily to endure poverty' (*Daybreak*, ¶200, p. 119). The power of rich people's wealth is a function of the value the poor attribute to it.

16. It was human beings' amorous complications that ended up making Epicurus' gods lose interest in human affairs and look for *ataraxía* in the *intermundia*. For an exemplary study of the attack on love in book 4 of *De Rerum Natura* and the legend of the madness that supposedly killed Lucretius, see Martha Nussbaum, *The Therapy of Desire* (Chapter 5). The representation of Cupid and the ravings of passionate love are the theme of some of the most moving passages of Erasmus's *The Praise of Folly* (esp. ¶19, pp. 90–92 and ¶67, pp. 206–08).

17. [Translator's note: these are lines from two songs by Brazilian

popular composers, Caetano Veloso (b. 1942), and Ari Barroso (1903–1964). 'Tabuleiro da baiana' is a tray of sweetmeats sold in the street by a woman from the state of Bahia.]
18. The logical counterpoint of promises like these can also be found in the enormous fund of experience collected and recreated aesthetically in Brazilian popular music. This is the tradition of lines like these: 'Only a madman loved as I love' ['Só louco amou como eu amei'] (Dorival Caymmi); 'Those lads, poor lads, ah!, if they knew what I know, they wouldn't fall in love, and wouldn't go through what I have' ['Esses moços, pobres moços, ah! se soubessem o que eu sei, não amavam, não passavam, aquilo que eu já passei'] (Lupicínio Rodrigues); 'Passion's solo only lasts a day before it caves in' ['O solo da paixão não dura mais que um dia antes de afundar'] (Antonio Cícero); and finally, why not?, 'I'm a good-for-nothing but I love you' ['Eu não presto mas eu te amo'] (Waldick Soriano). The phenomenon of self-deceived promising in the context of passionate love is treated by Socrates in his first speech in Plato's *Phaedrus*: 'He [the lover] was lavish with his promises [. . .] but when the time comes for fulfilling the promises, a new authority takes the place within him of the former ruler: love and passion are replaced by wisdom and temperance: he has become a different person [. . .] the erstwhile lover cannot for very shame bring himself to declare that he has become a new man, nor yet see his way to redeeming the solemn assurances and promises made under the old regime of folly'(241 *a*).
19. La Rochefoucauld, *Maxims*, ¶56, p. 44: see also 'The world more often rewards outward signs of merit than merit itself' (¶166, p. 58). The paradoxes of 'trying to make a good impression' are analysed by Elster in *Sour Grapes* (pp. 66–71). For a socio-biological approach to the care everyone takes with the impression he makes on others, see Wright, *The Moral Animal* (Chapter 13). The same theme is treated, but from a rhetorical perspective, by Michael Billig, in *Arguing and Thinking* (esp. pp. 231–33).
20. Montaigne, 'On the Art of Conversation' (*Essays*, p. 429). In

his essay for the collection *Eminent Economists*, the American
economist Kenneth Arrow says: 'I consider it essential to
honesty to look for the best arguments against a position that
one is holding. Commitments should always have tentative
quality' (p. 47). More provocatively, the Chicago economist
George Stigler, says: 'My lifetime as an observer of young
adults in college convinces me that a modest knowledge is all
that is needed for, or possibly even compatible with, strong
political views' (*Memoirs*, p. 138).

21. The tests and the results obtained in several experiments of
this kind are set out and discussed by Wright in *The Moral
Animal*, pp. 275–81. These results back up Malebranche's
thesis that 'all passions seek their own justification' and rarely
fail to find one (*The Search after Truth*, p. 399). As Nietzsche
says: 'There is an innocence in lying which is the sign of good
faith in a cause' (*Beyond Good and Evil*, ¶180, p. 93). In
Beliefs in Action (Chapters 6 and 7) I attempted to examine
this mechanism in the formation of beliefs in detail, and to
show its relevance in ordinary life.

22. Marshall, *Industry and Trade*, p. 724. For a collection of
recent examples illustrating Marshall's observation on protective blindness in the economic debate, see: Buchanan and
Burton, *The Consequences of Mr. Keynes*; Krugman, *Peddling
Prosperity*, and the articles 'The Dangerous Science' and 'The
Use and Abuse of Economics' in *The Economist*, 17 June 1989
and 25 November 1995.

23. Lenin, quoted in Arthur Koestler, *The Act of Creation*,
p. 194.

24. The co-option of Cicero in *Julius Caesar* originates from the
suggestion of Metellus Cimber: 'Oh let us have him, for his
silver hairs / Will purchase us a good opinion / And buy men's
voices to commend our deeds. / It shall be said his judgement
rul'd our hands; / Our youths and wildness shall no whit
appear, / But all be buried in his gravity' (I, 1, ll. 144–49;
see also I, 3, 157–60). The astonishing career of the leader
of the 'Supreme Truth', Shoko Asahara, and his relationship
with Buddhism are recounted in detail by Murray Sayle, an

Australian writer living in Japan, in 'Nerve Gas and the Four Noble Truths' (*New Yorker*, 1 April 1996, pp. 56–71). One of the worst abuses of Rousseau's political philosophy during the Great Terror was the transformation of the 'general will' (the interests that each citizen has in common with all the others) into the 'will of the people', understood as the right of the supposed majority to affirm their interests, to the point of persecuting and destroying certain individuals and groups (see Dent, *Rousseau Dictionary*, pp. 123–26). 'The *Social Contract*', warns Bertrand Russell, 'became the Bible of most of the leaders in the French Revolution, but no doubt, as is the fate of Bibles, it was not carefully read and was still less understood by many of its disciples' (*History of Western Philosophy*, p. 674). The quotation about the authority of the dead is attributed to Machado de Assis (with no source given) in Matos, *Machado de Assis*, p. 302.

25. Lenin, 'Philosophical Notebooks' (*Collected Works*, vol. 38, p. 180).
26. Nietzsche, *Beyond Good and Evil*, ¶290, p. 229. The tortured syntax and poor style peculiar to Hegel are analysed by Nietzsche in *Daybreak* (¶193, p. 114), following Leibniz's hint that 'only obscurity can serve as a defence for absurdity'. The expression 'bible of the working class' was created by a Swiss delegate at the Brussels congress of the First International, and cheerfully taken up by Marx and Engels (see Lafargue, 'Reminiscences of Marx', p. 85, and Stekloff, *First International*, p. 130 and p. 400, note).
27. This definition of communism appears in two speeches made by Lenin at the end of 1920 (*Collected Works*, vol. 31, pp. 408–26 and 487–518); the context and Lenin's unlimited enthusiasm for technology are discussed by Kuczynski and Nicholson, 'Lenin and the Energy Question' (*Labour Monthly* [1974], pp. 129–32). Lenin's reference to Marxism's 'complete scientific sobriety' was made in the pamphlet 'Against the boycott' (*Selected Works*, vol. 3, p. 414). When it comes to revolutionary promises, it would be hard to equal Trotsky's, in 1935, according to which the implantation of communism

would allow an 80% reduction in production costs in the US economy (see Kolakowski, *Main Currents of Marxism*, p. 212). The Pangloss-like belief quoted in this paragraph is from Marx's preface to his *Contribution to a Critique of Political Economy*: 'Mankind thus inevitably sets itself only such tasks as it is able to solve, since closer examination will always show that the problem itself arises only when the material conditions for its solution are already present or at least in the course of formation' (*Early Writings*, p. 426).

28. Engels' letter to Vera Sassoulitch (a militant in the Russian Marxist 'old guard' removed from the *Iskra* in 1903) is quoted by McLellan as the epigraph to Part 2 ('Russian Marxism') of *Marxism after Marx* (p. 63). In *The Rhetoric of Reaction*, Hirschman maps out a trio of strategies of 'reactionary' argumentation – the arguments from perversity, futility and threat – and tries to show that they have been used in public debate since 1789, always with the aim of preventing any kind of change in the status quo. Nothing, however, seems to have been more harmful to *progressive* causes in the whole modern period than the absurd blindness of reformers or revolutionaries of all persuasions when it comes to anticipating the difficulties in the way of the practical realisation of their goals. In overt opposition to Hirschman's thesis, the argument from self-deception reinforces this warning from Arrow: 'It is my view that most individuals underestimate the uncertainty of the world. This is almost as true of economists and other specialists as it is of the lay public. [. . .] vast ills have followed a belief in certainty, whether historical inevitability, grand diplomatic designs, or extreme views on economic policy' (*Eminent Economists*, p. 46). On the self-deceit typical of revolutionaries of all stripes, see also Russell's observation: 'They [some revolutionaries and other apostles of violence] are actuated, usually without their own knowledge, by hatred; the destruction of what they hate is their real purpose, and they are comparatively indifferent to the question of what is to come after it' (*The Conquest of Happiness*, p. 214).

29. This statement comes from an article written by Lenin towards

the end of his life about the difficulties the Russian Marxists had in inculcating their view of the world on a recalcitrant population, averse to atheism ('On the Relevance of Militant Materialism', *Selected Works*, vol. 11, p. 73). In 'Lenin's Moral Dilemmas', the Polish historian Isaac Deutscher discusses what he calls 'the one truly great and crushing moral crisis Lenin ever knew – the crisis at the end of his life.' At the beginning of the twenties, says Deutscher, Lenin began to realise that '[T]he administrative machine he created had little in common with the ideal model of it he had drawn in *State and Revolution*. [. . .] The new administration absorbed much of the old Tsarist bureaucracy [. . .] What was to have been a mere para-state was in fact a super-state. [. . .] He felt alienated from the state of his own making. At a party congress in April 1922, the last congress he attended, he strikingly expressed this sense of alienation. He said that often he had the uncanny sensation which a driver has when he suddenly becomes aware that his vehicle is not moving in the direction in which he steers it. [. . .] He began to succumb to a sense of guilt, and finally he found himself in the throes of a moral crisis, a crisis which was all the more cruel because it aggravated his mortal illness and was aggravated by it. ('The Moral Dilemmas of Lenin', pp. 170–71).

30. Goethe, *Maxims and Reflections*, ¶329.
31. Yeats, 'The Second Coming', from *Michael Robartes and the Dancer*. An analogous problem is discussed by Carlos Drummond de Andrade in 'Reflexões sobre o fanatismo' [Reflections on fanaticism]: 'It's not easy to decide if our age is characterised by an excess or a lack of belief' (*Obras*, p. 828). See also Baudelaire's confessions concerning politics in 'Mon coeur mis à nu': 'I have no convictions, as men of my century understand the world, because I have no ambition. There is no basis in me for a conviction. There is a certain cowardice, a certain weakness, rather, among respectable folk. Only brigands are convinced – of what? That they must succeed. And so they do succeed' (*Intimate Journals*, p. 58).

32. The principle of complementarity was proposed by the Danish physicist Niels Bohr and was created to deal with the apparently contradictory complexity of the world revealed by atomic and sub-atomic physics. Hölderlin's remark is from his novel *Hyperion* (1797); in the context of this work, dreaming is the moment of communion with the natural process of becoming, while reflection is self-consciousness, which fragments, separates and isolates the individual from nature (Hölderlin, *Fragments*, pp. 5–6). The problem of the natural unity, now lost but still dreamed of, in the German Romantic tradition and the intellectual context of that search in post-Kantian philosophy are analysed by Charles Taylor in *Hegel and Modern Society* (Part 1).

4. MORAL PARTIALITY AND HUMAN SOCIABILITY

1. The analysis of the relationship between distance and apparent size in visual perception was originally elaborated by George Berkeley in *An Essay towards a New Theory of Vision* (1709); for a review and critical commentary of this work, see Armstrong, *Berkeley's Theory of Vision*. The parallel between moral, sensory and perceptual partiality made throughout this chapter takes up and develops an analogous comparison made by Adam Smith in *Theory of Moral Sentiments* (pp. 134–39). In the unfinished essay 'Of the External Senses', Smith discusses the illusory distortions of the senses, their spontaneous character and indispensability to biological survival, and the relationship between distance and magnitude in visual experience (*Essays*, pp. 152–53).
2. The hypothalamus is a small organ at the base of the brain, whose principal function is to receive and process information concerning the internal state of the organism, and set in motion the necessary mechanisms to correct its deficiencies

and problems. It is in the nerve-cluster of the hypothalamus, that, for instance, organic shortages of substances like calcium, sodium, potassium and phosphate, and the demands of hormonal production, are registered and processed by the brain, and it is through it that automatic corrective processes are triggered, by means of glandular and muscular actions. Although it weighs no more than about four grams (0.3% of the encephalic mass), the hypothalamus is the organ in the brain that receives and sends most messages. It is presumed that a good part of the intellectual activities of the upper cortex, associated with conscious mental states, serve to moderate the primary impulses and drives determined by the hypothalamus, the central timekeeper of desire (Young, *Philosophy and the Brain*, pp. 178–80; *Oxford Companion to the Mind*, pp. 527–30).

3. Nietzsche, *The Anti-Christ*, ¶39, p. 15. On the same page, he says: '*In fact there have been no Christians at all. The "Christian", that which has been called a Christian for two millennia, is merely a psychological self-misunderstanding.*' The densely ambiguous relationships between Nietzsche, Socrates and Jesus Christ are penetratingly discussed by Michael Tanner in *Nietzsche* (pp. 78–79). The quotation from Machado de Assis is from Chapter CXIX of *Memórias póstumas de Brás Cubas* (translated as *Epitaph of a Small Winner* and *The Posthumous Memoirs of Brás Cubas*).

4. Unamuno, *The Tragic Sense of Life*, p. 90.

5. Erasmus, *The Praise of Folly*, ¶48, p. 143. Menippus was a Greek slave who became an exponent of philosophical cynicism in the third century BC. Although none of his writings have come down to us, he figures as central character and interlocutor in several of Lucian's satirical dialogues, such as the *Dialogue of the Dead* (the dead in Hades look out at the world and uncover the vanities and pretences of the living) and the *Icaromenippus* (Menippus goes up to the gods' celestial dwelling-place on an eagle's wings, and from there denounces the illusions and ambitions of the philosophers). In the rich tradition of radically external views of the human

condition in the history of ideas, we can single out: Bacon, *The Advancement of Learning* (p. 55); Hume 'The Sceptic' (*Essays*, p. 176); James, *Pragmatism* (p. 540); Russell, 'A free man's worship' (*A Free Man's Worship*, pp. 9–19), and Nagel, 'The Absurd' (*Mortal Questions*, pp. 11–23). A place of honour in the gallery of cosmic perspectives on the human animal is reserved for this picture, by the young Nietzsche:

'In some remote corner of the universe, flickering in the light of the countless solar systems into which it had been poured, there was once a planet on which clever animals invented cognition. It was the most arrogant and mendacious minute in the "history of the world"; but a minute was all it was. After nature had drawn just a few more breaths the planet froze and the clever animals had to die. Someone could invent a fable like this and yet they would still not have given a satisfactory illustration of just how pitiful, how insubstantial and transitory, how purposeless and arbitrary the human intellect looks within nature; there were eternities during which it did not exist; and when it has disappeared again, nothing will have happened. For this intellect has no further mission that might extend beyond the bounds of human life. Rather, the intellect is human, and only its own possessor and progenitor regards it with such pathos, as if it housed the axis around which the entire world revolved. But if we could communicate with a midge we would hear that it too floats through the air with the very same pathos, feeling that it too contains within itself the flying centre of this world.' (from 'On Truth and Lying in a Non-Moral Sense', in *The Birth of Tragedy and Other Writings*, p. 141).

6. From the Introduction to *Leviathan*, p. 5.
7. Guimarães Rosa, 'Famigerado'[Famous] (*Primeiras estórias* [The Third Bank of the River and Other Stories] (p. 9). The following comparison between the emotional impact of a tragedy distant from the centre of our emotional life and a lesser mishap closer to us, is based on the similar example (an

earthquake in China v. losing a finger) elaborated by Adam Smith in *Theory of Moral Sentiments* (pp. 136–37); in this important passage, Smith introduces an element of corrective rationality into the exercise of moral judgement which, he says, Hume ignored in his strictly naturalist treatment of the subject in Book 3 ('Of Morals') of *A Treatise of Human Nature*.

8. Hume, *Treatise*, p. 416. For an analysis of the 'Humean guillotine' and the limits Hume attributes to the role of the understanding in the exercise of moral judgement, see: Toulmin, *Reason in Ethics* (pp. 161–67) and Strawson, *Scepticism and Naturalism* (pp. 10–23); see also Chapter 2, note 12. On the evolution of Hume's thought on ethics, from its classical and French origins, see the detailed work of Jones, *Hume's Sentiments*.

9. Machado de Assis, *Dom Casmurro*, Ch. LXVII, p. 128. Another brilliant example of self-deception in Machado's work is the solution of the conflict of conscience brought about by the 'contradictory' actions of giving back a gold coin accidentally found in the street, and secretly appropriating a 'mysterious package' containing a very large sum of money, in *Memórias póstumas de Brás Cubas* (Chapters LI and LII): 'Thus I, Brás Cubas, discovered a sublime law, the Law of the Equivalence of Windows, and established the principle that the way to compensate for a closed window is to open another window, so that the conscience may always have plenty of air' (*Epitaph*, p.106). This modality of self-deception – the Law of the Equivalence of Windows – essentially corresponds to the thesis of the opportunistic adjustment of moral headlights according to the expected cost-benefit defined by circumstances, as in the example of the poem 'Travelling in a Comfortable Car' discussed in Chapter 2, Section 6.

10. In this letter to Lady Ottoline Morrell (27 August 1918), with whom he had a clandestine sexual affair for five years, Russell tells her that he would like to send the message quoted in the text to whoever might write his biography in the future. The passage was used as an epigraph in Caroline Moorehead's

biography of Russell. The opinions, not always flattering, of the philosopher's collaborators and ex-lovers concerning his conduct and character are collected in the chapter dedicated to him by Paul Johnson in *Intellectuals* (pp. 197–224). The curious thing, however, is that in his writings Russell preached something quite different from what, as he recognises, he practised throughout his life: 'I think that in general, apart from expert opinion, there is too much respect paid to the opinions of others, both in great matters and in small ones. One should as a rule respect public opinion in so far as is necessary to avoid starvation and to keep out of prison, but anything that goes beyond this is voluntary submission to an unnecessary tyranny' (*The Conquest of Happiness*, p. 136).

11. Fernando Pessoa, 'O problema da sinceridade do poeta' [The problem of the poet's sincerity] (*Obras em prosa*, p. 269). Nietzsche's aphorism quoted at the beginning of the paragraph is in *Daybreak*, ¶391, p. 173.

12. Butler, quoted in Bambrough, *Moral Scepticism*, pp. 27 and 82. The phrase quoted at the end of the paragraph appears in La Rochefoucauld, *Maxims*, ¶218, p. 65.

13. The fable of the ring that provides invisibility, found by the shepherd who became king by usurping the throne of Lydia, is recounted and discussed by Plato in the *Republic* (359–600). Reflections on the Platonic fable appear in: Cicero, *On Duties*, pp. 113–15; La Rochefoucauld, *Maxims*, ¶216, p. 65, and Hollis, *Invitation to Philosophy*, pp. 122–37. It is curious to note that the first organised lottery we know of, instituted in England by Queen Elizabeth in 1569, offered the winner, as well as the money prize, the benefit of complete immunity from imprisonment for a period of seven days, excepting major felonies (see Brenner and Brenner, *Gambling and Speculation*, p. 10). The effects of a sudden, generalised impunity are discussed in my *Vícios privados* (pp. 77–78). The fragment of Democritus (62) quoted in the text is discussed by Toulmin, *Reason in Ethics* (pp. 169–70).

14. Knight, quoted in Stigler, *Memoirs*, p. 23. A similar conclusion is defended by La Mettrie: 'I would say about truth in general

what M. de Fontenelle said about some truths in particular, namely that it must be sacrificed to suit society' (*Machine Man*, pp. 16–17). The conjecture of the transparency shock is an adaptation of analogous suggestions in Erasmus, *The Praise of Folly* (¶¶19–22, pp. 90–95) and Russell, *The Conquest of Happiness* (p. 114). The extension of the practice of social dissimulation nowadays can be evaluated by an enquiry on genetic paternity carried out in the 1990s by researchers at the University of Liverpool: one out of every five babies born in Liverpool was *not* conceived by the man who thought he was the father of the child ('Doing what Comes Naturally', *The Economist*, 5 January 1996, p. 103).
15. Carlyle, 'Chartism' (*Selected Writings*, p. 155). A diametrically opposed view is suggested by Baudelaire: 'The world only goes round by misunderstanding. It is by universal misunderstanding that all agree. For if, by ill luck, people understood each other, they would never agree' (*Intimate Journals*, p. 89).
16. Lecky, *History of European Morals*, vol. 1, p. 251. Isabel of Castile and her husband, Fernando of Aragon, were the main architects of the establishment of the Spanish Inquisition at the end of the fifteenth century and of the policy of racial persecution – 'limpieza de sangre' – that led to the expulsion of about 165,000 Jews and 275,000 *moriscos* from the Iberian peninsula. King Philip II, the absolute monarch of the vast and powerful Spanish empire in the second half of the sixteenth century, was famous for his coldness and the implacable determination with which he pursued his aims, rid himself of allies and eliminated enemies (even by false accusations of heresy and the cruel persecution of non-Catholics), always justifying his crimes and his unquestioning support for the Inquisition's bureaucratic machine with elaborate theological pretexts and the reasons of state of the Kingdom of God. Characterised by an unbounded zeal and an ascetic temperament, Philip II used to spend hours on end kneeling before Catholic saints and relics (see Kamen, *The Spanish Inquisition*, esp. p. 146, and Grimm, *The Reformation Era*, esp. p. 22) .

17. The subjective experience of the individual in front of a mirror, and the natural difficulty of dealing with one's own reflected image are penetratingly dealt with by Guimarães Rosa in 'O espelho' [The mirror] (*Primeiras estórias* [*The Third Bank of the River and Other Stories*] pp. 71–78). The observation on the neurology of tickling is based on the experimental research of the physicist Rodney Cotterill, of the Danish Technical University, on the relationships between self-awareness and voluntary muscular movement. As you extend your hand to pick up a glass, for example, three distinct and almost simultaneous flows of information are processed: *a) afference* (messages from the eyes and fingers to the brain); *b) efference* (messages from the brain to the fingers and eyes), and *c) copy of the efference* (messages disseminated through the brain informing and alerting the other receptive sensory areas of what the muscles are about to do and/or are doing). The copy of the efference is the one responsible for the co-ordination of the individual's actions, and it is because of it, it appears, that the attempt to tickle oneself fails ('Conscious machines', *The Economist*, 6 April 1996, p. 88).

18. The passage that probably inspired the proverb says: 'Both oligarchs and democrats have a hold on a sort of conception of justice; but they both fail to carry it far enough, and neither of them expresses the true conception of justice in the whole of its range. [. . .] The reason is that they are judging *in their own cause*; and most men, as a rule, are bad judges where their own interests are involved' (Aristotle, *Politics*, 1280 ª 15). The usual version, as can be seen, generalises and extends to *all* what Aristotle says of the *majority* of men.

19. La Rochefoucauld, *Maxims*, ¶567, p. 115. The research on American drivers' self-image is discussed by Rue, *By the Grace of Guile* (p. 161). Another example of asymmetry between the perception of oneself and of others is pointed out by the Epicurean poet Lucretius: 'And one man laughs at another, and urges him to appease Venus, since he is wallowing in a base passion, yet often, poor wretch, he cannot see his own

275

ills, far greater than the rest' (*De Rerum Natura*, Book 4, ll. 1155–59).

20. Smith, *Theory of Moral Sentiments*, p. 133. The lines quoted in this paragraph come from the poems of Álvaro de Campos (Fernando Pessoa, *Obra poética*, pp. 365 and 372).

21. Johnson, *Lives of the English Poets*, vol. 2, p. 207. Thucydides' account of the Athenian plague and Diderot's of the European adventure in the colonial tropics (see pp.220–21 and notes 36 and 37) give practical illustrations of this type of self-deception. The general principle is well formulated by the poet Lucretius: 'It is more fitting to watch a man in doubt and danger, and to learn of what manner he is in adversity; for then at last a real cry is wrung from the bottom of his heart: the mask is torn off, and the truth remains behind' (*De Rerum Natura*, Book 3, lines 54–57). On the same lines, Bacon says in 'Of Adversity': 'Prosperity doth best discover vice, but Adversity doth best discover virtue' (*Essays*, p. 14). On the effects of the intoxication produced by prosperity, and the revelatory shock of adversity in Bacon's own career, see Chapter 3, note 4.

22. Machiavelli, *The Prince*, pp. 36 and 56. The same principle applies to those governed. Consider, for example, the question of choice between *supporting*, *keeping quiet about*, or *resisting* an oppressive regime that comes to power. The integrity test usually brings surprising results, as the frank testimony of Jürgen Habermas, the Frankfurt school philosopher, shows: 'Historically, it is a fact that the logical positivists, and the juridical positivists [. . .] always kept their political integrity. In part they were Jews who were forced to emigrate, but they were already democrats before they were stigmatised as "enemies" by the Nazis [. . .] While, on the other hand, the Hegelians – and I say this against my own tradition – in great part became Nazi-supporters. The whole Kiel Law School [. . .] was Hegelian. It has to be recognised that there is in empiricism and positivism an element of rationality, that from our point of view may be insufficient, but that, at least at that time, probably immunised their supporters against

Nazism more effectively than, for example, the Hegelians [. . .] the Hegelians were always more vulnerable' (interview with Barbara Freitag and Sergio Paulo Rouanet, *Folha de São Paulo*, 30 April 1995, p. 6).

23. Darwin's oscillations concerning the importance of priority and his confession of self-deception, in a letter to his collaborator and confidant Joseph Hooker, were pointed out by Wright in *The Moral Animal* (p. 308). Darwin's preoccupation with the problem of self-deception in scientific research stands out clearly in his 'golden rule' discussed in Chapter 2 (p. 108). It is interesting to note that, introducing his *Autobiography*, Darwin says that he tried to write about his own life with the same distance as a dead man looking at his own past from the other world (echoes of Lucian: see note 5), and that his advanced age had made the task easier. However, judging by his change of attitude on the question of priority, it seems that Darwin's memory suppressed from conscious attention the critical experience he lived through when his life's work was almost eclipsed by Wallace's discovery.

24. A tough and conflict-ridden process of negotiation normally ends with each of the parties feeling they have the right to 'conjugate' their own verbs concerning the other: 'I am firm, you are stubborn, he is intractable; we are persistent, you are intransigent, they are pig-headed' (adapted from an analogous series suggested by Flew, *Thinking about Thinking*, p. 79).

25. More, *Utopia*, p. 6. On our natural propensity to distort the ideas of those we disagree with, or with whom we are in competition, see Nietzsche, *Daybreak* (¶431, p. 185), and Wright, *The Moral Animal* (p. 269). In the second part of *Beliefs in Action*, I tried to analyse the phenomenon of 'information entropy' in intellectual exchanges, and to classify the principal modalities of misunderstanding in the history of ideas.

26. Smith, *Theory of Moral Sentiments*, p. 155. Nietzsche, *The Anti-Christ* ¶55, p. 173. On Smith's definition of the politician – 'that insidious and crafty animal, vulgarly called a statesman or politician, whose councils are directed by the momentary

fluctuations of affairs' (*Wealth of Nations*, vol. 1, p. 468) – , and his attitude to the political scene of his time, see the excellent study by Donald Winch, *Adam Smith's Politics*.

27. Carlos Drummond de Andrade, 'Anedota búlgara' ['Bulgarian Anecdote'] (*Obras*, p. 71).

28. Novalis, 'Fragmentblatt' (*Pólen*, p. 61). The origins of the notion of the human individual as a complex and sometimes contradictory whole go back to a fragment of Democritus: 'Man, a microcosm' (34). In his magnificent interpretation of the conflict between the brothers Prometheus (in Greek: 'he who thinks before he acts') and Epimetheus ('he who acts before he thinks') in ancient mythology, Bacon elaborates the idea of man as a 'microcosm, or little world in himself' (*Essays*, p. 249). The theme also appears in Montaigne: 'We are entirely made up of bits and pieces, woven together so diversely and so shapelessly that each one of them pulls its own way at every moment. And there is as much difference between us and ourselves as there is between us and other people' (*Essays*, p. 380). Bismarck, for all he unified the German nation, apparently did not have the same success with his own mind: 'Faust complained that he had two souls in his breast. I have a whole squabbling crowd. It goes on as in a republic' (quoted in Elster, *The Multiple Self*, p. 197).

29. The examples of intertemporal anomalies given in this and the preceding paragraphs are adapted from Colin Price, *Time, Discounting and Value*, pp. 99–107. For a discussion of human impatience in the perception of time and the attribution of value, see the classic work of Irving Fisher, *Theory of Interest*.

30. Valéry, 'Remarks on Intelligence' (*Collected Works*, vol. 10, p. 157).

31. Hume, *Treatise*, p. 538.

32. Lucan (a Roman poet of the first century AD), *Pharsalia*, Book 1, l. 499. The examples listed in this paragraph were taken from the following sources: Levi, *The Drowned and the Saved*, p. 29; de Quincey, *Confessions*, p. 20; Gay, *Freud*,

p. 390 and Elster, *Ulysses and the Sirens*, p. 38. The problem of lack of self-control or of weakness of will (*akrasía*) in ordinary life was a central theme in Greek moral and psychological reflection (see A.W. Price, *Mental Conflict*); for an analysis of the problem from an intertemporal perspective, see Ainslie, *Picoeconomics*.

33. James, 'The Will' (*Selected Papers*, p. 72). The putting-off of tasks is another notable example, as Baudelaire shows: 'The devil, in spite of all my good resolutions, slinks every morning into my mind in the shape of this thought: "Why not rest for the moment in forgetfulness of all these things? This evening, at one fell swoop, I'll accomplish all the most urgent business." Then evening comes, and my mind reels at the sight of the multitude of things left undone; overwhelming depression induces incapacity, and then, the following day, the same old comedy starts off once more, with the same hopes and the same illusions' (letter of 19 February 1858, quoted in Starkie, *Baudelaire*, p. 536). Augustine's prayer is in *Confessions* (Book 8, ¶7, p. 169); as he explains in the next sentence, addressing himself to God: 'For I was afraid that you would answer my prayer at once and cure me too soon of the disease of lust, which I wanted satisfied, not quelled.' For an economic analysis of procrastination, see Akerlof, 'Procrastination and Obedience'.

34. 'Trabalhas sem alegria para um mundo caduco', Carlos Drummond de Andrade, 'Elegia 1938', from *Sentimento do mundo* (*Obra*, p. 115).

35. The central argument developed in this section, linking the propensity for self-deception and the necessity for impersonal rules, takes up and elaborates the points broached by Adam Smith in his *Theory of Moral Sentiments* (Part 3, Chapter 4). The parallel between language and moral codes is based on Plato, *Protagoras* (323 *a* – 328 *d*), and Quine, 'On the Nature of Moral Values' (pp. 61–62).

36. It should perhaps be made clear that the analysis of the *function* of rules should not be confused with the explanation of their *origin*. When a rabbit is seized by a predator, it lets

out a cry that alerts its companions and makes them run; the cause of the cry, however, is not the fact that it serves as an alarm. In the same manner, human beings have never had to know about the biological function of sex in reproduction to practise it. Attributing the role of cause to the function is to fall into the *functionalist fallacy*. The process that brings a given rule into being is different from the function and usefulness it may have in social interaction. The cause is the mother; the function the daughter. The whole discussion here is limited, of course, to the analysis of *one* of the basic functions of rules: the neutralisation of the effects of moral partiality in human social existence.

37. Thucydides, Book 2, ¶53, p. 128. The problem of moral regression in the Greek world is discussed by Dodds in *The Greeks and the Irrational* (pp. 179–95). On the passage quoted in the text, see also: Hume, 'The Sceptic' (*Essays*, p. 177), and the poetic reconstruction presented by Lucretius at the end of *De Rerum Natura* (Book 6, ll. 1138–286).

38. Diderot, 'Extracts from *Histoire des Deux Indes*' (*Political Writings*, p. 178). On the Latin maxim quoted in the text and its original, the Brazilian historian Sérgio Buarque de Holanda says: 'In the sixteenth century, the belief that beyond the Equator sin did not exist – *Ultra aequinoxialem non peccari* – was current in Europe. Barlaeus, who mentions the saying, comments on it, saying: 'As if the line which divides the world in two hemispheres also separated virtue from vice' (*Raízes do Brasil* [The Roots of Brazil], p. 198, note 40). Diderot's picture can be enriched by the stories and analyses presented by Buarque de Holanda and Paulo Prado on Brazil's cultural formation. 'It's possible to accompany all through our history', Buarque de Holanda says, 'the constant predominance of individual desires that find their ideal environment in closed circles, barely open to an impersonal ordering [. . .] Each individual [. . .] affirms himself in relation to his fellows, indifferent to the general rules, wherever these laws are opposed to his emotional urges, and gives attention merely to what distinguishes him from others [. . .] the individual

will almost never allow himself to be ordered about by a demanding, disciplinarian system' (*Raízes do Brasil*, pp. 146 and 155). A similar picture, though painted in stronger colours, emerges from Paulo Prado's *Retrato do Brasil*: 'In these pages we have suggested the deep mark left on the national psyche by the excesses of lust and greed [. . .] These influences developed in the licentious context of the most anarchic and disordered individualism, extending from the isolated, free existence of the colonist that landed on these shores, to the egotistical maunderings of poets suffering from unrequited love. [. . .] *Ubi bene, ibi patria* [Wherever one is happy, there is one's country], says our profound indifference [for communal life] [. . .] sporadic explosions of reaction and enthusiasm only serve to underline the day-to-day apathy' (pp. 195–96).

39. Machiavelli, *The Prince*, p. 52.

40. The role of interpersonal confidence in socio-economic life is analysed from an interdisciplinary point of view (biological, anthropological, economic, political, and ethical) in the collection *Trust*, organised by Diego Gambetta. On this point, it is worth recalling, also, the observation of the German sociologist Georg Simmel: 'In a richer and larger cultural life, [. . .] existence rests on a thousand premises which the single individual cannot trace and verify to their roots at all, but must be taken on faith. Our modern life is based to a much larger extent than is usually realised upon faith in the honesty of the other' (quoted in Rue, *By the Grace of Guile*, p. 154). The financial economist Harry Markowitz adds: 'Laws and law enforcement are needed to assure me that the meal I buy is not poisoned and the airplane I fly on is well maintained; that those who manufacture things for my use pay their full costs, including the costs of cleaning up the mess they make; that if I deposit money with a bank or pay an insurance premium to an insurance company the banker or insurer will not go to Las Vegas to gamble with my money' ('Markets and Morality', *Wall Street Journal*, 14 May 1992. p. A22).

41. Solon, quoted in Plutarch, 'Solon' (*Lives*, vol. 1, p. 142).

Solon's concern with the legitimacy of laws appears clearly in two of his replies, reproduced by Plutarch: 'And when he was afterwards asked if he had left the Athenians the best laws that could be given, he replied, "The best they could receive." [. . .] being asked what city was best modelled, "That", said he, "where those that are not injured try and punish the unjust as much as those that are"' (*Lives*, vol. 1, pp. 130 and 133). When he had completed his constitutional work, Solon, courted by everyone, preferred to leave Athens for a long voluntary exile, saying that the application of the laws was not his responsibility, but that of the citizens of Athens (see Zoja, *Growth and Guilt*, p. 58). On Solon, see also Chapter 1, note 40, and Chapter 2, note 14.

42. The proverb was attributed to St. Bernard by St. Francis de Sales: 'The proverb taken from our St. Bernard, "Hell is full of good intentions and desires"' (Letter 74). It's possible that its origin may be related to the debacle of the Second Crusade, the principal failure in St. Bernard's life: 'Zeal without knowledge', he points out, 'is always less useful and effective than regulated zeal, and very often it is highly dangerous' (see *Oxford Dictionary of Saints*, pp. 44–45).

BIBLIOGRAPHY

Ainslie, G. 'Beyond Microeconomics: Conflict among Interests in a Multiple Self as a Determinant of Value'. In J. Elster, ed., *Multiple Self*. Cambridge: Cambridge U.P., 1986.

——. *Picoeconomics*. Cambridge: Cambridge U.P., 1992.

Akerlof, G. A. 'Procrastination and Obedience'. *American Economic Review* 81 (1991), 1–19.

Amann, P. *Paul Gauguin*. San Diego, 1990.

Aristotle, *Politics*. Tr. E. Baker. Oxford: Oxford U.P., 1946.

——. *Historia animalium*. Tr. D. Ross. Oxford: Oxford U.P., 1980.

Armstrong, D. M. *Berkeley's Theory of Vision*. Melbourne: Parkville, 1960.

Arrow, K. *The Limits of Organization*. New York: Norton, 1974.

——. 'I Know a Hawk from a Handsaw'. In M. Szenberg, ed., *Eminent Economists*. Cambridge: Cambridge U.P., 1992.

Augustine, St. *Confessions*. Tr. R.S. Pine-Coffin. Harmondsworth: Penguin, 1961.

Machado de Assis, Joaquim Maria, *Dom Casmurro*. Tr. John Gledson. New York: Oxford University Press, 1998.

Epitaph of a Small Winner (Memórias póstumas de Brás Cubas). Tr. William Grossman. London: Bloomsbury, 1997.

283

Bacon, F. 'The Wisdom of the Ancients'. In *Essays*. London: Henry G. Bohn, 1854.
——. *Novum organum*. Ed. T. Fowler. Oxford: Clarendon Press, 1889.
——. 'Of Great Place' and 'Of Adversity'. In *Essays*. London: Collins, 1913.
——. 'Cogitata et visa'. In B. Farrington, ed., *The Philosophy of Francis Bacon*. Liverpool: Liverpool U.P., 1964.
——. *The advancement of learning*. Ed. A. Johnston. Oxford: Clarendon Press, 1974.
Bailey, C. *Epicurus: The Extant Remains*. Oxford: Clarendon Press, 1926.
——. *The Greek Atomists and Epicurus*. Oxford: Clarendon Press, 1928.
Bambrough, J. R. *Moral Scepticism and Moral Knowledge*. London: Routledge and Kegan Paul, 1979.
Baudelaire, C. *Intimate Journals*. Tr. C. Isherwood. San Francisco: City Lights Books, 1983.
——. *The Poems in Prose*. Tr. Francis Scarfe. London: Anvil Press Poetry, 1989.
Bernstein, P. *Against the Gods*. Oxford: Wiley, 1996.
Billig, M. *Arguing and Thinking*. Cambridge: Cambridge U.P., 1987.
Blake, W. *The Complete Poems*. Ed. A. Ostriker. Harmondsworth: Penguin, 1977.
Bok, S. *Lying*. New York: Pantheon, 1978.
——. *Secrets*. Oxford: Oxford U.P., 1984.
Borges, J. L. *Elogio de la sombra*. In *Obra poética*. Buenos Aires/Madrid: Alianza/Emecé, 1975.
Brenner, R. and Brenner, G.A. *Gambling and Speculation*. Cambridge: Cambridge U.P., 1987.
Broad, C.D. *The Philosophy of Francis Bacon*. Cambridge: Cambridge U.P., 1926.
Buarque de Holanda, S. *Raízes do Brasil*. São Paulo: Companhia das Letras, 1995.
Buchanan, J. and Burton, J. R. *The Consequences of Mr Keynes*. London: I.E.A., 1978.

BIBLIOGRAPHY

Burnet, J. *Early Greek Philosophy*. London: A. and C. Black, 1930.

Burtt, E. A. *The Metaphysical Foundations of Modern Science*. London: Kegan Paul, 1932.

Butler, J. 'Upon Self-deceit' and 'Upon Forgiveness of Injuries'. In *The Analogy of Religion*. London: Everyman, 1889.

Cahn, S. M. *Fate, Logic and Time*. New Haven: Yale U.P., 1967.

Carlyle, T. 'Chartism'. In *Selected Writings*. Ed. A. Shelston. Harmondsworth: Penguin, 1971.

Castro, R. O *anjo pornográfico*. São Paulo: Companhia das Letras, 1992.

Charlton, W. *Weakness of Will*. Oxford: Blackwell, 1988.

Churchland, P. *Matter and Consciousness*. Cambridge, Mass.: MIT Press, 1986.

Cicero. *On Duties*. Tr. M. Griffin and E. Atkins. Cambridge: Cambridge U.P., 1991.

Cícero, A. *O mundo desde o fim*. Rio de Janeiro: Francisco Alves, 1995.

Citati, P. *Goethe*. São Paulo: Companhia das Letras, 1996.

Clark, S. *The Moral Status of Animals*. Oxford: Clarendon Press, 1984.

Cornford, F. M. *Before and After Socrates*. Cambridge: Cambridge U.P., 1932.

———. *Principium sapentiae*. Cambridge: Cambridge U.P., 1952.

———. *Plato's Theory of Knowledge*. London: Routledge and Kegan Paul, 1960.

Cranston, M. *John Locke*. Oxford: Oxford U.P., 1985.

Curtius, E. R. *European Literature and the Latin Middle Ages*. Tr. W. R. Trask. New York: Pantheon, 1953.

Damasio, A. R. *Descartes' Error: Emotion, Reason and the Human Brain*. London: Picador, 1995.

Darwin, C. *Life and Letters*. Ed. F. Darwin. London: Murray, 1887.

———. *Autobiography*. Ed. N. Barlow. London: Collins, 1958.

———. *On the Origin of Species*. Ed. E. Mayr. Cambridge, Mass., 1964.

———. *Early Writings*. Ed. P. H. Barret. Chicago: Chicago U.P., 1974.

Dawkins, R., 'Universal Darwinism'. In D. S. Bendall, ed., *Evolution from Molecules to Men*. Cambridge: Cambridge U.P., 1983.

Dent, N. J. H. *A Rousseau Dictionary*. Oxford: Blackwell, 1992.

Descartes, R. *Philosophical Works*. Tr. E. S. Haldane and G. Ross. Cambridge: Cambridge U. P., 1931. vol. 1.

——. *Philosophical Letters*. Tr. A. Kenny. Oxford: Blackwell, 1970.

——. *Meditations on First Philosophy*. Tr. J. Cottingham. Cambridge: Cambridge U.P., 1986.

Deutscher, I. 'The Moral Dilemmas of Lenin'. London: Oxford U.P., 1966.

Diderot, D. *Political Writings*. Tr. J. H. Mason and R. Wokler. Cambridge: Cambridge U.P., 1992.

——. *Selected Writings on Art and Literature*. Tr. G. Bremner. Harmondsworth: Penguin, 1994.

Dijksterhuis, E. J. *The Mechanization of the World Picture*. Tr. C. Dikshoorn. Princeton: Princeton U.P., 1986.

Diogenes Laertius. 'Pyrrho' and 'Democritus'. In *Lives of Eminent Philosophers*. Tr. R.D. Hicks. London/ New York: Loeb, 1925, vol. 2.

Dodds, E. R. *The Greeks and the Irrational*. Berkeley: California U.P., 1951.

Dostoevsky, F. M. *Notes from the Underground*. Tr. J. Coulson. Harmondsworth: Penguin, 1972.

——. *The Diary of a Writer*. Tr. B. Brasol. Surrey: Haslemere, 1984.

Drummond de Andrade, C. *Obras completas*. Rio de Janeiro: Aguilar, 1977.

——. *A paixão medida*. Rio de Janeiro: José Olympio, 1980.

Elster, J. *Sour Grapes*. Cambridge: Cambridge U.P., 1983.

——. *Ulysses and the Sirens*. Cambridge: Cambridge U.P., 1984.

——. ed. *The Multiple Self*. Cambridge: Cambridge U.P., 1986.

——. *The Cement of Society*. Cambridge: Cambridge U.P., 1989.

Emerson, R. W. 'Nature'. In *Complete Works*. Ed. A. C. Hern. Edinburgh: Waverly, 1907.

Epictetus. 'Encheiridion'. In *Epictetus*. Tr. W. A. Oldfather. Cambridge, Mass., 1978, vol. 2.

Erasmus, Desiderius. *The Praise of Folly*. Tr. Betty Radice. Harmondsworth: Penguin, 1971.

Euripides. *Bacchae*. Tr. E. R. Dodds. Oxford: Clarendon Press, 1960.

——. *Medea*. Tr. Rex Warner. In *Complete Plays*. vol. 1. Chicago: Chicago U.P., 1959.

Farrington, B. *Francis Bacon*. London, 1951.

Ferguson, A. *An Essay on the History of Civil Society*. Ed. D. Forbes. Edinburgh: Edinburgh U.P., 1966.

Fest, J. C. *The Face of the Third Reich*. Tr. M. Bullock. Harmondsworth: Penguin, 1979.

Findlay, J. N. *Hegel: a Re-examination*. London: Allen and Unwin, 1958.

Fingarette, H. *Self-deception*. London: Routledge and Kegan Paul, 1969.

Fisher, I. *The Theory of Interest*. New York: Kelley, 1930.

Flew, A. *Thinking about Thinking*. London: Fontana, 1975.

Fontenelle, B. le B. de. *Nouveaux dialogues des morts*. Ed. J. Dagen. Paris: Librairie Marcel Didier, 1971.

Freud, S. 'Creative Writers and Day-Dreaming', *Standard Edition*, vol. 9. London: Hogarth Press, 1959.

Furbank, P. N. *Diderot*. London: Secker and Warburg, 1992.

Gambetta, D., ed. *Trust: Making and Breaking Cooperative Relations*. Oxford: Blackwell, 1988.

Gaukroger, S. *Descartes*. Oxford: Clarendon Press, 1995.

Gay, P. *Freud*. New York: Doubleday, 1989.

Gellner, E. *Legitimation of Belief* Cambridge: Cambridge U.P., 1974.

Giannetti da Fonseca, E. 'Comportamento individual: alternativas ao homem econômico'.*Estudos Econômicos* 20 (1990) 5–37.

——. *Beliefs in Action*. Cambridge: Cambridge U.P., 1991.

——. *Vícios provados, benefícios públicos?* São Paulo: Companhia das Letras, 1993.

Glacken, C. J. *Traces on the Rhodian Shore*. Berkeley: California U.P., 1967.

Goethe. J.W. von. *Faust. Part Two*. Tr. Philip Wayne. Harmondsworth: Penguin, 1981.

——. *Maximen und Reflexionen* [*Maxims and Reflections*], Weimar, 1907.

——. *The Autobiography of Goethe* [*Dichtung und Wahrheit*]. Tr. John Oxenford. London: Sidgwick and Jackson, 1971.

Grimm, H. J. *The Reformation Era*: 1500–1650. New York, 1965.

Gruber, H. E. *Darwin on Man*. Chicago: Chicago U.P., 1981.

Guthrie, W. K. C. *The Sophists*. Cambridge: Cambridge U.P., 1971.

——. *Socrates*. Cambridge: Cambridge U.P., 1971.

Habermas, J. 'A história negativa' (interview given to Barbara Freitag and Sergio Paulo Rouanet). In *Folha de São Paulo*, 30 April 1995. pp. 5–7.

Hamburger, M. 'Brecht and his Successors'. In *Art as Second Nature*. Manchester: Carcanet, 1979.

Hayman, R. *Nietzsche: a Critical Life*. London: Weidenfeld and Nicolson, 1980.

Hegel, G. W. F. *The Philosophy of History*. Tr. J. Sibree. New York: Dover, 1956.

——. 'The Preface to the *Phenomenology*'. In *Hegel*. Ed. W. Kauffmann. New York: Doubleday, 1966.

——. *The Philosophy of Nature*. Tr. M. J. Petry. London: Allen and Unwin, 1969.

Hirschman, A.O. *The Rhetoric of Reaction*. Cambridge, Mass.: Harvard U.P., 1991.

——. *A Propensity to Self-Subversion*. Cambridge, Mass.: Harvard U.P., 1995.

Hobbes. T. *Leviathan*. Ed. M. Oakeshott. Oxford: Blackwell, 1955.

——. 'De Cive'. In *Man and Citizen* (Tr. Thomas Hobbes) Ed. Bernard Gert. Gloucester, Mass.: Peter Smith, 1978.

Hölderlin, F. *Poems and Fragments*. Tr. M. Hamburger. Cambridge: Cambridge U.P., 1980.

Hollingdale, R. J. *Nietzsche*. London: Routledge and Kegan Paul, 1985.

Hollis, M. *Invitation to Philosophy*. Oxford: Blackwell, 1985.

Horace, Q. *Satires and Epistles*. Tr. N. Rudd. Harmondsworth: Penguin, 1979.

Hume, D. *An Enquiry concerning Human Understanding* [First] and *An Enquiry concerning the Principles of Morals* [Second]. Ed. L. A. Selby-Bigge. Oxford: Clarendon Press, 1975.

———. *Dialogues concerning Natural Religion.* Ed. J. V. Price. Oxford: Clarendon Press, 1976.

———. *A Treatise of Human Nature.* Ed. L. A. Selby-Bigge. Oxford: Clarendon Press, 1978.

———. *The History of England.* Ed. W. B. Todd. Indianapolis: Liberty Fund, 1983, vol. 6.

———. *Essays Moral, Political and Literary.* Ed. E. F. Miller. Indianapolis: Liberty Fund, 1985.

Huxley, T. H. 'The *Origin of Species*'. In *Darwiniana*. London: Macmillan, 1899, vol. 2.

Jacob, F. *La Logique du vivant.* Paris: Gallimard, 1970.

James, W. *The Varieties of Religious Experience.* New York: Longmans, 1916.

———. 'The will'. In *Selected Papers on Philosophy*. London: Everyman, 1975.

———. *Pragmatism.* Cambridge, Mass.: Harvard U.P., 1975.

Johnson, P. *Intellectuals.* London: Wiedenfeld and Nicolson, 1988.

Johnson, S. *Lives of the English Poets.* London: Dent, 1925, vol. 2.

Jones, E. *The Life and Work of Sigmund Freud.* New York: Basic Books, 1955, vol. 2.

Jones, P. *Hume's Sentiments.* Edinburgh: Edinburgh U.P., 1982.

Kamen, H. *The Spanish Inquisition.* London: Weidenfeld and Nicolson, 1965.

Kaufmann, W. *Hegel.* New York: Doubleday, 1966.

Keynes, J. M. *The General Theory of Employment, Interest and Money.* London: Macmillan, 1973.

———. *Collected Writings.* Ed. D. E. Moggridge. London: Macmillan, 1971–82.

Knight, F. H. 'Freedom as Fact and Criterion'. In *Freedom and Reform*, New York: Harper, 1982.

Koestler, A. *The Act of Creation.* London: Hutchinson, 1964.

Kolakowski, L. *Main Currents of Marxism.* Oxford: Clarendon Press, 1978.

LIES WE LIVE BY

Krebs, J. R. and Dawkins, R. 'Animal Signals: mind reading and manipulation'. In *Behavioural ecology*. Eds. J. R. Krebs and N. B. Davies. Oxford: Clarendon Press, 1984.

Krugman, P. *Peddling Prosperity*. New York: Norton, 1994.

Kuhn, T. S. 'Logic of Discovery or Psychology of Research' and 'Mathematical versus Experimental Traditions in the Development of Physical Science'. In *The Essential Tension*. Chicago: Chicago U.P., 1977.

Lafargue, P. 'Reminiscences of Marx'. In *Reminiscences of Marx and Engels*. Moscow: Foreign Language Publishing House, 1959.

La Mettrie, J. O. de. *Man Machine*. Tr. Ann Thomson. Cambridge: Cambridge U.P., 1996.

Lange, F. A. *The History of Materialism*. Tr. E. C. Thomas. London: Kegan Paul, 1925.

Laplace, P. S. de. *A Philosophical Essay on Probabilities*. Tr. E. Bell. New York: Dover, 1951.

Larmore, F. 'Descartes' Empirical Epistemology'. In *Descartes: Philosophy, Mathematics and Physics*. Ed. S. Gaukroger. Brighton: Harvester 1980.

La Rochefoucauld, Duc de. *Maxims*. Tr. L. Tancock. Harmondsworth: Penguin, 1967.

Larson, J. L. *Reason and Experience*. Berkeley: California U.P., 1971.

Lautréamont [Isidore Ducasse]. *Poésies*. Tr. A. Lykiard. London: Allison and Busby, 1978.

Lecky, W. E. H. *History of European Morals*. London: Longmans, 1890, vol.1.

Lenin, V. I. *Selected Works*. New York, s. d., vols. 3 and 11.

——. *Collected Works*. London: Lawrence and Wishart, 1957–61, vols.31 and 38.

Levi, P. *The Drowned and the Saved*. Tr. R. Rosenthal. London: Abacus, 1989.

Lewis, C. S. *Studies in Words*. Cambridge: Cambridge U.P., 1967.

Lloyd, G. E. R. *Early Greek Science*. London: Chatto and Windus, 1970.

290

Locke, J. *An Essay concerning Human Understanding*. Ed. P. Nidditch. Oxford: Clarendon Press, 1975.

Lovejoy, A. O. *Primitivism and Related Ideas in Antiquity*. Baltimore: Johns Hopkins U.P., 1935.

———. *The Great Chain of Being*. Cambridge, Mass.: Harvard U.P., 1964.

Lucian of Samosata. *Dialogue of the Dead*. Tr. H.W. Fowler and I.G. Fowler, Oxford, 1905.

Lucretius. *De rerum natura*. Tr. C. Bailey. Oxford: Oxford Library of Translation, 1910.

Lukács, G. *The Young Hegel*. Tr. R. Livingstone. London: Merlin Press, 1975.

Macaulay, T. B. 'Lord Bacon'. In *Essays*. London: Longmans, 1920.

Macdonell, J. *A Survey of Political Economy*. Edinburgh: Edmonston and Douglas, 1871.

Machiavelli, N. *The Prince*. Tr. N. H. Thomson. Oxford: Oxford Library of Translation, 1913.

Malcolm, N. *Ludwig Wittgenstein*. Oxford: Oxford U.P., 1984.

Malebranche, N. *The Search after Truth*. Tr. T. Lennon and P. Olscamp. Columbus: Ohio State U.P., 1980.

Mandeville, B. de. *The Fable of the Bees*. Ed. F. B. Kaye. Oxford: Clarendon Press, 1924.

Manser, A. 'Pain and Private Language'. In *Studies in the Philosophy of Wittgenstein*. Ed. P. Winch. London: Routledge and Kegan Paul, 1969.

Marcus Aurelius. *Meditations*. Tr. M. Stanniforth. Harmondsworth: Penguin, 1964.

Marshall, A. *Industry and Trade*. London: Macmillan, 1919.

———. *Principles of Economics*. London: Macmillan, 1949.

Marx, K. *Early Writings*. Tr. R. Livingstone and G. Benton. London: Penguin/New Left Review, 1975.

Masson, J. and McCarthy, S. *When Elephants Weep*. London: Vintage, 1996.

Matos, M. *Machado de Assis*. São Paulo: Editora Nacional, 1939.

McLellan, D. *Marxism after Marx*. London: Macmillan, 1979.

Mill, J. S. 'Nature'. In *Collected Works*. Ed. J. M. Robson. Toronto: Toronto U.P., 1978.

Monk, R. *Wittgenstein*. London: Cape, 1990.

Montaigne, M. de. *The Complete Essays*. Tr. M. A. Screech. Harmondsworth: Penguin, 1991.

——. *The Essayes*. Tr. John Florio. London: Routledge and Sons, 1885.

Moore, G. E. 'A Defence of Common Sense' and 'Certainty'. In *Selected writings*. Ed. T. Baldwin. London: Routledge, 1993.

Moorehead, C. *Bertrand Russell*. London: Sinclair-Stevenson, 1992.

More, T. *Utopia*. Ed. G. M. Logan and R. M. Adams. Cambridge: Cambridge U.P., 1989.

Murdoch, I. *The Sovereignty of Good*. London: Routledge and Kegan Paul, 1970.

Nagel, T. 'What is like to be a Bat?' and 'The Absurd'. In *Mortal Questions*. Cambridge: Cambridge U.P., 1979.

——. *The View from Nowhere*. New York: Oxford U.P., 1986.

——. *What does it all Mean?* New York: Oxford U.P., 1987.

——. 'Moral luck' and 'Williams: One Thought too Many'. In *Other minds*. Oxford, 1995.

Nietzsche, F. *The Anti-Christ*. Tr. R. J. Hollingdale. Harmondsworth: Penguin, 1968.

——. *On the Genealogy of Morals and Ecce Homo*. Tr. W. Kaufmann and R. J. Hollingdale. New York: Vintage, 1969.

——. *The Gay Science*. Tr. W. Kaufmann. New York: Vintage, 1974.

——. *Daybreak*. Tr. R. J. Hollingdale. Cambridge: Cambridge U.P., 1982.

——. *Selected letters*. Tr. A. N. Ludovici. London: Soho Book Co., 1985.

——. *Human All too Human*. Tr. R. J. Hollingdale. Cambridge: Cambridge U.P., 1986.

——. *The Birth of Tragedy and Other Writings*. Tr. R Speirs, Cambridge: Cambridge U.P., 1999.

——. *Beyond Good and Evil*. Tr. W Kaufmann. New York: Vintage, 1966.

Novalis [F. von Hardenberg]. *Pólen.* Tr. Rubens R. Torrez Filho. São Paulo: Iluminuraz, 1988.

Nussbaum, M. *The Therapy of Desire.* Princeton: Princeton U.P., 1994.

Oxford Classical Dictionary. Eds. N. G. L. Hammond and H. H. Scullard. Oxford: Oxford U.P., 1970.

Oxford Companion to Animal Behaviour. Ed. D. McFarland. Oxford: Oxford U.P., 1987.

Oxford Companion to the Mind. Ed. R. L. Gregory. Oxford: Oxford U.P., 1987.

Paz, O. *Versiones y diversiones.* Mexico, 1978.

Penguin Dictionary of English History. Ed. E. N. Williams. Harmondsworth: Penguin, 1980.

Pessoa, F. *Obra em prosa.* Rio de Janeiro: Aguilar, 1974.

——. *Obra poética.* Rio de Janeiro: Aguilar, 1974.

Peters, R. *Hobbes.* Harmondsworth: Penguin, 1956.

Piaget, J., *The Moral Judgement of the Child.* London: Routledge and Kegan Paul, 1960.

Plato, *Laws* . Tr. A. E. Taylor. London: Dent, 1934.

——. *Apology.* Tr. R. W. Livingstone. Oxford: Clarendon Press, 1938.

——. *Republic.* Tr. F. M. Cornford. Oxford: Clarendon Press, 1941.

——. *Phaedo.* Tr. R. S. Buck. London: Routledge and Kegan Paul, 1955.

——. *Theaetetus.* Tr. F. M. Cornford. London: Routledge and Kegan Paul, 1960.

——. *Phaedrus.* Tr. R. Hackforth. Cambridge: Cambridge U.P., 1972.

——. *Protagoras.* Tr. C. C. W. Taylor. Oxford: Clarendon Press, 1976.

——. *First Alcibiades.* Tr. W. Lamb. Cambridge, Mass.: Loeb, 1986.

Plutarch, 'Solon'. In *Lives.* Tr. A. H. Clough. London: Dent, 1910.

Popper, K. R. *The Open Society and its Enemies.* London: Routledge and Kegan Paul, 1963.

——. and Eccles, J. *The Self and its Brain*. London: Routledge, 1983.

Porphyry. 'On the Life of Plotinus and the Arrangement of his Work'. In *The Enneads*. Ed. S. Mackenna. London, 1930.

Prado, P. *Retrato do Brasil*. Ed. Carlos Augusto Calil. São Paulo: Companhia das Letras, 1997.

Price, A. W. *Mental Conflict*. London: Routledge, 1995.

Price, C. *Time, Discounting and Value*. Oxford: Blackwell, 1993.

Quincey, T. de. *Confessions of an English Opium-Eater*. London: Grant Richards, 1907.

Quine, W. V. 'On the Nature of Moral Values'. In *Theories and Things*. Cambridge, Mass.: Harvard U.P., 1981.

——. *Quidditaies*. Cambridge, Mass.: Harvard U.P., 1987.

Rée, J. *Philosophical Tales*. London: Methuen, 1987.

Rhees, R. ed. *Recollections of Wittgenstein*. Oxford: Oxford U.P., 1984.

Rogow, A. A. *Thomas Hobbes*. New York: Norton, 1986.

Rosa, J. Guimarães. 'O espelho' and 'Famigerado'. In *Primeiras estórias*. Rio de Janeiro: José Olympio, 1962.

Rousseau, J.J. *Reveries of the Solitary Walker*. Tr. P. France. Harmondsworth: Penguin, 1979.

Rue, L. *By the Grace of Guile*. Oxford: Oxford U.P., 1994.

Ruskin, J. *Unto this Last*. Orpington: Alan, 1862.

Russell, B. *The Problems of Philosophy*. London: Allen and Unwin, 1912.

——. *The Conquest of Happiness*. London: Allen and Unwin, 1930.

——. 'Ideas that have Harmed Mankind'. In *Unpopular Essays*. London: Allen and Unwin, 1950.

——. *History of Western Philosophy*. London: Allen and Unwin, 1961.

——. 'A Free Man's Worship'. In *A Free Man's Worship*. London, 1976.

——. *Power*. London: Basic Books, 1940.

Sacks, O. *The Man who Mistook his Wife for a Hat*. London: Pan, 1986.

Sambursky, S. *The Physical World of the Greeks*. Tr. M. Dagut.

London: Routledge and Kegan Paul, 1956.

Sartre, J. P. *Baudelaire*. Tr. M. Turnell. London: Horizon, 1949.

——. *Being and Nothingness*. Tr. Hazel E. Barnes. London: Methuen, 1969.

Schelling, T. 'The Intimate Contest for Self-Command'. In *Choice and Consequence*. Cambridge, Mass.: Harvard U.P., 1984.

——. 'The Mind as a Consuming Organ'. In J. Elster, ed., *The Multiple Self*. Cambridge: Cambridge U.P.,1986.

Seneca, *Minor Dialogues*. Tr. A Stewart. London: Bohn's Classical Library, 1889.

Schopenhauer, A. *The World as Will and Representation*. Tr. E. Payne. New York: Dover, 1969.

Sherrington, C. *Man on his Nature*. Harmondsworth: Penguin, 1955.

Smith, A. *The Theory of Moral Sentiments*. Eds. D. D. Raphael and A. L. Macfie. Oxford: Clarendon Press, 1976.

——. *A Inquiry into the Nature and the Causes of the Wealth of Nations*. Eds. R. H. Campbell and A. S. Skinner. Oxford: Clarendon Press, 1976.

——. *Essays on Philosophical Subjects*. Eds. W. P. D. Wightman, J. C. Bryce and I. S. Ross. Oxford: Clarendon Press, 1980.

Spinoza, B. de. *Ethics* and *On the Improvement of the Understanding*. Tr. R. Elwes. New York: Dover, 1955.

Starkie, E. *Baudelaire*. London: Faber, 1958.

Stekllof, G. M. *The History of the First International*. Tr. E. Paul and C. Paul. London: Martin Lawrence, 1928.

Stevens, W. *Opus Posthumous*. Ed. M. Bates. New York: Knopf, 1990.

Stigler, G. *Memoirs of an Unregulated Economist*. New York: Basic Books, 1988.

Strawson, P. *Scepticism and Naturalism*. London: Methuen, 1975.

Tanner, M. *Nietzsche*. Oxford: Oxford U.P., 1994.

Taylor, C. T. *Hegel and Modern Society*. Cambridge: Cambridge U.P., 1979.

Taylor, A. E. *Plato*. London: Methuen, 1960.

Thomas, L. *The Medusa and the Snail: More Notes of a Biology Watcher*. London: Lane, 1980.

Toulmin, S. *Reason in Ethics*. Cambridge: Cambridge U.P., 1968.

Thucydides. *Thucydides*. Tr. B. Jowett. Oxford: Clarendon Press, 1881.

Unamuno, M. de. *The Tragic Sense of Life*. Tr. E.C. Flitch. New York: Dover, 1954.

Valéry, P. 'Remarks on intelligence'. In *Collected Works*. Ed. J. Matthews. London, 1973, vol. 10.

Walker, S. *Animal Thought*. London: Routledge and Kegan Paul, 1985.

Wasianski, K. 'The Last Days of Kant'. In *Last Days of Immanuel Kant*. Tr. T.de Quincey. Edinburgh: Adam and Charles Black, 1867.

Watson, G. ed. *Free Will*. Oxford: Oxford U.P., 1982.

Whitehead, A. N. *Science and the Modern World*. Cambridge: Cambridge U.P., 1926.

Williams, B. 'Moral luck'. In *Moral Luck*. Cambridge: Cambridge U.P., 1981.

Williams, R. *Keywords*. London: Croom Helm, 1976.

Winch, D. *Adam Smith's Politics*. Cambridge: Cambridge U.P., 1978.

Wittgenstein, L. *On Certainty*. Tr. D. Paul and G. E. M. Anscombe. Oxford: Blackwell, 1979.

——. *Remarks on Frazer's 'Golden Bough'*. Tr. A. C. Miles. Retford: Brywell, 1979.

——. *Culture and Value*. Tr. P. Winch. Oxford: Blackwell, 1980.

Woodbridge, F. J. E. *Aristotle's Vision of Nature*. New York: Columbia U.P., 1965.

Wright, R. *The Moral Animal*. New York: Pantheon, 1994.

Young, J. Z. *Philosophy and the Brain*. Oxford: Oxford U.P., 1986.

Zajonc, A. *Catching the Light*. Oxford: Oxford U.P., 1993.

Zoja, L. *Growth and Guilt*. Tr. H. Martin. London: Routledge, 1995.

GLOSSARY

Fernando Pessoa (1888–1935): p. xi
Portuguese poet, born in South Africa and who wrote poetry in English as well as Portuguese. He is most famous for the creation of a number of 'heteronyms', best described as aspects of his personality and attitude to life, of whom Álvaro de Campos (see p. 48) is one.

Mário de Andrade (1893–1945): p. xii
Brazilian intellectual, poet, essayist, fiction-writer and musicologist. He was one of the leaders of the modernist movement in Brazilian letters, which began in the early 1920s. Although the movement was in large part nationalist in inspiration, Mário's position was always one of enthusiasm mixed with healthy scepticism.

Machado de Assis (1839–1908): p. 28
Brazilian novelist, short-story writer, poet, journalist. The first indisputably great novelist to write in Latin America, author of *The Posthumous Memoirs of Brás Cubas, Dom*

Casmurro etc. His works, almost always set in Rio de Janeiro, have an unconventional, curiously modern tone and style, and are informed both by subtle realist observation and a sharp, apparently cynical pessimism.

Álvaro de Campos: p. 48
One of the heteronyms of Fernando Pessoa (see p. xi). He is the most 'advanced' of Pessoa's personalities, and his earlier poetry has something of the enthusiasm of Walt Whitman, to whom 'he' wrote an ode. In his later poetry, notably 'Tabacaria', that enthusiasm is considerably toned down, and affected by a growing self-consciousness and frustration.

João Guimarães Rosa (1908–1967): p. 112
One of the most important and ambitious Brazilian writers of the twentieth century. His masterpiece is *Grande sertão: veredas* [*The Devil to Pay in the Backlands*], a Faustian tale set amongst the cowboys of the Brazilian interior, and told in language which is deliberately poetic and experimental, almost Joycean. His short stories, notably those of *Primeiras estórias* [*The Third Bank of the River and Other Stories*] have many of the same characteristics.

Carlos Drummond de Andrade (1902–1987): p. 116
Almost universally thought of as the greatest Brazilian poet, Drummond was a member of the modernist movement. His poetry, which touches on many subjects and whose style evolved considerably over his long career, in the late 1930s and '40s took on a tone of (somewhat self-doubting) political commitment. He was also a prolific journalist.

Caetano Veloso (b. 1942): p. 149
Brazilian popular singer and composer. He was the founder
of the Tropicalist movement, which in the late 1960s
broke with traditional popular music, and used a clash-
ing, aggressive style, making use of 'foreign' instruments
like electric guitars to convey something of the country's
contradictions. The language of his lyrics is highly wrought
and often intensely poetic.

Ari Barroso (1903–1964): p. 149
Brazilian popular composer, of an earlier generation than
Caetano Veloso, and much more traditional in style. The
author of a large number of songs of all kinds, he is
most famous as the composer of Brazil's 'second national
anthem', 'Aquarela do Brasil' [literally 'A Brazilian Water-
colour', but usually rendered as 'Brazil, Brazil'].

INDEX

300

INDEX

organic deception 24–5
Orpheus 204

partiality, individual 164–72; *see also* moral partiality
party politics, and moral partiality 196
past, certainty of 134
perception 164–5
Pessoa, Fernando 43, 47, 48–9, 180
Phaedo 87
Phaedrus 86
phantom limb experience 30–1
Philip II, of Spain 187
philosophy, Socrates' view of goal of 83
physical deception 24–5
Piaget, Jean 27–8
plants, and deception in natural world 5–6
Plato 49, 50, 85, 229
poets, as self-deceivers 133–4
political leadership, and need for belief 153–4
political power, and moral partiality 200–201
politics, and self-deception 153–4
polygraph 94
power, abuse of 200–201
primates, and deception in natural world 10–14; and language 12–14
Prometheus 22
promises, 149–50; as evidence of doubt 143–4
prophecies, self–fulfilling 141
Protagoras 39–40
protozoa 3
psychology, and self-deception 38–41, 102–112

Quincy, Thomas de 122

rationalism, Cartesian 71–5
rationality, limits of 59–61
reason, and self-deception 48–50
religion, and self deception 108–9
reproduction, and partiality 167; imperative of 1
reputation 219; concern for 182–3; *see also* self-image
reveries 30
revolutionaries, and self-deception 155–59
revolutions, nature of 157–9
Robespierre, Maximilien 155, 156
Rochefoucauld, Duc de La 123, 152, 191
roles, living false 40–1

Rosa, Guimaraes 112
Rousseau, Jean Jacques 15, 132–3
rules: breakdown of 219–20; as necessary evil 229; as restrainers of moral partiality 214–25
Ruskin, John 133
Russell, Bertrand 179

Sartre, Jean Paul 90
scepticism 65
Schopenhauer, Arthur 15
science, and knowing 66–7; limitations of 76–83
scientific knowledge, basis of 69–75
Scriptures, interpretation of 22–3
self 219; and moral judgement 186–9; as obstacle to self–knowledge 89–100; difficulty of observing 93; opinion of 104–5; view of 38–9, 190
self-belief, and success in public arena 152–3
self-centredness 164–72; impossibility of denying 168; impossibility of escaping from 181; limits of 173–77, 179–80; and moral judgement 188–90; necessity of 167, 172; resistance to excessive 181
self-deception, and: attempts at conscious 121, 126–33; belief in one's own deceits 40–1; benefits of 45–57; collective 42, 108–9, 110; difference from deliberate deceit 123; explanation of 38–41; fiction 35–6; fulcrum of 105; intellectual life 106–8; introspection 89–100; involuntary nature of 124; limits of 120–21; logic of 118–63; memory 102–4; paradox of 118–120; passionate love 147–51; passive nature of 122;
protection against 102; psychology 102–112; realisation of 44–5; religion 108–9; requirements for successful 133; rising from bed 141–5; roots of 38–41; self–centredness 177–80; sensory 164–5; social dissimulation 182–90; theatre 36–41; types of 43–5, 122; unpremeditated nature of 123; *see also* hypocrisy, moral partiality
self-image 102, and: flexibility of 110–112; moral partiality 200; opinion of others 104–5, 182–3
self-importance, *see* self-centredness
self-knowledge 57–9; and, basic questions of 90; dangers of 59–61; difficulties in

LIES WE LIVE BY

achieving 91–5; difficulties in validating
101; doubt 113; ethical life 84; illusory
conviction of 113; impossibility of
objective comparison 99; limits of scientific method 76–83; need for 84–5;
problem of introspection 89–100; provisional nature of 113; Socratic meaning of 88; subjective nature of 101;
uncertainty principle 101–2
self–love 116; *see also* self–centredness
senses, and individual viewpoint 164–5
sex, and self-deception 148
Shakespeare, William 149–50
sight, and individual viewpoint 164–5;
objective description of 77–8; subjective
meaning of 79–81
Sirens, the 203–7
situational transference 129–30, 131
sleep, and self-deception 141–5
sleeping sickness 4
Smith, Adam 47–8, 192, 196
social sanctions 218–19
society, and necessity for laws 214–25
Socrates 83–8; and self–knowledge 84;
and goal of philosophy 83; and doubt
86; and dialogic method 85–6, 88
Socratic dialogues 85–6, 88
Socratic philosophy, goal of 87–8
Solon 225
Sophocles 105
Stalin, Josef 114–15, 159
Stalin paradox, the 114–15
Stevens, Wallace 37
subjectivity, elimination of in search
for knowledge 69–75
success, attribution of and partiality
191
suffering, and moral partiality 213; and
self-centredness 175

survival, imperatives of 1; and partiality
167; and value of self-deception 54–6

temptation 203–12
Theaetetus 86
theatre, and self-deception 36–41
Thucydides 219–20, 225
time, and desire 206–12; human perception of 137–8; subjective experience
of 201–2
time travel, paradoxes of 138–40
traffic system, and moral partiality 191,
194–5; and regulation of 214–16
transparency, interpersonal, shock of 184
truth, and self-deception 144–5, 149–50;
false standards of 160–62; types of
68
trypanosome 4

Ulysses 204–6
Unamuno, Miguel de 169
uncertainty principle 93; and self–knowledge 101–2
Uriah 197–200
utopias, merit of 228–9

Valéry, Paul 202–3
vanity 114–16
Veloso, Caetano 149
Venus fly-trap 4
viruses 3
voice-recognition 94–5

Wallace, Alfred 193
war, and moral partiality 196
Wittgenstein, Ludwig Josef Johann 52, 90,
107, 132

Xenophanes 169

304